Muriel Spark, Existentialism and the Art of Death

For Max and Christine Roach

Muriel Spark, Existentialism and the Art of Death

Cairns Craig

EDINBURGH
University Press

Edinburgh University Press is one of the leading university presses in the UK. We publish academic books and journals in our selected subject areas across the humanities and social sciences, combining cutting-edge scholarship with high editorial and production values to produce academic works of lasting importance. For more information visit our website: edinburghuniversitypress.com

Edinburgh University Press Ltd
The Tun – Holyrood Road
12(2f) Jackson's Entry
Edinburgh EH8 8PJ

First published in hardback by Edinburgh University Press 2019

Typeset in 11/14 Adobe Sabon by
IDSUK (DataConnection) Ltd

A CIP record for this book is available from the British Library

ISBN 978 1 4744 4720 1 (hardback)
ISBN 978 1 4744 4721 8 (paperback)
ISBN 978 1 4744 4722 5 (webready PDF)
ISBN 978 1 4744 4723 2 (epub)

Contents

Preface

In my book on *The Modern Scottish Novel* (1999), I devoted considerable space to the work of Muriel Spark, but I have long wanted to write something more substantial on her novels, both because she seems to me the most important Scottish novelist of the second half of the twentieth century – despite the many demurrals about whether she can really be counted as Scottish – and because her reputation as a novelist is often undermined by a sense that she is clever and witty rather than profound, and that, if she is the most important British novelist of the period, that is, at least in part, because the British novel is itself so insignificant. I originally set out to write a book on Spark as a Scottish novelist in the tradition of Stevenson and Barrie, and elements of that will be found occasionally in this book, but my interest in Spark here is in Spark as a theologically and philosophically informed writer, profoundly influenced by the works of Kierkegaard – as Chapter 1 suggests, the plots of her early novels reflect aspects of Kierkegaard's life and writings – and also with the consequences of the post-war existentialisms for which Kierkegaard had been a major inspiration.

Some of the original research for this book was done while I was Director of the AHRC Centre for Irish and Scottish Studies at the University of Aberdeen, and I am grateful to the AHRC for the support they then provided, and to the School of Language, Literature, Music and Visual Culture at Aberdeen for the sabbatical which allowed me to complete this project. My thanks, too, to the staff at the libraries of the universities of Aberdeen and Edinburgh and at the National Library of Scotland where most of the research was carried out. And, as always, my thanks to Linda and Conan for their patience during what sometimes seemed a project that was consuming their lives as well as mine.

Abbreviations

Works by Muriel Spark

AA *Aiding and Abetting* (London: Viking, 2000)
AC *The Abbess of Crew* (London: Macmillan, 1974)
B *The Bachelors* (London: Macmillan, 1960)
BPR *The Ballad of Peckham Rye* (London: Macmillan, 1960)
C *The Comforters* (London: Macmillan, 1957)
CSS *The Complete Short Stories* (London: Viking, 2001)
DS *The Driver's Seat* (London: Macmillan, 1970)
FCK *A Far Cray from Kensington* (London: Constable, 1988)
FS *The Finishing School* (London: Viking, 2004)
GF *The Golden Fleece*, ed. Penelope Jardine (Manchester: Carcanet, 2014)
GSM *The Girls of Slender Means* (London: Macmillan, 1963)
HBER *The Hothouse by the East River* (London: Macmillan, 1973)
LI *Loitering with Intent* (London: Bodley Head, 1981)
MG *The Mandelbaum Gate* (London: Macmillan, 1965)
MM *Memento Mori* (London: Macmillan, 1959)
PI *The Public Image* (London: Macmillan, 1968)
PJB *The Prime of Miss Jean Brodie* (London: Macmillan, 1961)
R *Robinson* (London: Macmillan, 1958)
S *Symposium* (London: Constable, 1990)
TOP *The Only Problem* (London: Bodley Head, 1984)
TR *Territorial Rights* (London: Macmillan, 1979)

Works by Søren Kierkegaard

CUP *Concluding Unscientific Postscript to* Philosophical Fragments, trans. Howard V. and Edna H. Hong (1846; Princeton: Princeton University Press, 1992)

E/O *Either/Or*, vol. 1 trans. David F. Swenson and Lillian M. Swenson; vol. 2 trans. Walter Lowrie (1843; 2 vols, Princeton: Princeton University Press, 1944)

F&T *Fear and Trembling: A Dialectical Lyric*, trans. Walter Lowrie (1843; Princeton: Princeton University Press, 1941)

J *The Journals of Søren Kierkegaard*, trans. Alexander Dru (Oxford: Oxford University Press, 1938)

Rep *Repetition: An Essay in Experimental Psychology*, trans. Walter Lowrie (1843; Princeton: Princeton University Press, 1942)

SLW *Stages on Life's Way*, trans. Walter Lowrie (1845; Princeton: Princeton University Press, 1940)

SUD *Sickness unto Death*, trans. Walter Lowrie (1849; Princeton: Princeton University Press, 1941)

Works by Jean-Paul Sartre

B&N *Being and Nothingness: An Essay on Phenomenological Ontology*, trans. Hazel E. Barnes (1943; New York: The Philosophical Library, 1956)

WIL *What is Literature?*, trans. Bernard Frechtman (1947; New York: The Philosophical Library, 1949)

Other Works

RN Ian Watt, *The Rise of the Novel* (Harmondsworth: Penguin, 1963; 1957)

Introduction

That Muriel Spark was a Catholic convert was the burden of much of the early criticism of her work;[1] that she was an avant-garde innovator in a new, minimalist style of narrative that had much in common with the French *nouveau roman* has been the assertion of 'theoretical' approaches to her work;[2] that she resisted binary conceptions of sexuality long before the emergence of the LGBT reconfigurations of the sexual made her seem presciently aware of some of the directions in which Western societies were travelling;[3] and that she was a literary exile – a Scotswoman living and writing in London, New York and in Italy – has both provoked efforts to reincorporate her into specifically Scottish traditions of writing[4] and, on the other hand, to see her as representative of the diasporic experience of global displacements of population in the twentieth century.[5] Despite Spark's apparent importance in these various contexts, there continues to linger the sense that she is not quite a 'serious' novelist: perhaps the best *British* novelist of the second half of the twentieth century but only because the British novel is, in itself, so poor in comparison with the novel in the United States or in France.

The doubleness of the critical reception of Spark is caught by Ali Smith when she describes *A Far Cry from Kensington* as being 'mercurially funny, playful and mischievous',[6] but based on 'a cheap detective mystery',[7] that somehow manages to imply that 'the lightness of things is always a serious business'.[8] For some, however, the 'serious business' is what seems to be lacking in Spark: even those who admire her works have reservations about what Jenny Turner describes as its 'Ealingish melodrama' – a reference to the 'Carry On' comedies shot at the Ealing Studios, full of camp farce – which, Turner suggests, 'is a feature of many Spark novels and, generally speaking, [. . .] isn't ageing well'.[9] Equally, Alan Taylor, general editor of the new edition of Spark's novels published by Polygon, notes that many have, in the words of Carol Shields, 'mistaken Spark's amusing style for a lightness of subject matter'.[10] David Lodge is perhaps the most notable author-critic who found even Spark's most popular work – *The Prime of Miss Jean Brodie* – problematic: as he noted in an article in the *New York Review of Books* in 2010, when he first reviewed Spark's novel in 1961, 'I declared myself "beguiled [. . .] but not really stirred or involved or enlightened." It was some time before I realized that the disappointment was entirely my own fault and that the novel was a masterpiece.'[11] Spark's novels are so deceptively 'light' – deceptively like genre fiction, whether detective novels or romantic comedy – that they seem to carry no intellectual substance: as Frank Kermode commented in a review of *The Only Problem*, the notion that she was the best novelist of the age was one which was not 'widely shared' because her works are not 'thought serious enough'.[12] Leo Robson, worrying about what he considered to be the 'toy like contraptions' of Spark's novels, in which her 'virtuosity is suspiciously sweatless – brilliance as a form of complacency', suggested that,

> For Spark, the novel was a frivolous, earthbound endeavour – in the words of her contemporary Philip Larkin, 'a quite unlosable game'. And while it would be preposterous to argue, in the face of *The Prime of Miss Jean Brodie* and *The Ballad of Peckham Rye*, that Spark's gifts were in any sense unrealised, the shortcomings of her work ought to disqualify her from being even an interesting writer. She was incapable of picturing real heartbreak or malice; she preferred types to characters, and telling to showing; she was excessively fond of formulae and gimmicks; she offered little in the way of verbal reward; she was manipulative and coercive; she alerted the reader to how little was at stake in reading a novel rather than encouraging what Coleridge called 'the willing suspension of disbelief'.[13]

For some, it is Spark's Catholicism which gives weight to her writing – Thomas Mallon, for instance, suggests that Catholicism 'is the joker in the pack of her early and best novels, the antic sabotage without which the books might have become mere entertaining additions to the postwar comic realism of writers like Kingsley Amis and Angus Wilson'[14] – while for others it is her formal innovations that give weight to her fiction, and, in particular, her introduction into the anglophone novel of the experimental strategies of the French *nouveau roman*.[15] I want to suggest, however, that both Catholicism and the *nouveau roman* are outcomes of a much more pervasive intellectual context in which Spark was developing her art in the late 1940s and early 1950s – that of the anglophone reception of existentialism, and, in particular, the conflict between 'Christian existentialism', as developed in and from the works of Søren Kierkegaard, and the contemporary atheistic existentialism represented by Jean-Paul Sartre, Albert Camus and Simone de Beauvoir. Existentialism, I suggest, was key both to Spark's religious convictions and to her aesthetic innovations and provides the undertow of intellectual depth which so many have found absent in her work.

Existentialism was a pervasive concern of the poetic and intellectual circles in which Spark moved in London after the Second World War: Derek Stanford, Spark's sometime lover, co-author and co-editor, recalls, for instance, evenings spent debating whether 'existential fiction was now the all-important thing' and the 'great status of Camus and Sartre';[16] Reyner Heppenstall, who would later commission Spark to write for the BBC, published in 1946 an introduction to the translation of Guido De Ruggiero's *Existentialism*, an attack on the 'atheistical' existentialism that had emerged in France during the Second World War; and one of Spark's supporters in the Poetry Society was fellow Scot G. S. Fraser, whose translation of *The Mystery of Being* by the Christian existentialist Gabriel Marcel appeared in 1950.[17] Though Sartre's atheistic philosophy came to dominate the public understanding of existentialism,[18] it is important to recall that Christian thinkers such as Marcel and Karl Jaspers had developed a Christian existentialism many years before the era of Sartre, Camus and de Beauvoir, and if some of them would later distance themselves from the term 'existentialism' as understood by the general public, they continued to argue the case for a Christian existentialism against the powerful assertion of Sartre's atheistic version. The poet Kathleen Raine, whom Spark published both in *The Poetry Review* which she edited for the Poetry Society, and in her own short-lived journal *Forum*, translated Paul Foulquié's *Existentialism* in 1948, in which Foulquié emphasised the Christian origins of existentialism:

> There is no cause for astonishment in the Christian origins of modern existentialism. Christianity – in its philosophy and dogma no less than its morality and mysticism – gives rise in those who practice it

> to a state of the soul which corresponds to the existentialist attitude, the sense of existence, of responsibility, of anguish, of astonishment in the face of the irrational.[19]

He went on:

> The Incarnation notably reinforces the existential character of the Christian religion. In fact, our nature being what it is, it is a matter that gives us the strongest impression of reality, so that, for us, nothing gives us such a strong sense of existence as those things that we can touch. In becoming Incarnate, the Word has assumed this mode of being, and at the same time has made it possible for us to re-live its life, that is, to become conscious of the existence lived by the Word. This is what the liturgical cycle in particular, that played such a large part in Christian society in the past, helps us to do.[20]

That this hinterland of existentialism is a part of Muriel Spark's intellectual and literary development in the late 1940s and early 1950s is confirmed in *The Mandelbaum Gate*, in which existentialism both underpins and undermines the friendship between half-Jewish Barbara Vaughan and the head teacher of the school in which she works, Miss Rickward:

> Ricky could discourse for hours on the history and development of the existentialist philosophy. It had been pleasant for Barbara, it had given her a remote sense that she was doing something in life, if only mentally, to sit and listen, with an occasional comment, while Ricky expounded the doctrine that existence precedes essence. (*MG*, 161)

Barbara Vaughan might question, 'could Ricky apply this notion to the world she existed in? To Barbara? Herself?' (*MG*, 162), but even if it is unlikely that two unmarried women, seemingly drifting towards sharing a house in their retirement, could be living examples of the 'doctrine that existence precedes essence', it is clearly part of their intellectual and rhetorical environment. In *The Girls of Slender Means*, on the other hand, Nicholas Farringdon's conversion and subsequent 'martyrdom' in Haiti (*GSM*, 5) derives originally from a lack of ability to choose – in other words to fulfil what the philosophy of existentialism would require of him: 'he could never make up his mind between suicide and an equally drastic course of action known as Father D'Arcy [. . .] a Jesuit philosopher who had the monopoly for converting the English intellectuals' (*GSM*, 63). Significantly, one of the early anglophone accounts of existentialism, Ralph Harper's *Existentialism: A Theory of Man*, published in 1949, notes in its acknowledgements the author's debt to 'the Very Reverend M. C. D'Arcy, S.J. formerly of Oxford University, for opening up to me the prospect of an existentialism not of nihilism but of love'.[21] The potentialities of this alternative existentialism are played out in Nicholas's transformation from someone perennially 'undecided' on every issue (*GSM*, 63), to one who has accepted the need to step across the threshold into commitment to Christianity and, in the end, to a martyr's death.

The interactions between the atheistic and theistic existentialisms of the 1940s and 1950s, both among Spark's literary acquaintances and among the characters in her novels, were made possible because of the belated influence, in the 1920s and 30s, of the works of Søren Kierkegaard, unknown till the early years of the century to anyone outside Denmark but rapidly translated into German and French around the First World War and then into English in the 1930s and 1940s. Almost all accounts of existentialism in the 1940s and 1950s trace its origins to Kierkegaard, and Ralph Harper, for instance, finds in Kierkegaard a turning point in which Christianity rediscovers the real meaning of its origins:

> One hundred years ago, in opposition to one kind of philosophical relativism, that of Hegel, Kierkegaard referred men back to a starting-point of which they could be certain, their own existence [. . .] It is easy to forget – and Kierkegaard never forgot this – that he was but one of a long line of Christian witnesses of a respect for the self. Genuine self-knowledge first came into Western civilization through Judaism, and hosts of religious folk in taking the words of the Psalmist to their hearts have been testifying to a concern for themselves which no Greek philosopher could share. 'Save me, O my God' . . . One cannot imagine Aristotle groaning, 'Out of the depths have I cried unto thee, O Lord.' . . . And just as one cannot imagine Plato affirming, 'My heart is glad, and my glory rejoiceth: my flesh also shall rest in hope,' so one cannot hear even Socrates confessing with Job, 'For I know that my redeemer liveth . . . and though after my skin worms destroy this body, yet in my flesh shall I see God.' As we would now say, Socrates could not take his flesh that seriously.[22]

Atheistic existentialism took from Kierkegaard his insistence on the need for human beings to exert the freedom of choice which was fundamental to their nature but excised his insistence that the most important choice was the choice of Christian belief. The significance of this aspect of Kierkegaard's philosophy was underlined by the initial publication of selections from Kierkegaard's *Journals*, which were translated into English by Alexander Dru in 1938: the *Journals* chart Kierkegaard's personal struggles to come to terms with the meaning of Christianity and are full of a sense of the dramatic nature and the historical significance of what he aims to achieve by his writings:

> 'The individual'; that category has only been used once before and then by Socrates, in a dialectical and decisive way, to disintegrate paganism. In Christianity it will be used once again – in order to make men (the Christians) into Christians. It is not the category which missionaries can use in dealing with heathens when they preach the Gospel, but the category of a missionary in Christendom itself, so as to make the change, which lies in being and becoming a Christian, a more inward change. (*J*, '723', 228)[23]

For Kierkegaard making modern Christians into real Christians was the purpose of his writings, a purpose which could only be achieved by choosing faith in a full awareness of the fallen nature of man: 'The real proportions are these: if I were not conscious of being a sinner I should be scandalised by Christianity. The consciousness of sin silences me so that in spite of the possibility of scandal I choose faith' (*J*, '820', 264). Kierkegaard's insistence on the 'choice' of faith is made on the basis that there can never be an adequate argument or reasoned case for belief in God: faith cannot be proven, but follows from the act of choice which is then validated in its everyday enactment and in its everyday consequences. The atheistic existentialism of Sartre insisted on human beings' ability to choose as the proof of man's freedom in an otherwise absurd world, but for Kierkegaard it is not freedom but faith that follows from choice:

> Socrates did not first of all get together some proofs of the immortality of the soul in order then to live in that belief, on the strength of the proofs. The very reverse is the case; he said: the possibility of there being an immortality occupies me to such a degree that

> I unquestioningly stake my whole life upon it as though it were the most certain of all things. And so he lived – and his life is proof of the immortality of the soul. He did not believe merely on the strength of the proofs and then live: no, his life is the proof, and only with his martyr's death is the proof complete. (*J*, '1044', 367)

Belief arises from the act of choosing and not as the outcome of reasoning or reflection, and the example of Socrates shapes Kierkegaard's own beliefs: 'And so I say to myself: I choose; that historical fact means so much to me that I decide to stake my whole life upon that if' (*J*, '1044', 368). The necessary consequence of such a choice, however, is that belief is never a settled matter – it is a continuous and ongoing test of what one has chosen, of what one must again choose on a daily basis: 'without risk faith is an impossibility. *To be related to spirit means to undergo a test*; to believe, to wish to believe, is to change one's life into a trial; daily test is the trial of faith' (*J*, '1044', 368).

The biblical exemplar of this faith is Job, and the case of Job echoes through the *Journals* – '801', '895', '930', '1233' – as it was to be the central concern of Kierkegaard's *Repetition* (1843): Job reveals that faith is a test which must be endured even when it seems to entail nothing but loss, and that the believer can only maintain his belief by resisting the possible reliefs offered by his 'comforters', who try to lure him back into the world of ordinary purposes and values:

> The secret of the story of Job, the vital force, the core, the idea is: that Job, despite everything, is in the right. This claim makes him an exception to all human consideration; his endurance and strength prove his authority, his warrant. Every human explanation is simply a misunderstanding to him, and all his distress is to him, in relation to God, a mere sophism that he knows he cannot solve himself, but which he has confidence that God can solve. Every *argumentum ad hominem* is used against him, yet he is undaunted in his conviction. (*R*, 65)

Job is the symbol of faith as a daily trial and as a daily refusal of the temptations offered by his 'comforters'. The Book of Job was to be equally important to Spark: her first novel was titled *The Comforters*, enigmatically invoking Job as the context for a narrative of religious conversion, and a later novel, *The Only Problem*, is focused on a character, Harvey Gotham, who is writing a study of the Book of Job and comes increasingly to see his own life as a modern version of the biblical story. Writing about that novel, Spark recalls how,

> Years ago I started to study the Book of Job, which is surely one of the loveliest, most intricate and most ambiguous books of the Bible. Uncountable works have been written on Job, and although textual and interpretive scholarship has progressively helped us with the details, it remains unmanageable as a rational narrative, and yet hypnotic as a poem. I intended to write a critical book. In 1954 I wrote a few essays and many notes on the Book of Job, and put away the subject to get on with my life. (*GF*, 191)

For Spark, the Book of Job is a great poetic engagement with the fact that 'suffering is indivisible from life itself. It is insoluble, a mystery' (*GF*, 192) and, as she quotes in a review of Raymond P. Scheindlin's translation of Job in 1998:

> The author [of Job] does not make the simplistic claim that life's delights are commensurate with or compensation for life's sorrows. He does not make any argument at all. All arguments have been rendered nil by the book's premise. Since the narrative presents Job's complaint as rational and correct, there is no room left for a rational solution. Rather, poetry is used to shift the ground from reason, where life must lose, to emotion, where it at least has a chance. (*GF*, 198–9)

Poetry makes reason irrelevant just as, for Kierkegaard, 'The problem is not to understand Christianity but to understand that it cannot be understood. That is the holiness of faith [. . .]' (*J*, '813', 261). For Spark, Kierkegaard's 'philosophy', if indeed one could extract such a singular statement from his writings, is not as important as the fact, often ignored by atheistic existentialists, that 'Kierkegaard's religious, and especially Christian, thought [is] the central factor in his life and writings' (*GF*, 201). In her review of T. H. Croxall's *Meditations from Kierkegaard* she insists that what is important to modern readers are 'certain isolated but luminous fragments' which reveal the foundations of a 'Christian existentialist philosophy' (*GF*, 201).[24]

That a Protestant philosopher might have been one of the guides to Spark's conversion to Catholicism is less strange than it might be if one recalls Kierkegaard's struggles against the Lutheran church in Denmark: as he notes in a diary entry of 6 April 1838,

> There are after all few men equal to bearing the Protestant view of life, and if it is really to be a source of strength to the average man it must either constitute itself into a smaller community (separatism, conventicles etc.), or become more like Catholicism, so as in both cases to promote a communal bearing of the burden of life in society, which only the most gifted individuals can afford to be without. Christ certainly died for all men, and also for me; but that 'for me' must be understood in the sense that he only died for me in so far as I belong to the many. (*J*, '192', 57)

E. L. Allen, in one of the earliest accounts of Kierkegaard in English, suggested that, when confronted with the needs of modern society, Kierkegaard's 'steps would have turned in the direction of Catholicism',[25] a view which echoes a comment by Regine Olsen, Kierkegaard's fiancée, recorded in the *Journal* of 1848: 'Her words about me were prophetic: you will end by becoming a Jesuit' (*J*, '789', 250). In fact, the Christian existentialism which flowed from engagement with Kierkegaard's works was largely Catholic – Jacques Maritain, Gabriel Marcel, Emmanuel Mounier – and saw in Kierkegaard's existentialism a justification for faith, and in that justification a foundation for a renewed Catholicism.

Spark was clearly aware of Kierkegaard's writings by the time she came to write her first novels – her review of Croxall's edition starts confidently, 'Few scholars have done better service to Kierkegaard than Dr T. H. Croxall, who is one of the minority of writers on the subject with a knowledge of both the Danish language and the philosophical environment to which Kierkegaard's Christianity was a corrective' (*GF*, 201); the reference to 'existence before essence' in *The Mandelbaum Gate* also points to her familiarity with Sartre's existentialism, a knowledge of which is likely to have been enhanced by *The Tablet*, a journal in which Spark published a poem, 'Sisera', in August 1953,[26] and which reviewed Spark and Stanford's *My Best Mary: Selected Letters of Mary Shelley* on 6 June 1953, their *Emily Brontë* on 26 December 1953, and their edition of *Letters of*

John Henry Newman on 24 August 1957. *The Tablet* carried regularly articles and reviews both on existentialism in general – on 22 March 1952 there was a review of H. J. Blackham's *Six Existentialist Thinkers* – and, more specifically, on Christian existentialists, from 'A Study of Gabriel Marcel' by John Durkan on 25 October 1947 to *Kierkegaard as Theologian* by Louis Dupré on 18 January 1964, as well as regular reviews of Sartre's works. This environment of debate between atheistic and Christian existentialism, between existentialism as a philosophy of crisis and the ordinary world in which most human beings have to make their way, shapes the intellectual hinterland that inspires the dynamics of Spark's plots and the forms of her fiction. Spark was not just a Catholic convert, she was a convert to an existential Christianity. Some of Spark's critics have complained about the lack of information she provides in her autobiography, *Curriculum Vitae*, about what seems to have been a key moment in her life, her conversion; what she tells us is,

> When I am asked about my conversion, why I became a Catholic, I can only say that the answer is both too easy and too difficult. The simple explanation is that I felt the Roman Catholic faith corresponded to what I had always felt and known and believed; there was no blinding revelation in my case. The more difficult explanation would involve the step by step building up of a conviction; as Newman himself pointed out, when asked about his conversion, it was not a thing one could propound 'between the soup and the fish' at a dinner party. 'Let them be to the trouble that I have been to,' said Newman. Indeed, the existential quality of a religious experience cannot be simply summed up in general terms. (*CV*, 202)

The 'existential quality of a religious experience' points not merely to the 'lived' nature of that experience but the lived nature of the Christian existentialism with which she was familiar in Kierkegaard. It also reflects her resistance to the atheistic existentialism which had become so prominent in her contemporary cultural environment. Because the division between Christian and atheistic existentialism has largely disappeared from accounts of the intellectual context in which Spark came to her belated creative maturity in the 1950s, it is assumed that 'Catholic' and 'existential' represent the terms of an opposition rather than, as they were for Marcel or Jaspers, a reconciliation, a reconciliation made possible by the recovery and exploration of the works of Kierkegaard. 'The existential quality of a religious experience' is, in effect, the experience of a religious existentialism, which is founded on Kierkegaard's notion of the *paradox* of faith:

> Immanently (in the fantastic medium of abstraction) God does not *exist*, he only is – God only *exists* for an existing man *i.e.* he can only exist *in faith*. Providence, atonement, etc. only exist for an existing man. When all things are accomplished providence rests in consummation, when all things are accomplished the atonement comes to rest in equilibrium, but they do not *exist*. Faith is therefore the anticipation of the eternal which holds the factors together, the cleavages in existence. When an existing individual has not got faith God *is* not, neither does God *exist*, although understood from an eternal point of view God is eternally. (*J*, '605', 173)

Only in and through the relation between an existing human being and God can God *exist* rather than merely 'be' eternally because it is faith that creates the intersection between the eternal and time that defies the categories of reason. For Kierkegaard, the crisis of his own time was that of the Hegelian 'System' in which existing individuals would simply play their part in some vast historical process that had nothing to do with the individual's specific experiences and individual choices: those choices would be absorbed into the higher development of the System as whole. But, Kierkegaard insists, it is only as an existing human being, and not as a function in an abstract philosophy or a rational theology, that one can encounter God; one can only encounter God as an existing human being who has to confront the coming of his or her own death – not death in general or death as an abstract category but his or her specific death – and only in that context does faith make sense. In the *Concluding Unscientific Postscript*, Kierkegaard mocks those who have a general knowledge of death:

> For example, *what it means to die*. On that topic I know what people ordinarily know: that if I swallow a dose of sulfuric acid I will die, likewise by drowning myself or sleeping in coal gas etc. I know that Napoleon always carried poison with him, that Shakespeare's Juliet took it, that the Stoics regarded suicide as a courageous act and others regard it as cowardice, that one can die from such a

> ludicrous trifle that the most solemn person cannot help laughing at death, that one can avoid certain death, etc. I know that the tragic hero dies in the fifth act and that death here gains infinite reality [*Realitet*] in pathos but has no such pathos when an alehouse keeper dies. In know that the poet interprets death in a variety of moods to the point of verging on the comic; I pledge myself to produce in prose the same variety of effects in mood. Moreover, I know what the clergy usually say; I know the stock themes dealt with at funerals. (*CUP*, 165–6)

All such knowledge is, however, entirely theoretical, because if 'the uncertainty of death is something in general, then my dying is also something in general' (*CUP*, 167) but *my* death is not something in general:

> That difficulty can also be expressed in this way: is it so that the living person cannot approach death at all, since he, experimenting, cannot come close enough without comically becoming a victim of his own experiment, and since he, as experiencing, cannot exercise any restraint but learns nothing from the experience, since he cannot pull himself back out of the experience and have the benefit of it later but remains stuck in the experience. (*CUP*, 168)

Whatever experiments I make 'I am, even if my life were at stake, very far indeed from having comprehended death, and even less have I existentially carried out my task' (*CUP*, 170). The problem of death is also the problem of immortality – it can have no general or communal meaning:

> several families can join together for a box at the theatre, and three single gentlemen can join together for a riding horse so that each one rides every third day. But this is not the way it is with immortality: the consciousness of my immortality belongs simply and solely to me. The very moment I am conscious of my immortality, I am completely subjective, and I cannot become immortal in partnership in rotation with two single gentlemen. (*CUP*, 173–4)

The need to interrogate such issues from the point of view of the *existing* person and not from the point of view of some abstract philosophical system is what drives Kierkegaard's philosophising and what makes it an *existential* philosophy, a philosophy whose conclusion is not an abstract proposition but is the intimate experience of a living being confronted by a death which cannot be 'drawn up into an idea' (*CUP*, 168) but must remain always beyond the boundary of what can be known conceptually. It is at this point that one must make what has come to be known as the 'leap to faith'[27] and discover what faith can reveal about the self and its relation to God: 'God is spirit – only one who is dead can speak that language at all. If you do not desire to die then neither can you love God, you talk of quite different things from him' (*J*, '1266', 470). Spark's 'leap to faith' was a leap to a Christian existentialism, to the 'existential quality of a religious experience', and existentialism profoundly shaped the fiction which flowed from that leap.

Notes

1. See, for instance, Ruth Wittaker, *The Faith and Fiction of Muriel Spark* (London: Macmillan, 1982).
2. See Martin McQuillan (ed.), *Theorizing Muriel Spark: Gender, Race, Deconstruction* (Basingstoke: Palgrave, 2002).
3. See Len Gutkin, 'Muriel Spark's Camp Metafiction', *Contemporary Literature*, Volume 58, Number 1, Spring 2017, 53–81.
4. See my own discussion of Spark's novels in *The Modern Scottish Novel* (Edinburgh: Edinburgh University Press, 1999).
5. See Bryan Cheyette, *Muriel Spark* (Tavistock: Northcote House, 2000). Cheyette sees Spark's diasporic status as opposed to her Scottishness, but given the huge proportion of the Scottish population which emigrated in the twentieth century, it might be more appropriate to see a diasporic perspective as itself inherently Scottish.
6. 'Introduction', Muriel Spark, *A Far Cry from Kensington* (London: Virago, 2009), v.
7. Ibid. vii.
8. Ibid. ix.
9. Jenny Turner, 'On My Way Rejoicing', *The Guardian*, Saturday, 21 April 2007; https://www.theguardian.com/books/2007/apr/21/fiction.murielspark, accessed 26 April 2018.
10. https://fivebooks.com/best-books/muriel-spark-best-novels; accessed 19 August 2018.
11. David Lodge, 'The Prime of Muriel Spark', *The New York Review of Books*, 19 August 2010; https://www.nybooks.com/articles/2010/08/19/prime-muriel-spark/, accessed 19 April 2018.
12. Quoted Lodge, ibid.

13. Leo Robson, 'Muriel Spark: The Biography', *New Statesman*, 6 August 2009; https://www.newstatesman.com/books/2009/08/spark-fiction-work-stannard, accessed 21 April 2018.
14. Thomas Mallon, 'Transfigured: How Muriel Spark rose to join the crème de la crème of British fiction', *New York Review of Books*, 5 April 2010; https://www.newyorker.com/magazine/2010/04/05/transfigured, accessed 20 April 2018.
15. See Aidan Day, 'Parodying Postmodernism: Muriel Spark (*The Driver's Seat*) and Robbe-Grillet (*Jealousy*), *English: Journal of the English Association*, Volume 56, Issue 216, 1 October 2007, 321–7, https://doi.org/10.1093/english/56.216.321.
16. Derek Stanford, *Inside the Forties: Literary Memoirs, 1937–1957* (London: Sidgwick & Jackson, 1977), 173.
17. Gabriel Marcel, *The Mystery of Being*, Vol. 1, *Reflection & Mystery* (London: Harvill Press, 1950); this was the first of two series of Gifford Lectures delivered by Marcel at the University of Aberdeen in 1949 and 1950.
18. Edith Kern dates the emergence of atheistic existentialism to 1946 when, after listening to Jean Wahl's account of the history of existentialism, a meeting of French philosophers 'agreed that only Sartre, Simone de Beauvoir and Merleau-Ponty – the philosophers sometimes known as the Paris school — could be called existentialists, because they alone had willingly accepted the term which had been thrust upon them'; Edith Kern, *Existential Thought and Fictional Technique: Kierkegaard, Sartre, Beckett* (New Haven: Yale University Press, 1970), 1.
19. Paul Foulquié, *Existentialism*, trans. Kathleen Raine (London: Dennis Dobson Ltd, 1948), 96.
20. Ibid. 96–7.
21. Ralph Harper, *Existentialism: A Theory of Man* (Cambridge, MA: Harvard University Press, 1949), viii.
22. Harper, *Existentialism*, 6–7.
23. Alexander Dru (ed.), *The Journals of Søren Kierkegaard* (Oxford: Oxford University Press, 1938), '723', 228; the number in inverted commas is the number of the entry, followed by the page; hereafter cited in the text as *J*.
24. Spark's possible understanding of Kierkegaard is suggested by Ruth Whitaker in a passing reference in *The Faith and Fiction of Muriel Spark* (London: Macmillan, 1982) to Kierkegaard's notion of the 'absurd' in *F&T*, 80–1.
25. E. L. Allen, *Kierkegaard: His Life and Thought* (London: Stanley Nott Ltd, 1935), 143.

26. *The Tablet*, 29 August 1953, 7, accessed at archive.thetablet.co.uk, 6 February 2018.
27. This is often presented as a 'leap *of* faith', but the leap precedes the faith rather than following on from it. See M. Jamie Ferreira, 'Faith and the Kierkegaardian Leap' in Alastair Hannay and Gordon D. Marion (eds), *The Cambridge Companion to Kierkegaard* (Cambridge: Cambridge University Press, 1998), 207–34.

Chapter 1

Living Next Door to Death

In Muriel Spark's story 'Bang-Bang You're Dead' (1961), the central character, Sybil, discovers as a child that there is another girl in her neighbourhood who looks disturbingly like her, and who will later be mistaken for her by their schoolteachers: 'Sybil suddenly felt she was walking past her own reflection in the long looking-glass' (*CSS*, 60). Many years later, films of Sybil's life in Africa are being shown to some of her friends, who make the same mistake:

> The new reel was fixed. 'Put out the lights,' he said.
>
> It was the stoep again. Through the French windows came a dark girl in shorts followed by a frisky young Alsatian.
>
> 'Lovely dog,' commented Sybil's host. 'He seems to be asking Sybil for a game.'
>
> 'That is someone else,' Sybil said very quickly.
>
> 'The girl there, with the dog?'
>
> 'Yes, of course. Don't you see me walking across the lawn by the trees?'
>
> 'Oh, of course, of course. She did look like you, Sybil, that girl with the dog' (*CSS*, 60)

The two girls are framed together in the film, their resemblance seemingly attracting them into parallel lives. When Désirée Coleman's family decide to move house, it is into the same square where Sybil's family live and together the children become playmates of the Dobell brothers who live nearby; as adults they discover they have both moved with their husbands to the same part of Africa. The magnetism which draws them together is also, however, a repulsion: playing war games with the Dobell brothers, Sybil discovers that Désirée

> lacked mental stamina, could not keep up an imaginative game for long, was shrill and apt to kick her playmates unaccountably and on the sly; the Dobells reacted to this with simple resignation. Perhaps the lack of opposition was the reason that Désirée continually shot Sybil dead, contrary to the rules, whenever she felt like it. (*CSS*, 62)

Despite wishing to retaliate against 'the repeated daily massacre of herself before the time was ripe' (*CSS*, 62), Sybil submits to Désirée's version of the game – 'That's the rule' (*CSS*, 63) – just as, following her own husband's death after he is mauled by a lion, Sybil submits to playing her assigned part in Désirée's relationship with her husband, Barry: 'It was like a game for three players. According to the rules she was to be in love, unconsciously, with Barry, and tortured by the contemplation of Désirée's married bliss' (*CSS*, 75). Sybil had tried to get the Dobells to play without Désirée but they insisted 'you need four people for the game' (*CSS*, 63), and the adult players find the same when Barry's business manager, David Carter, is drawn into their 'magnetic field' (*CSS*, 71). Barry is suspicious of a relationship between David and Désirée but it is Sybil who has an affair with David, as though the women can simply substitute for one another. As in the film in which Désirée is mistaken for Sybil, which was 'shot' immediately after Sybil had ended the affair with David, David is confused by the similarity of the two women and, when he tries to take revenge on Sybil, kills Désirée with a handgun before shooting himself: 'David lingered a moment enough to roll his eyes in Sybil's direction as she rose from Désirée's body. He knows, thought Sybil quite lucidly, that he got the wrong woman' (*CSS*, 83). In that sentence the simplicity of 'got the wrong woman', as so often in Spark's writings, opens up a complex interplay of possibilities. He 'got' the wrong woman in his affair with Sybil because, in fact, she has little sexual appetite – 'I am not predominantly a sexual being' (*CSS*, 69) she tells herself – and having been saved by her husband's death from an unhappy marriage – 'It was plain to her that must have separated had he lived' (*CSS*, 66) – she does not want to be married again. The woman he should have 'got' was Désirée, both desiring and desired, but instead he 'got' her with the single shot that he intended for Sybil. In the game of life, Sybil lives next door to death: in their childhood games, Désirée used their proximity to play-act Sybil's killing many times but as Sybil watches the film of her earlier life, sent to her by

Barry a month before he died in action in North Africa, she is the only survivor of the game for four, still living next door to others' deaths.

Living next door to death is a theme played out with many variations in Spark's fiction: in *Robinson*, January Marlow survives an air crash only to find herself on an island whose owner, it later appears, has been murdered by one of her fellow survivors; in *Memento Mori*, Miss Taylor, confined to an old folks' home, insists that 'Being over seventy is like being engaged in a war. All our friends are gone and we survive amongst the dead and dying as on a battlefield' (*MM*, 34); in *The Ballad of Peckham Rye*, Dougal Douglas's disruption of the local community results in the murder of Merle Coverdale by her employer Mr Druce: 'He came towards her with the corkscrew and stabbed it into her long neck nine times and killed her. Then he took his hat and went home to his wife' (*BPR*, 193); in *The Hothouse by the East River*, Elsa – who has in fact been dead for more than twenty years – 'sits by the window, speaking to him against the purr of the airconditioner, but looking away – out across the East River as if he were standing in the air beyond the window pane' (*HER*, 5–6); in *The Girls of Slender Means*, the residents of the May of Teck Club are literally living next door to death since there is an unexploded, but undetected, German bomb in the garden of their building, which, when it goes off, leaves a group of girls trapped on the top floor, hoping for an escape through a bricked-up skylight; in *Symposium*, Margaret Murchie is so regularly in close vicinity to sudden deaths that people begin to fear she might be a witch: 'Margaret's capacity for being near the scene of tragedy was truly inexplicable in any reasonable terms' (*S*, 142); while in *The Abbess of Crewe*, Alexandra oversees the devotions of her nuns while seated in the chapel next to the last resting place of her predecessor, and, similarly, *Loitering with Intent* opens with Fleur seated 'in an old graveyard which had not yet been demolished' (*L*, 1). In one of Spark's last novels, *Aiding and Abetting*, the real Lord Lucan, on the run after having killed his nanny when he intended to kill his wife, has hired a double named Walker, whose deliberate appearances in different parts of the world are meant to confuse the authorities in their search for Lucan, except that, in the end, in Africa, the two are mistaken for each other, and the 'men clubbed him to death, only it wasn't Walker, it was Lucan' (*AA*, 181).

In Spark's fiction, life produces strange doubles who live next door to one another, whether physically, like Sybil and Désirée in 'Bang-Bang You're Dead', or psychologically, like Dougal Douglas and Douglas Dougal in *The Ballad of Peckham Rye*, or as a matter of deception, as in the case of Lucan and Walker, doubles whose defiance of the notion of a uniquely individual human being seems to attract death as the necessary re-establishment of the natural order. In other cases, Spark's characters live next door to death because the dead have not departed, as in the case of the short story 'The Executor' (*CSS*, 177), in which Susan's uncle, a famous author who left a manuscript incomplete at his death, writes messages for her in an empty notebook, chiding her for retaining the manuscript in the hope of profiting from it; or discover themselves to have passed unawares through that door, as in 'The Girl I Left behind Me' (*CSS*, 196), in which the narrator fears she has left something undone at work and returns to her office to discover her own strangled body on the floor; or, as in 'Portobello Road' (*CSS*, 35), in which the narrator is already dead when she accosts her murderer in a Saturday market. The door of death is a swing door which can be opened from the direction of life or from the direction of death. It is a doubleness enacted in *The Driver's Seat*, in which Lise has planned how she will die, and is, in effect, already looking at herself from beyond life, and merely in need of identifying the man who will be capable of killing her and whom, indeed, she finds sitting next to her on her plane that will fly her to meet that death. Lise travels next to the murderer who will make real the death she has already envisaged, needing only to find the man who can open that door for her.

Being next door to death is a condition that drives the action of many of Spark's plots as her characters seek by the rewriting of wills (like Lettie Colston, Lisa Brooke and Granny Barnacle in *Memento Mori*), or through blackmail (like Tom Wells in *Robinson* or Robert Leaver in *Territorial Rights*), or more directly by murder (like Patrick Seton in *The Bachelors* or Lord Lucan in *Aiding and Abetting*) to gain power over the events which will follow from their own or someone else's death. Many of Spark's plots are about those who plot to shape life to their own advantage when death comes knocking at the door. Such plotters seek to achieve, through their actions, the kind of control over events which an author has over her plot: in effect, they are trying to escape from the condition of being characters in someone else's plot to being the authors of their own plots, putting into question the ontological relation between author and character, between what happens in the time of the narrative and what causes or controls those happenings.

If, however, the characters who attempt, by their plots, to control the lives of those around them are evil, what then of the author who subjects all characters to the impositions of her own imaginings? Is the novelist a human being usurping the role of God, or someone faithfully representing a world whose ultimate cause is God? From the beginning of her career as a novelist, Spark's novels put at issue both the status of the novel as a representation of the world as it is experienced by human beings and the status of the author as a potentially demonic force transforming reality in her own image. Her plots allow competing ontological levels to intersect with each other in ways that disrupt the relations of past, present and future but also the relations of the natural and the supernatural. In *Robinson*, the three survivors of a plane crash on the isolated island called, like its owner, Robinson, discover that the man who has saved them has apparently been murdered. The central character and narrator, January Marlow, is confronted by having to decide between the possible causes of this death: has it been done by one of her fellow survivors – 'he has been killed by Jimmie or Tom Wells', or might it be a plot organised 'by both together'? (*R*, 111); Wells and Jimmie, however, have alternative explanations: Wells suggests that 'A supernatural force [. . .] had done away with Robinson, in revenge for some sacrilege done to the lucky charms which Robinson had confiscated' (*R*, 111–12), whereas Jimmie declares, 'Ah me! Man is born, he suffers, he dies' (*R*, 112), as if individual processes of causation are irrelevant to the final outcomes of existence. January is haunted by the problem of cause: when the boy to whom Robinson has given a home apparently disappears when January has gone to explore the island with him she is tormented by multiple alternative possibilities:

> I did not really think he could have jumped into the sea in the few moments that my eyes had been turned from him. I did not really think he would be so foolish. I was sure Miguel was somewhere safe but I was disturbed by having no reason for this certainty. For a moment I thought perhaps my other companions, too, had disappeared. I thought perhaps they had never existed, that Robinson and his household were a dead woman's dream, that I was indeed dead as my family believed and the newspapers had now reported. (*R*, 34)

Is the 'cause' of Miguel's disappearance *within* the framework of the events she is experiencing? Or is there some 'supernatural' cause at work that undermines her immediate experience, either a supernatural power on the island or the fact that she is, in fact, already dead and beyond the causality of ordinary existence? Her own Catholicism insists on the possibility of supernatural interventions, and while Tom Wells's supposedly magical trinkets are, to an ironic January, said to be 'vibrating with luck' (*R*, 59), they are to Robinson charged with 'evil properties' (*R*, 61) which can disrupt the future. When Robinson tears up the proofs of the next issue of Tom's newspaper *Your Future*, which offers its readers predictions of their futures, he is attempting to negate the 'proofs' of Tom's occult view of causation, to which Tom replies,

> There are countless methods of probing the mysteries of the universe. I number among my acquaintances distinguished psychometrists, clairvoyants, divine healers, astral radiesthetists, saliva prognosticators, and so on and so on. It's the quality of the medium that counts. I go in for quality. All my friends are of high esoteric quality. (*R*, 57)

Wells's publications proliferate with 'proofs' of alternative causations that allow the prediction of the future; Robinson's religion insists on the reality of an eternal evil which can also intervene in the events of time; the unpublished issue of *Your Future* poses the question, what is the appropriate *medium* for revealing the truth about the causes which shape the world? However, the cause of the medium in which we, as readers, encounter the story of Robinson, is given a different explanation when January notices in one of the adverts in Wells's newspaper an advertisement for the powers of

> MURIEL THE MARVEL with her X-ray eyes. *Can read your very soul.* Scores of satisfied clients. (*R*, 62)

and

> CONSULT BROTHER DEREK. Troubled? Anxious. Is that well-paid job just out of your reach? Write to Brother Derek. (*R*, 62)

Though January, within the text, regards Wells's newspaper as full of falsehood, it points truly, if ironically, towards the causal source of this text – Muriel-the-marvellous-Spark-of-insight who reads souls but anxiously looks for support from the co-author of her account of Emily Brontë, 'brother' Derek [Stanford]. Wells's 'proofs' open up a path to a transcendent reality even if it is not the reality that Wells is in search of. The doubtful assertions of Wells's fake beliefs point truly towards the causal origins of the book we are reading, but in doing so imply that the imagination which is the cause of the book may be no more trustworthy than the fake claims of *Your Future*. January's name suggests the Roman god of doorways, and the plane crash has opened, for January, many different doors into the nature and causes of the world in which she discovers herself.

It is in *Memento Mori*, however, a novel full of characters who are trying to control the consequences of their coming deaths, that Spark introduces her most surreal intersection between the world of time and material causation and the possible intervention in that world of the supernatural, an intervention which takes the form of repeated phone calls warning the characters, sometimes in a male voice, sometimes a female, sometimes by someone sounding young and sometimes old, that they should remember they 'must die', an announcement that is both distant – no one knows or can trace who is at the end of the telephone line or where the call has come from – and, at the same time, as close as the orifice of their own ear. Suspicion of secular causes – the calls may be organised by Dame Lettie Colston's estranged son Eric, working in collusion with the retired police detective Mortimer (*MM*, 193), or may form part of Alec Warner's 'research' into the effects of old age (*MM*, 68–9) – gives way to psychological possibilities – Warner himself queries whether the calls are a case of 'mass-hysteria' (*MM*, 152) – which in turn are displaced by supernatural explanations: Jean Taylor tells Dame Lettie that 'the author of the anonymous telephone calls is Death himself, as you might say [. . .] If you don't remember Death, Death reminds you to do so' (*MM*, 195). That Death should use the modern medium of the telephone to make the pronouncement that the listener ought to remember their own coming death gives the novel the surreal supernaturalism which is typical of many of Spark's narrative inventions – her first successful short story was, after all, about Samuel Cramer, 'who was going strong in Paris early in the nineteenth century, and when I met him in 1946 he was still going strong' (*CSS*, 85).

Spark's early fiction often operates on the boundary between the natural and the supernatural, but the notion of the supernatural telephone line had also appeared in an essay which self-consciously opposed any notion of supernatural intervention in human affairs, Jean-Paul Sartre's 'The Humanism of Existentialism' (1946), an essay which provocatively tried to harness existentialism to an atheism that saw the universe as 'absurd' in its lack of any significance except that given to it by human beings themselves. Existentialism was a word which had become fashionable in post-war Paris, but neither Sartre nor his lover and co-activist Simone de Beauvoir had regarded themselves as 'existentialists' during the war years. Even the publication of Sartre's *Being and Nothingness* of 1943 was seen, as its subtitle 'An Essay on Phenomenological Ontology' suggested, as a development of Husserl's phenomenological method rather than a contribution to an existential tradition in European thought. Existentialism in 1945 was viewed primarily as a Christian philosophy which had been developed in Germany by Karl Jaspers and in France by Gabriel Marcel. When Sartre and Beauvoir accepted the term 'existentialism' as a description of their philosophies, they set out to establish its atheistic rather than theistic credentials, and to insist that only an atheistic existentialism could address the fundamental condition of mankind in the second half of the twentieth century.[1] 'The Humanism of Existentialism' was Sartre's declaration that his own philosophy was indeed an existentialism – but an existentialism very different in tenor from the existentialism that had become the commonplace of current journalism and which meant that 'even the work of a musician or a painter is being called existentialist'.[2] For Sartre, existentialism required that 'man is nothing else but what he makes himself to be';[3] he is not pre-defined by nature or by God to fulfil a particular purpose or identity – his identity is what he becomes as a consequence of his own choices: 'there is no determinism, man is free, man is freedom'.[4] In the course of his exposition of existentialism, Sartre contrasts its insistence on freedom and on choice with traditional Judaeo-Christian accounts of faith as being unprovable and does so by comparing belief in supernatural interventions in human life to the experiences of someone who has lost their sanity:

> A certain mad woman who suffered from hallucinations said that people were telephoning to her, and giving her orders. The doctor asked, 'But who is it that speaks to you?' She replied: 'He says it is God.' And what, indeed, could prove to her that it was God? If

> an angel appears to me, what is the proof that it is an angel; or, if I hear voices, who can prove that they proceed from heaven and not from hell, or from my own subconsciousness or some pathological condition? Who can prove that they are really addressed to me?[5]

The supernatural phone call of Sartre's essay becomes a very real – if troublingly untraceable – phone call in Spark's novel. as though she has taken Sartre's sceptical denial of the possibility that God – or Death – might intervene in the temporal life of human beings to remind them of their own mortality, and turned it from a sceptical fantasy into a 'real' interaction between the eternal and the temporal. The atheistic existentialism for which divine intervention can be nothing but a fiction or a madness is turned inside-out to challenge the world of time with the demands of an eternity from which it seeks to conceal itself. The novel is, as it were, a gesture of resistance on behalf of Christian belief against its atheistic alternative, and an assertion of the ability of the eternal to intervene in the world of time. The importance of this brief passage in Sartre's essay to Spark's imaginative conception of the purposes of her own writing is underlined by the fact that the other two examples in Sartre's account of the absurdity of giving credence to the supernatural are both re-envisaged in Spark's early fiction as justifications for belief. Thus Sartre's 'angel' who, if it 'appears to me, what is the proof that it is an angel?', foretells Spark's first success as a writer, her story 'The Seraph and the Zambezi', in which the long-lived Cramer, whom 'Baudelaire wrote about' (*CSS*, 87), himself writes a Nativity Masque which attracts the apparently real presence of a heavenly Seraph who can travel 'at about seventy miles an hour and skimming the tarmac strips with two of his six wings in swift motion, two folded over his face, and two covering his feet' (*CSS*, 91). The eternal makes itself present in time in defiance of the sceptic's lack of 'proof that it is an angel'. Equally, the dubious voices which might 'proceed from heaven and not from hell, or from my own subconsciousness or some pathological condition' also prefigure the voices which haunt Caroline Rose in Spark's first novel, *The Comforters*: 'She feared it more; she feared that those sounds, so real that they seemed to have come from the other side of the wall, were hallucinations sent forth from her own mind' (*C*, 48). Sartre's challenge to the possibility of communication with a higher reality, his refusal to accept that there can be a message or messenger from the eternal, proleptically anticipates Spark's dramatisations of just such interventions into the world of time by the timeless.

The philosophical and theological source of Spark's opposition to Sartre's atheistic scepticism is revealed in the event which transforms Sybil's life in 'Bang-Bang You're Dead': trapped in a marriage in which she finds herself increasingly estranged from a husband who 'had ceased to evolve on the day he obtained his degree', she

> lay in bed in the mornings reading the translation of Kierkegaard's *Journals*, newly arrived from England in their first, revelatory month of publication. She felt like a desert which had not realized its own aridity till the rain began to fall upon it. (*CSS*, 66)

The transformation of the desert is itself an image taken from Kierkegaard's *Journal*, at a point when he declares that simply adding to his knowledge is not enough and that faith is quite different from knowledge:

> I certainly do not deny that I still recognise an *imperative of understanding* and that through it one can work upon men, *but it must be taken up into my life*, and *that is* what I now recognise as the most important thing. That is what my soul longs after, as the African desert thirsts for water. (*J*, '22', 15)

Sybil and Kierkegaard, one geographically and the other metaphorically, live in an African desert of the spirit, and Kierkegaard is, for Sybil, the water for which the desert thirsts. Equally, it is Kierkegaard's insistence on thinking every day about death which informs Jean Taylor's assertion in *Memento Mori* that 'If you don't remember Death, Death reminds you to do so' (*MM*, 195): in 1847, Kierkegaard noted in his *Journal* that, 'It is really not worth bothering oneself with men except with those who have given their life for something or at least have religious or desperate energy enough to think of death every day' (*J*, '677', 213). Kierkegaard, the non-philosopher who establishes a new way of philosophising which challenges existing Christianity and yet gives a new justification for faith, is, for Sybil, 'revelatory'. And this transformation is possible because Kierkegaard, too, lived next door to death: in a journal entry he imagines himself as 'a galley-slave, chained to death; every time life moves the chains rattle and death withers everything – *and that happens every minute*' (*J*, '136', 47). In part, this was because he expected, like several older members of his family, to die at the age of thirty-four, and was astounded when he reached his thirty-fifth birthday: 'It is quite incomprehensible to me; I was so sure of dying before or on that birthday that I am almost tempted to suppose that my birthday was incorrectly registered, and that I may still die on the 34th' (*J*, '655', 202). Not only did he live in the continual consciousness of death, but his response to it produced the kind of double life that is imaged not only in Sybil's relationship with Désirée but by many of Spark's characters – the Dougal Douglas become Douglas Dougal in *The Ballad of Peckham Rye*, or the female Jekyll and Hyde that is Margaret Murchie in *Symposium*: in Kierkegaard's case he spent his days obsessively writing out of his profound melancholy while, in the evenings, he disported himself in the social world 'incognito, as a *flâneur* [who] appeared to be lively and frivolous, wit itself: nobody could grasp its true seriousness' (*J*, '965', 332). Reading Kierkegaard allows Sybil, whose surname after her marriage is 'Greeves', to cease to grieve over her previous choices and to learn 'those arts of leading a double life and listening to people ambiguously, which enabled her to mix without losing identity, and to listen without boredom' (*CSS*, 69). Kierkegaard not only enhances her life – he allows her entry into a double life, a life both secularly sociable and, at the same time, profoundly spiritual.

As Sybil is haunted by the 'revelatory' discovery of Kierkegaard, so Kierkegaard haunts Spark's early fiction, her plots replicating aspects of Kierkegaard's life and writings. Her first novel, the enigmatically titled *The Comforters*, focuses on a recent Catholic convert, Caroline Rose, who suffers both from the judgements of the Catholics she has joined – who regard her as having 'a lot of the Protestant about you still' (*C*, 34) – and the values of the secular world, represented by her lover, Laurence Manders, who tries to maintain their relationship and their possible future together despite her desire to withdraw into a religious life. It is a situation which directly parallels the central event of Kierkegaard's life, his breaking-off of his engagement with Regine Olsen and his retreat from the possibilities of married life into a commitment to become a writer. Caroline's refusal to commit herself to Laurence and to the secular world is, to her acquaintances, as unreasonable and apparently self-destructive as Kierkegaard's rejection of his planned marriage to Regine Olsen:

> this terrible anxiety – as though at every moment I wished to convince myself whether or not it was possible to turn back to her, O God give me the courage. It is so hard, I had set my last hope in life upon her and I must deprive myself of it. How strange, I had never really thought of being married, but I never thought it would come to pass in this way, and leave so deep a wound behind. (*J*, '383', 99)

Caroline's 'voices' and the prophetic typewriter that foretells her inmost thoughts suggest that her life is the product of an author who is not herself and who is determined to punish her for her decision to choose religion rather than love and marriage; Kierkegaard, equally, was haunted by the life which he might have lived but which he had rejected, so that almost all of his writings in one way or another recapitulate his relationship with Regine, a relationship summarised by Walter Lowrie as 'an amazing love-story':

> It began idyllically with love at first sight – the first love, and for a girl who is only 14; three tormented years of waiting until she was approaching her 18th year; then (1) a sudden and successful wooing; (2) a lovers' quarrel, which was swiftly resolved (3) by her all too devoted attachment, while he perceives (4) that they must separate. He sends her back the ring; but (5) she fights like a lioness to retain him, beseeching him in the name of Christ and by the memory of his deceased father not to desert her, so that, to save her life and reason, the hero feels himself obliged to pretend that he is only a mean scoundrel who has been playing with her affections – and after two months of this cruel deceit (cruel most of all to himself) she lets him go.[6]

This is a story which Kierkegaard retells in a variety of ways in the works which flowed from his pen after he had given up the possibility of marriage: having chosen authorship over marriage his productivity in the following years – he published in 1843 no less than six volumes[7] – was testimony to the stimulus that his rejection of marriage – or his guilt over that rejection – gave to his creativity. Indeed, his first major publication, *Either/Or*, is a disquisition on the disadvantages and advantages of marriage that was read, in Copenhagen, as an autobiographical account of its author's 'betrayal' of his fiancée. That betrayal Kierkegaard himself found prefigured in a passage in Aristotle which he cites in *Fear and Trembling*, a passage about a bridegroom who '*suddenly changes his plan at the decisive moment when he comes to fetch the bride* – he will not celebrate the wedding' (*F&T*, 135), and it is an event which Spark makes central to the plot of *The Ballad of Peckham Rye*, in which Dougal Douglas tutors Humphrey – 'he was a sinister goggling bridegroom. "No," he declared to the ceiling, "I won't quite frankly"' (*BPR*, 158) – in how to refuse to commit to the marriage vows:

> There was Dixie come up to the altar with her wide flouncy dress and her nose, a little red from her cold, tilted towards the minister.
> 'Wilt thou have this woman to thy wedded wife?'
> 'No, to be frank,' Humphrey said, 'I won't.' (*BPR*, 200)

That Spark's 'nay-saying' bridegroom is one of many echoes of Kierkegaard's life and writings in her early novels is underlined by the fact that Kierkegaard's discussion of Aristotle is immediately followed by the story of a merman who is a seducer (*F&T*, 144), while Dougal's conversation with Humphrey is juxtaposed with a story of a 'lately caught and highly accomplished young mermaid' (*BPR*, 27) that Dougal has discovered in a history of Peckham.

If Kierkegaard was 'revelatory' for Sybil in 'Bang-Bang You're Dead', he seems to have been no less revelatory for the author of that story, his Christian existentialism being not only an antidote to Sartre's atheistic version but his life story revelatory of how the refusal of marriage could be the route to combining religion and authorship. The 'revelatory' Kierkegaard pointed the way to an individual and existential religious experience which 'cannot be simply summed up in general terms' but which also explains the relationship of the different Christian traditions Spark had inherited from her Edinburgh Presbyterian education and her profound engagement both with T. S. Eliot's Anglo-Catholicism (her review of Eliot's *The Confidential Clerk* was 'so good that Eliot himself was astonished'[8]) and with Cardinal Newman's conversion to Catholicism (together with Stanford she edited the *Letters of John Henry Newman*, published in 1957). For Kierkegaard there is a mutual dependence between Protestantism and Catholicism that makes it impossible to choose one and dismiss the other: 'Are not Catholicism and Protestantism,' he asks, 'related to each other like – it may seem extraordinary but it is really so physically – like a building which cannot stand, to a buttress which cannot stand alone, whereas the whole is even very firm and secure, so long as they keep together, the building and the buttress which supports it' (*J*, '1327', 509). Catholicism and Protestantism form a dialectic in which each is in need of the other: the lack of such a dialectic will prove to be the undoing of Jean Brodie:

> she was by temperament suited only to the Roman Catholic Church; possibly it could have embraced, even while it disciplined, her soaring and diving spirit, it might have normalized her. But perhaps this was the reason she shunned it, lover of Italy though she was, bringing to her support a rigid Edinburgh-born side of herself when the Catholic Church was in question. (*PJB*, 112–13)

Spark's Catholicism, like Kierkegaard's continued commitment to the Lutheran church, is not so much an answer to life's dilemmas as it is the particular medium through which an existential discovery of faith can find institutional expression. Nevertheless, instituted Christianity was for Kierkegaard, 'a scandal' (*J*, '820', 264), and it is presented as such in many of Spark's novels – in *The Prime of Miss Jean Brodie* we are told that Sandy, on entering the Catholic Church, 'had found quite a number of Fascists much less agreeable than Miss Brodie' (*PJB*, 168); in *The Abbess of Crewe* we are told of the nuns in the Abbey that 'a less edifying crowd of human life it would have been difficult to find; either they have become so or they always were so; at any rate, they are in fact a very poor lot, all the more since they do not think so for a moment' (*AC*, 61); and in *Symposium* Margaret Murchie discovers 'that of those nine nuns of St Pancras only three were of vital interest, and that those three were fairly unprincipled. The remaining six were devout and dutiful, and two of them very sweet and trusting, but all those six were dreary as hell' (*S*, 103).

Equally telling about Spark's attitude to the *institution* of Roman Catholicism is her attack on the papacy for the way it treated Golda Meir on her visit to the Vatican in 1973, in which Spark makes no bones about the difference between Catholic belief and Catholic hierarchy:

> It was probably unnecessary to ask, once more, if he thought the Pope had spoken for the whole of Christianity. However, this Scottish Churchman drily replied, 'The Pope speaks only for the Roman Catholics.'

> And not always for the Roman Catholics. In Rome the people like to do things in style. The natural Italian sense of hospitality was afflicted by what went on behind the high sheltering walls of the Vatican. Whatever their feelings about the Middle East, Italians felt the incident set a poor example in ethics and taste. 'She would never have been treated like that if she had gone to visit King Hussein,' was one of their more memorable remarks. (*GF*, 210–11)

To be committed to an institutional religion is not the same as finding religious fulfilment in it, since the ultimate religious fulfilment comes, according to Kierkegaard, from rising beyond the institutional structures of religion to an individual relationship between the self and God. This is the underlying irony of *The Abbess of Crewe*, for the Abbess is in post to run a Catholic institution but she asserts her preference for Sextus Propertius over St Francis of Assisi because he, too, not only belonged to Assisi but 'was a contemporary of Jesus and a spiritual forerunner of Hamlet, Werther, Rousseau and Kierkegaard' (*AC*, 49). The institution is not enough for the achievement of a truly Christian faith – one has to go beyond it, one has to defy it, one has to become the Kierkegaardian 'individual' whose aim is to 'make men (the Christians) into Christians' (*J*, '723', 228). Indeed, far from making her Catholic characters mouthpieces for her own Catholicism, Spark uses them – as Kierkegaard used the Lutheran pastors of his own Danish community – as examples of how fallen is the established Christianity in the contemporary world. Caroline Rose's experiences of her fellow Catholics – 'The wonderful thing about being a Catholic is that it makes life so easy. Everything easy for salvation and you can have a happy life' (*C*, 43) – underline her Kierkegaardian commitment to faith as a 'trial' rather than a consolation:

> Caroline thought, 'The demands of the Christian religion are exorbitant, they are outrageous. Christians who don't realize that from the start are not faithful. They are dishonest; and their teachers are talking in their sleep . . .' (*C*, 42)

It is a thought which precisely echoes Kierkegaard:

> Christianity has been made much too much into a *consolation*, people have forgotten that it is a *demand*. Alas, the vapid speakers! The result is that it falls all the harder on those who have to proclaim Christianity again. (*J*, '999', 347)

To proclaim Christianity is to acknowledge that most of those who already claim to be Christian have failed to recognise the *demand* that it makes on belief and on the believer. They can only become truly Christian when, like Barbara in *The Mandelbaum Gate*, they are prepared to undergo the 'trial' of their faith:

> 'Well, either religious faith penetrates everything in life or it doesn't. There are some experiences that seem to make nonsense of all separations of sacred from profane – they seem childish. Either the whole of life is unified under God or everything falls apart.' (*MG*, 307–8)

The echoes of Kierkegaard's *Either/Or* in these sentences – '*either* religious penetrates every in life *or* it doesn't . . . *Either* the whole of life is unified under God *or* . . .' – is symptomatic of the paradox in which Barbara is caught: she cannot *not* be a Jew (it is her blood) and cannot *not* be a Christian (it is her faith), with the result that reason and rational reflection are incapable of providing a decision for her predicament, an indecision that Kierkegaard saw as necessary prelude to the discovery – or recovery – of faith:

> I, a rational being, must act in a case where my reason, my powers of reflection, tell me: you can just as well do one thing as the other, that is to say where my reason, my powers of reflection tell me [. . .] you cannot act – and yet here is where I have to act. But that is the case every time I have to act really decisively: because I am then caught up in an infinite passion, and that is just where the incongruity between action and reflection becomes evident. In the routine of everyday I do not notice the secret of reflection, and so imagine that I am acting upon reflection in spite of the fact that nothing is more impossible – because reflection is the equilibrium of possibilities.
>
> The absurd, or to act by virtue of the absurd, is to act upon faith, trusting in God. It is perfectly simple. I must act, but reflection has closed the road, so I take one of the possibilities and turn to God saying: This is what I do, bless my actions. (*J*, '871', 291)

Barbara's actions – entering Jordan to see the holy sites, trusting herself to Suzi Mendez, whose father is an informer to more than one government, and disguising herself as a Muslim servant – are absurd, but they assert that she acts 'upon faith, trusting in God', a trust which will, in the end, be justified.

Kierkegaard's conception of faith was premised on his profound opposition to any philosophy – and here he thought principally of Hegel's 'system' – which failed to acknowledge that all philosophical or theological thought is the product of a living being for whom knowledge of the universe must be knowledge from a particular place and from a particular time, a particularity which makes impossible any kind systematic knowledge of the world that could claim the status of a universal truth.

> A system of existence [*Tilværelsens System*] cannot be given. Is there, then, no such system? That is not at all the case. Neither is this implied in what has been said. Existence itself is a system – for God, but it cannot be a system for any existing [*existerende*] spirit. System and conclusiveness correspond to each other, but existence is the very opposite. Abstractly viewed, system and existence cannot be thought conjointly, because in order to think existence, systematic thought must think it annulled and consequently not as existing. Existence is the spacing that holds apart, the systematic is the conclusiveness that combines. (*CUP*, 118)

Existence is that which cannot be incorporated into a system. In the Hegelian system contradictions are overcome by the process of mediation in which a thesis and its antithesis are transformed into a synthesis which resolves the contradiction in new unity. Such a resolution is to Kierkegaard, however, the destruction of both the thesis and its antithesis, and when applied to human beings requires the effective erasure of the individual, whose meaning is not founded in the fact of his or her own existence but in the part they play in the higher order system to which they contribute. For Kierkegaard, thesis and antithesis are unresolvable; they are contradictions which must be lived through and lived with, and Christian faith is precisely such an unresolvable contradiction because it involves what no other religion proposes, that 'The eternal truth has come into existence in time' (*CUP*, 209). This unresolvable contradiction – how can the eternal *be* in time? – is the 'paradox' (*CUP*, 209) on which Christianity is founded: 'that the eternal truth has come into existence in time, that God has come into existence, has been born, has grown up, etc. has come into existence exactly as an individual human being, indistinguishable from any other human being' (*CUP*, 210). It is a paradox which is repeated in every act of Christian belief, for 'When the eternal truth relates itself to an existing person it becomes the paradox' (*CUP*, 209). The most universal truth becomes a 'paradox' when it can only come into existence through an individually existing, time-determined human being – a fact ignored by Hegelian systematisers who must forget that their system was produced by an actual, living, existent human being. It is this paradox which makes a rational account of faith impossible: it is absurd and one can only reach it by a leap beyond reason, a leap to a faith which can only be known existentially in the experience of the believer.

To situate the paradox of existential faith in relation to the ordinary existence of human communities, Kierkegaard divides human experience into three categories or stages – the aesthetic, the ethical and the religious. The 'aesthetic' is the immersion in the everyday, the realm of immediate sensation in which 'the judgment of the world is not *moral* at all (naturally not, or it would not be the world) but *aesthetic*: admires everything that has power, cunning, selfishness – and luck, *i.e.* so that it wins money, honour, respect' (*J*, '1081', 385); 'the aesthetic' is countered by the 'ethical', which encourages human beings to live their lives in the light of universal truths applicable to everyone, and therefore in relation to God as the source of such universal truths. The ethical, however, has its limitations:

> The ethical is the universal and as such, it is again the divine. One has therefore a right to say that fundamentally every duty is a duty toward God; but if one cannot say more, then one affirms at the same time that properly I have no duty toward God. Duty becomes duty by being referred to God, but in duty itself I do not come into relation with God. Thus it is a duty to love one's neighbour: but in performing this duty I do not come into relation with God but with the neighbour whom I love. (*F&T*, 102)

To enter into a relation with God is to pass from the ethical into the religious, into faith, which will often, as in the case of Abraham when instructed to sacrifice Isaac, result in a contradiction between the requirements of the ethical – fathers should not murder their children – and the requirements of faith – one should obey God. For Kierkegaard, this is not a resolvable dialectic of the Hegelian kind: it is an unresolvable contradiction to which only faith can give an answer – a faith which defies the universal in its commitment to the individual's relationship to God:

> The paradox of faith is this, that the individual is higher than the universal, that the individual (to recall a dogmatic distinction now rather seldom heard) determines his relation to the universal by his relation to the absolute, not his relation to the absolute by his relation to the universal. (*F&T*, 105)

Faith is above and beyond the ethical; it transcends the ethical, and Abraham is the symbol of faith precisely because his faith was justified by the outcome when God offers an alternative sacrifice; otherwise Abraham would simply have been a murderer: 'So either there is a paradox, that the individual stands in an absolute relation to the absolute/or Abraham is lost' (*F&T*, 187). To Jean-Paul Sartre, the figure of Abraham symbolises delusion, as in the case of the mad woman who takes telephone calls from God:

> You know the story: An angel commanded Abraham to sacrifice his son; and obedience was obligatory, if it really was an angel who had appeared and said, 'Thou, Abraham, shalt sacrifice thy son.' But anyone in such a case would wonder, first, whether it was indeed an angel and secondly, whether I am really Abraham. Where are the proofs?[9]

But, for Kierkegaard, Abraham symbolises the ultimate paradox of religion, in that to discover faith we have to rise above the demands of the apparent universality of the ethical and to stand alone with God:

> Now we reach the paradox. Either the individual as individual is able to stand in an absolute relation to the absolute (and then the ethical is not the highest)/or Abraham is lost – he is neither a tragic hero, nor an aesthetic hero. (*F&T*, 175)

For Kierkegaard, Abraham represents a dialectic between the ethical and the individual in which the individual reveals itself as superior to the ethical: Sartre may ask 'where are the proofs?' but this is to remain within the ambit of the ethical as the application of universalisable judgements; indeed, Sartre is insufficiently *existential* in Kierkegaard's terms because there are no proofs, there can be no proofs, there is only the lived experience of choice that creates a directly personal relationship to God. Abraham is the symbol of a religious consciousness in which we have to rise beyond universal judgements to make ourselves truly 'individual' determiners of our own fate through our personal relationship with God. To become 'the individual' requires that one be 'alone, alone in the whole world, alone – before God: then it will be easy to obey', because 'ultimately all doubt has its stronghold in the illusions of temporal existence' (*J*, '723', 228). Kierkegaard's 'existentialism' rests on the individual's ability to defy incorporation into pseudo-universal systems or, when necessary, to resist conforming to apparently universal truths – including Christian truths – in order to establish a purely personal relationship with God.

Kierkegaard's influence on Spark can be traced in early stories such as 'The House of the Famous Poet' (1952), in which a real event in Spark's life – the fact that she spent a night in the house of Louis MacNeice – is incorporated into a story about a chance encounter during an overnight train journey with a girl called Elise, who turns out to be the servant in the house of the famous poet, but also with a strange soldier who offers them both cigarettes:

> This was a private soldier who was awake to a greater degree than most people are when they are not sleeping. He was smoking cigarettes one after the other with long, calm puffs. I thought he looked excessively evil – an atavistic type. His forehead must have been less than two inches high above dark, thick eyebrows, which met. His jaw was not large, but it was apelike: so was his small nose and so were his deep, close-set eyes. I thought there must have been some consanguinity in the parents. He was quite a throwback. (*CSS*, 297)

An apparently threatening version of Stevenson's Mr Hyde, this 'throwback' turns out not to be the threat that his appearance suggests, but to be 'extremely gentle and kind' (*CSS*, 237). Nonetheless, he is a real threat of a very different kind for, despite his seeming physicality, he is a ghostly apparition – 'I'm only a notion of myself' (*CSS*, 244) – whose business, like the supernatural phone caller in *Memento Mori*, is to remind people of their coming death and to sell them in advance an 'an abstract funeral' (*CSS*, 242), a funeral which, like death in Kierkegaard's account of the Hegelian system, has no reality – it is simply 'the idea of a funeral' (*CSS*, 243). The narrator is persuaded to purchase this bulky piece of paperwork, only then to realise that it is not an abstract funeral but 'a real funeral I want' (*CSS*, 244). The soldier points out, however, that her funeral cannot ever be 'real' to her, since it cannot be a part of her experience:

> 'Your own funeral?' he said. 'You want to write it up?
> 'Yes,' I said.
> 'But,' said he. 'you're only human. Nobody reports on their own funeral. It's got to be abstract.' (*CSS*, 244)

You may get a telephone call to remind you that you should reflect on your coming death but that death will be incommunicable: it is speechless. When the narrator of 'The House of the Famous Poet' phones to thank the servant who put her up for the night what she hears is 'the high, long hoot which means that the telephone at the other end is not functioning' (*CSS*, 244), and it is not functioning because the house has been demolished by 'a flying bomb' that has killed both its owner, the famous poet, and his servant, both previous purchasers, it turns out, of the ghostly soldier's 'abstract funeral' – 'No complaints. It was just what he wanted – the idea of a funeral' (*CSS*, 243). Spark's story adopts Kierkegaard's existential challenge to the abstraction of philosophical system-makers to insist that one's death cannot be an idea that will play its part in some grand scheme of reality: 'In the summer of 1944 a great many people were harshly and suddenly killed' (*CSS*, 244). One lives, of necessity, next door to death because one can never live through it.

Notes

1. It was Beauvoir who had first 'discovered' and been influenced by Kierkegaard's existentialism; see Ronald M. Green and Mary Jean Green, 'Simone de Beauvoir: A Founding Feminist's Appreciation of Kierkegaard', in Jon Stewart (ed.), *Kierkegaard and Existentialism* (Farnham, Surrey: Ashgate, 2011), 1–22.

2. Jean-Paul Sartre, 'The Humanism of Existentialism', trans. Bernard Frechtman, from 'L'Existentialisme est un humanisme' (1947), in Wade Baskin (ed.), *Jean-Paul Sartre: Essays in Existentialism* (New York: Citadel Press, 1965), 33.
3. Ibid. 36.
4. Ibid. 41.
5. Ibid. 38–9.
6. Walter Lowrie, *Kierkegaard* (London: Oxford University Press, 1938), 192.
7. See 'Historical Introduction', in Søren Kierkegaard, *Stages on Life's Way: Studies by Various Persons*, ed. and trans. Howard V. Hong and Edna N. Hong (Princeton: Princeton University Press, 1988), xiii–xiv.
8. Martin Stannard, *Muriel Spark: The Biography* (London: Weidenfeld & Nicolson, 2009), 145.
9. Sartre, 'The Humanism of Existentialism', 39.

Chapter 2

Resisting Realism

Sartre's 'The Humanism of Existentialism', the text of a lecture he gave in 1945,[1] did not provide an existentialist account of art or of literature, but it did use art and literature as a means of establishing what is distinctive about existentialism's approach to the human condition. If man 'is condemned every moment to invent man',[2] then man is himself like a work of art, something created, and the artist is thus an appropriate analogy for the man who makes himself, for in creating a work of art,

> It is clearly understood that there is no definite painting to be made, that the artist is engaged in the making of his painting, and that the painting to be made is precisely the painting he will have made. It is clearly understood that there are no *a priori* aesthetic values, but that there are values which appear subsequently in the coherence of the painting, in the correspondence between what the artist intended and the result. Nobody can tell what the painting of tomorrow will be like. Painting can only be judged after it has once been made.[3]

This reciprocity between existentialism and art was to be developed into a full-scale theory of literature with the publication of *Qu'est-ce que la littérature* (*What is Literature?*) in 1947.[4] Sartre, like Spark, was a late developer as a writer, at least in terms of published work, but by 1947 his reputation as one of the leading writers of the age had been consolidated by the publication of the first two volumes of *Roads to Freedom*, what was intended to be a four-volume account of the French experience of the Second World War, and of the search for personal and political freedom in the context of military defeat and totalitarian ideologies. For Sartre, the freedom which existentialism proposes as being central to the fact of being human has to be equally central to literature – literature can exist only in and through the freedom of the writer and the reader:

> For, since the one who writes recognizes, by the very fact that he takes the trouble to write, the freedom of his readers, and since the one who reads, by the mere fact of his opening the book, recognizes the freedom of the writer, the work of art, from whichever side you approach it, is an act of confidence in the freedom of men. And since readers, like the author, recognize this freedom only to demand that it manifest itself, the work can be defined as an imaginary presentation of the world insofar as it demands human freedom. (*WIL*, 63)

For Sartre, freedom is both the necessary condition of literature and a demand that is made upon the writer – writing must be undertaken in order to extend and maximise personal and political freedom. The necessity underpinning this relationship Sartre ascribes to the fact that language is a tool for transforming the world, and the writer has to be 'engaged' in that transformation: 'The "engaged" writer knows that words are action. He knows that to reveal is to change and that one can reveal only by planning to change' (*WIL*, 23). The urgency of asserting the need for political engagement among writers rises from the fact that there is a particular class of writers and a particular tradition of writing which refuses to make use of this potential of language – poets, who deploy language as though it were paint or music:

> Notes, colours, and forms are not signs. They refer to nothing exterior to themselves. To be sure, it is quite impossible to reduce them strictly to themselves, and the idea of a pure sound, for example, is an abstraction. As Merleau-Ponty has pointed out in *The Phenomenology of Perception*, there is no quality of sensation so bare that it is not penetrated with signification. But the dim little meaning which dwells within it, a light joy, a timid sadness, remains immanent or trembles about it like a heat mist [. . .] (*WIL*, 7)

The poet is someone working with language but refusing to make use of its fundamental purpose: poetry 'uses words as does prose [. . .] but it does not use them in same way':

> Poets are men who refuse to utilize language. Now, since the quest for truth takes place in and by language conceived as a certain kind of instrument, it is unnecessary to imagine that they aim to discern

> or expound the true. Nor do they dream of naming the world, and, this being the case, they name nothing at all, for naming implies a perpetual sacrifice of the name to the object named [. . .] (*WIL*, 12)

The purpose of language is to name, identify and consequently allow us to change the world; the poet, on the other hand, 'has withdrawn from language-instrument in a single movement. Once and for all he has chosen the poetic attitude which considers words as things and not as signs' (*WIL*, 12). Sartre's aesthetic theory privileges the novel over poetry and privileges the realist novel over all other kinds of writing as the one most capable of *engaging* with and thus changing the world. Indeed, Sartre had first come to prominence by challenging what he saw as François Mauriac's failure to fulfil the requirements of the realist novel by using authorial omniscience as a means of commenting on and summarising the nature of his characters and prefiguring their futures. The novelist must never, Sartre argued, seem to know more than his characters: 'the theory of relativity', he argued, 'is wholly applicable to the world of the novel, and that, in a real novel, as in the universe of Einstein, there is no place for a privileged observer'.[5] This first rule of the world of the novel had been undermined by the influence of poetry: 'If the contamination of a certain kind of prose by poetry had not confused the ideas of our critics, would they dream of attacking us on the matter of form, when we have never spoken of anything but the content?' (*WIL*, 26). There is, however, a paradox at the heart of Sartre's view of the novel as founded upon and as an augmentation of human freedom: if a character must seem to be free in order for the reader, out of his or her own freedom, to identify with that character – to project, as it were, the reader's freedom on to the character – nonetheless it is impossible for characters in novels ever to make 'authentic' choices because they exist in a medium over which the novelist has absolute control; characters in a novel perform the roles assigned to them by the choice of the novelist rather than by their own choices. If the world were actually structured like a novel, each of us would live in a predetermined narrative where all of our choices and their subsequent consequences had already been planned in advance by the God who rules over that world: the freedom of choice upon which existentialism insists is effectively unrepresentable in the literary form which Sartre claims to be a primary proof of our freedom, for choice, at the level of the characters represented, is alien to the very nature of the medium in which the world of the novel is constructed. The novel, as Sartre conceives it, is subject to the same paradox that Sandy Stranger finds in Jean Brodie: 'She thinks she is Providence, thought Sandy, she sees the beginning and the end' (*PJB*, 161). The medium of the novel, in which the end is already there, waiting for us, as we read, cannot be a representation of our world if our world is indeed a world of freedom and choice. Characters can be represented as making choices – the choice of a life partner is, after all, at the crux of most romances – but the character has no freedom over a choice that has already been determined in advance by the author. In the final chapter of the first book of Sartre's trilogy *Roads to Freedom*, Mathieu discovers in his isolation that the breaking of his relationship with Marcelle has not set him free:

> 'I remain alone.' Alone but no freer than before. He had said to himself last evening: 'If only Marcelle did not exist.' But in so saying he deceived himself. 'No one has interfered with my freedom; my life has drained it dry.'[6]

As a character, Mathieu has failed to fulfil the freedom with which he was endowed by the very fact of being human, but as a 'character-in-a-novel' his freedom has been 'interfered with' from the beginning: his psychological sense of having lost his freedom corresponds to his ontological reality – as a 'character-in-a-novel' he may be a representation of a free human being but it is a representation which lacks, precisely, the category of freedom, of *being* free.

It is this paradox into which Caroline Rose falls in *The Comforters*: instead of being the author of a critical book on *Form in the Modern Novel*, she has become the medium – as though she were the vehicle of a supernatural power – through which an external agency is writing her life with a clear knowledge of her future: she tells her priest,

> 'It's exactly as if someone were watching me closely, able to read my thoughts; it's as if the person is waiting to pounce on some insignificant thought or action, in order to make it signify in a strange and distorted way. And how does it know about Laurence and my friends? And then there was the strange coincidence the other day. Laurence and I sent each other a wire with exactly the same words, at the same time. It was horrifying. Like predestination.' (C, 68–9)

Caroline's horror at having been reduced to a character in a novel is mirrored in her sudden awareness of the character of her friend Eleanor, whose 'fascination' to Caroline is 'her entire submersion in whatever role she had to play' (*C*, 95). Eleanor lives her life as a series of fictional characters: 'There did not seem to be any question of Eleanor's choosing her part, it was forced on her, she was enslaved by it' (*C*, 95). The existential freedom which characterises human beings for Sartre has, for Eleanor, been transformed by a necessity of the kind that governs characters in a novel – she lives as though performing in a script:

> She would change her personality like dresses according to occasion, and it had been fun to watch [. . .] But she had lost her small portion of detachment: now, to watch her was like watching doom. As a child Caroline, pulling a face, had been warned, 'If you keep doing that it will stick one day.' She felt, looking at Eleanor, that this was actually happening to the woman. Her assumed personalities were beginning to cling: soon one of them would stick, grotesque and ineradicable. (*C*, 95–6)

Eleanor's various personalities have the appearance of being choices, assertions of freedom, but in fact they have become a 'doom' that will deprive her of the possibility of freedom, trapped forever in one of her inauthentic poses. Caroline's understanding of Eleanor is in part, however, the product of a hyper-sensitivity produced by her own disturbed state of mind, in which she has come to believe her 'theory about the author making a book out of their lives' (*C*, 103), an author who has already predetermined the future of Caroline and her friends. The chanting voices that she hears announce that Caroline and Laurence will travel '*. . . next day by car, though Laurence's M.G. was due for repair, instead of going by train. This was owing to their getting up late and frittering the day in talk, first about poor Eleanor, as they agreed she was, then about themselves*' (*C*, 102). The following afternoon she discovers that she and Laurence have done exactly what the voices predicted, 'chatted about Eleanor', 'about themselves', 'frittered the day' and she therefore declares 'we must go by train' because 'it's a matter of asserting free will' (*C*, 107). Only by defying the omniscient narrator for whom she has become a medium of communication about her future can she assert her freedom as a human being, but that defiance fails because of the duties of a religious observance – it is All Saints' Day and she must attend Mass (*C*, 109) – so that she and Laurence do indeed travel by car, and during the journey she provides an analysis of what she believes to be Laurence's condition:

> It's clear that you are getting these ideas into your head through the influence of a novelist, who is contriving some phoney plot. I can see clearly that your mind is working under the pressure of someone else's necessity, and under the suggestive power of some irresponsible writer you are allowing yourself to become an amateur sleuth in a cheap mystery piece. (*C*, 113–14)

Of course, Caroline is right – they *are* characters in a narrative in which 'there's an attempt being made to organize our lives into a convenient slick plot' (*C*, 114), an irony underlined when Willi Stock provides his analysis of Caroline's condition:

> 'I told you of her experience with the voices and the typewriter. Now she has developed the idea that these voices represent the thoughts of a disembodied novelist, if you follow, who is writing a book on his typewriter. Caroline is apparently a character in this book and so, my dears, am I.' (*C*, 177–8)

To the reader of the novel, however, Willi has simply spoken the truth – he is nothing more than 'a character in this book', typed into existence by the author of the novel in which he appears. Indeed, his surname is 'Stock' and he is a stock character, 'one of a type' in both senses of that word: 'I know your type', Mrs Hogg tells Caroline (*C*, 34). As the letters on the typewriter reduce the multiplicity of the sounds of people's voices to a uniform and restricted set of characters, so the multiplicity of human experience is reduced by plot – Caroline 'said a good deal more against the plot (*C*, 116) – to a set of 'types', like the case notes that Alec Warner is keeping in *Memento Mori*, and which translate his friends into 'characters' – 'Thus, Charmian was, in the second set of cards, "Gladys"' (*MM*, 61) – who become, as a result of the 'neat network of codes and numbers relating to various passages in the books around the walls, on the subjects of gerontology and senescence' (*MM*, 61), simply illustrations of general patterns of bodily decay. So, too, the old women in the Maud Long Medical Ward in *Memento Mori* are universally addressed as 'Granny', the individuality of their earlier lives worn down into the sameness of age. Spark's early novels, in defiance of Sartre's efforts to represent freedom, continually underline not only that her characters are not free but that they are what they appear to be, the products of artifice.

Spark's novels thus defiantly refuse Sartre's existential insistence on the representational virtues of novelistic realism in order to insist, like Robert Louis Stevenson in his debate with Henry James, on the distance between art and reality:

> Life is monstrous, infinite, illogical, abrupt and poignant; a work of art, in comparison, is neat, finite, self-contained, rational, flowing and emasculate. Life imposes by brute energy, like inarticulate thunder; art catches the ear, among the far louder noises of experience, like an air artificially made by a discreet musician. A proposition of geometry does not compete with life; and a proposition of geometry is a fair and luminous parallel for a work of art. Both are reasonable, both untrue to crude fact; both inhere in nature, neither represents it.[7]

Far from trying to fulfil an art which 'represents' the real, Spark constructs her plots as parodies of various existing types of novel in order to underline their inherent artificiality. In *The Comforters*, for instance, the plot develops through a complicated series of improbable interconnections between the characters – Eleanor has been married to Mervin Hogarth who was previously married to Mrs Hogg but, because of her Catholicism, they have never been divorced; Mervyn and Mrs Hogg's crippled son are smuggling diamonds in the plaster statues of saints acquired on trips to various Catholic shrines on the Continent in search of a cure for him; the diamonds are then transferred by Mr Webster the baker, hidden in loaves of bread, to Laurence's grandmother, Louisa Jepp – who, in a mocking irony of fiction's use of names to define characters, lives in a house named 'Smuggler's Retreat' – and from there the diamonds are distributed to Willi Stock concealed in tins of home-made food. As Caroline insists to Laurence, 'Your grandmother being a gangster, it's taking things too far. She's an implausible character' (*C*, 115). A reader of Kierkegaard's *Journals* would, however, know that in the modern world,

> one must live, and live in style. And so one has arranged one's life. For example, secretly one is the leader of a little gang of thieves, to which one gives up a certain amount of time, secretly directing its affairs and from which one gets 30 to 50 per cent of the swag. There is really nothing else to do . . . (*J*, '1201', 434)

The 'implausibility' of the plot of *The Comforters* is compounded by what appears to be a miracle, when Hogarth's son seems to have been cured at a Roman Catholic shrine, a miraculous intervention in the world of causality which is repeated by his mother's apparent disappearance out of the body of the text, for when she 'stepped into her room, she disappeared, she simply disappeared', because 'she had no private life whatever' (*C*, 156). Her private life cannot be articulated in the text and so she ceases to exist: asleep in the back of Helena's car, Mrs Hogg drops out of existence:

> '[. . .] And when I turned to reach for the matches, I couldn't see Georgina.'
>
> 'Why, what had happened?'
>
> 'She simply wasn't there,' Helena declared. 'I said to Willi, "Heavens where's Georgina?" and Willi said, "My God! She's gone!" Well, just as he said this, we saw Georgina again. She suddenly appeared before our eyes, sitting in the same position and blinking, as if she'd just woken up. It was as if there's been a black-out at the films. (*C*, 185)

The mechanism of the realist novel, like the snapping of a reel of film, has broken down: the characters act in a world where the supernatural is as 'real' as the natural, thus defying the limits of the traditional realism at which Caroline, in her book on the modern novel, has got into difficulty: Caroline has been turned from being a character in a novel to being the medium through which an author on another, transcendent, level of being is shaping her life. As Gabriel Marcel, the Christian existentialist, put it in his challenge to the Sartrean version of existentialism in *The Philosophy of Existence* (1948),

> I would suggest in conclusion that existentialism stands to-day at a parting of the ways: it is, in the last analysis, obliged either to deny or to transcend itself. It denies itself quite simply when it falls to the level of infra-dialectical materialism. It transcends itself, or it tends to transcend itself, when it opens itself out to the experience of the

> supra-human, an experience which can hardly be ours in a genuine and lasting way this side of death, but of which the reality is attested by mystics, and of which the possibility is warranted by any philosophy which refuses to be immured in the postulate of absolute immanence or to subscribe in advance to the denial of the beyond and of the unique and veritable transcendence. Not that there is anything in this which, in our itinerant condition, we can invest like capital; this absolute life can be apprehended by us only in flashes and by virtue of a hidden initiative which can be nothing other than grace.[8]

The structure of *The Comforters* allows Caroline to 'voice' a transcendent reality (the supra-human novelist beyond the novel) as she attempts to realise in her own life the act of transcendence made possible by her new-found faith. Her fear of the transcendent novelist is the retroactive effect of her fear of the supra-human transcendence to which her faith has committed her. In the kind of Christian existentialism presented by Gabriel Marcel, the intervention of the supra-human is the guarantee that we live in world where 'grace' is as real as a car crash; it is a world that a novel can only imitate by pointing to the limitations of its own medium, just as faith must acknowledge the limitations of a fallen world in which grandmothers can be leaders of gangs amassing material comforts. *The Comforters* is aimed at breaking open the closed world of realism in order to reveal the possibility of a 'unique and veritable transcendence', one that is the true basis of our freedom in the world. Marcel, who had converted to Catholicism in 1928, accused Sartre of the 'the systematic vilification of man', which might 'seem to be a paradox, for does not Sartre ceaselessly exalt man and his freedom in the face of the radical absurdity of the universe?'; but, Marcel suggests, 'etymologically, to vilify a thing is to take away its value, its price. This can be done in the case of merchandise by flooding the market, and this just what Sartre does to freedom: he debases it by putting it on every stall.'[9] Real freedom requires the possibility of a real encounter with transcendence; as Marcel puts it in *The Mystery of Being*, 'not only does the word "transcendent" *not* mean "transcending experience", but on the contrary there must exist a possibility of having an experience *of* the transcendent, and unless that possibility exists the word can have no meaning.'[10] Caroline's religious conversion offers her access to transcendence (however problematic in its Kierkegaardian 'trial') but it is also her – and her author's – access to a transcendence of the limits of the realist novel.

The realisation of transcendence, however, also requires that we acknowledge that the world we live in is, in Marcel's terms, a 'broken world', a fallen world, the antithesis of all that transcendence implies: for anyone who 'accepts the dogma of the Fall', Marcel suggests, 'is there not implicit in that acceptance an admission that the world is, in fact, broken', and not 'merely *historically* broken' but broken from its very origins.[11] The possibility of encountering transcendence is also, therefore, the necessity of encountering evil, an evil which Willi, in *The Comforters*, believes is revealed in the 'diabolism' of Mervyn Hogarth, but the real evil in the novel is not Hogarth but his wife, with whom Caroline will end up struggling when she and Mrs Hogg fall into the canal and Hogg refuses to let go of Caroline even if it means they will both die. Caroline survives, Hogg drowns: 'God knows where she went' (*C*, 217), the narrator ambiguously opines, balancing Mrs Hogg's physical and spiritual ends, and balancing, too, the colloquial implication that where she went is unknown to anyone against the Christian assertion that God will indeed know where she went. The name 'Hogg', however, gestures to the Scottish author James Hogg, much neglected by readers in the nineteenth century and the first half of the twentieth but whose reputation was revived in 1947 when his *Private Memoirs and Confessions of a Justified Sinner* was published with a new introduction by André Gide. In Hogg's tale of a Christian fanatic who is drawn into doing the Devil's work, Gide saw a version of the dilemmas of the generations of the 1920s and 30s, who had sought in fascism and communism a means of salvation which could lead only to their historical damnation. Hogg's novel raises many of the same issues about religious belief that Spark attributes to her characters in *The Comforters*: Mrs Hogg, like James Hogg's Robert Wringhim, believes that her acts of evil are justified or erased by her faith; she suffers, as Laurence describes it, from 'chronic righteousness' (*C*, 28), and believes the events of her life are directed by interventions in which 'Our Lady always speaks to me' (*C*, 37) and produces 'a miracle' (*C*, 36) to help her out of her difficulties. Threats of blackmail are used by her to gain power over those whose secrets she uncovers, as when she opens a letter from Laurence to Caroline that reveals his suspicions about his grandmother's criminal gang (*C*, 80), information which Mrs Hogg then uses to attempt to extort from Louisa an offer of employment (*C*, 122). Equally, Caroline's consciousness of the author in whose plot she is trapped repeats the double narrative of Hogg's novel, in which Robert Wringhim is trapped both in the machinations of his 'friend' the Devil, and in the retelling of his story by the nineteenth-century editor of his 'confessions': Wringhim's 'confession' is thus both an account of his haunting by the Devil, who instructs him as to which actions he should undertake, and his haunting by an alternative interpretation of his life which does not accept the possibility of the Devil's interventions in ordinary life. Hogg's novel implies that the 'demand' of Christianity is acknowledgement of the reality of evil but such an acknowledgement is precisely what is unimaginable to a scientifically informed view of the modern world: 'in this day, and with the present generation, it will not go down, that a man should be daily tempted by the devil, in the semblance of a fellow-creature'.[12] Equally, Caroline's awareness of her Typing Ghost may imply a capacity for intuiting the possibilities of transcendence, but to those who inhabit a secular modernity it is simply a sign, as Laurence thinks, that 'she really is mad, after all. There's no help for it, Caroline is mad' (*C*, 116). Recognition of the reality of evil is the necessary complement to the possibility of transcendence – as Nicholas Farringdon discovers in *The Girls of Slender Means*, in his realisation 'that a vision of evil may be as effective to conversion as a vision of good' (*GSM*, 180). The reality of evil confirms indirectly the validity of the transcendence to which it is opposed, a fact that Caroline almost grasps when, in her distress, she encounters and suppresses 'the shapeless notion that Mrs Hogg was somehow in league with her invisible persecutor' (*C*, 112).

Transcendence and evil are intertwined in a mutually defining dialectic that results in the corruption of all the media of communication which link the characters in *The Comforters*: thus our 'daily bread' is the medium not of God's beneficence but of trafficking in diamonds (*C*, 28); the Church is the medium not of eventual acceptance into the 'bosom of Abraham' but of confrontation with the unsupported and unsupportive bosom of Mrs Hogg (*C*, 34); Mervyn Hogarth, the failed artist, can tell himself 'I have it in me to be a sculptor if I find the right medium' (*C*, 155) but he is defeated by Mrs Hogg – 'he had married Georgina instead of hacking out her image in stone' (*C*, 155) – who herself cannot find a medium by which to rein in that fleshly excess of which the Manders boys are so conscious (*C*, 150–1), and both Mervyn and Georgina use their son as the medium by which they can gain revenge on the other (*C*, 158–60). Corrupt media proliferate across the narrative: a children's book becomes the medium for transmitting codes to eastern Europe (*C*, 54); trafficking in diamonds is, for Louisa, 'sport' (*C*, 193, 195), just as, for Laurence, being a detective is a holiday game equivalent to the sports on which he is a radio commentator (*C*, 18); the Baron is obsessed with the implications of the 'black mass' rather than its true version (*C*, 93) while Eleanor, who is appalled by the Baron's interest and thinks it may be the cause of Caroline's being 'haunted' by spirits (*C*, 96), treats her own identity, as we have seen, merely as a medium which she can change 'like dresses according to the occasion' (*C*, 95). The Royal Mail, too, proves an unreliable medium of communication when Laurence's letter to Caroline about his grandmother's activities arrives in Mrs Hogg's hands and can be used, corruptly, as *black*mail (*C*, 81); Louisa takes no such chances, sending her messages by pigeon-post (*C*, 123) and her smuggled goods in tins of her own prepared foods ('I never liked to have the diamonds carried loose' (*C*, 202), receipt of which the Baron acknowledges by return in an equally perverted medium – 'The contents of your tin were more delicate than oysters, rarer than . . .' (*C*, 171). Throughout, the corruption of communicative media is the surface effect of the reality of the corruption of human relations:

> At the first pub, after they had left, a friend of Laurence had said, 'That's Larry's form of perversion – beautiful neurotic women. They have to be neurotic.'
>
> It was understood that every close association between two people was a perversion. Caroline sensed the idea they had left behind them when they left this pub. Laurence, of course, knew it, but he didn't mind; he accepted that, for instance, 'perversion' was his friends' code-word for anyone's personal taste in love. (*C*, 86)

The use of the word 'perversion' to describe others' relationships is itself an index of how perverse the world is – whether the real world of the early 1950s in which the characters are assumed to live, or the fictional world that reduces them to these character types. Laurence and Caroline are not people in a relationship but mere types of a recognisable 'perversion', mere types recognisable from certain kinds of novel – in Laurence's case the ever-popular novel of the 'amateur sleuth in a cheap mystery piece' (*C*, 114); in Caroline's case the recently popular form, like Graham Greene's *The End of the Affair*

(1951), of Catholic conversion and modern miracles. Spark's novel forces readers to acknowledge that its characters are products of their medium, types typographically inscribed on paper, but at the same time drawing attention to its own limitations as a medium, as when a tape recorder repeats a presumably lewd suggestion made by Laurence to Caroline which the narrator notes cannot be recorded in print because it is 'unprintable' (*C*, 70); so, too, the hospital ward in which Caroline is treated after the car crash goes unrecorded by the 'Typing Ghost' because 'the author doesn't know how to describe a hospital ward' (*C*, 176).

The limitations of the author's ability to represent the world defies what had been central to European aesthetics from Aristotle's account of tragedy in the *Poetics* to Sartre's existential realism – the notion of art's fundamentally mimetic purpose, a purpose which had been given a profound and scholarly exposition in Erich Auerbach's *Mimesis: The Representation of Reality in Western Literature*, an account of the changing nature of 'realism' from Homer to Virginia Woolf. The English translation of Auerbach's masterpiece dates from 1953,[13] and so may have been the context of Caroline's difficulties 'with the chapter on realism' in her book on *Form in the Modern Novel* (*C*, 62), but the nature of realism is put under stress from a variety of different directions in all of Spark's early novels. In Chapter Seven of her fifth novel, *The Ballad of Peckham Rye*, we are offered the following description:

> At the back of Hollie's Hamburgers at Elephant and Castle was a room furnished with a fitted grey carpet, a red upholstered modern suite comprising a sofa and two cubic armchairs, a television receiver on a light wood stand, a low glass-topped coffee table on which stood an electric portable gramophone and a tape recorder, a light wood bureau desk, a standard lamp, and several ash-trays on stands. Two of the walls were papered with a wide grey stripe. The other two were covered with a pattern of gold stars on red. Fixed to the walls were a number of white brackets containing pots of indoor ivy. The curtains, which were striped red and white, were drawn. This cheerful interior was lit by a couple of red-shaded wall-lamps. (*BPR*, 124–5)

The description stands out because it is so rare for Muriel Spark to provide this level of 'solidity of specification' (as Henry James called it)[14] about the physical environment in which the action of her novels is set. Spark's technique is usually minimalist, giving us only such information as is absolutely essential to advancing her narrative. Here, the description is, despite the banality of the environment, luxuriously unnecessary: for the purposes of the plot the colour and pattern of the wallpaper or of the curtains are no more relevant than the existence of the standard lamp. This description comes, however, immediately before a list that is read out from one of the stolen notebooks of Dougal Douglas:

> I thrilled to his touch.
> I was too young at the time to understand why my mother was crying.
> As he entered the room a shudder went through my frame.
> In the moment of silent communion we renewed our shattered faith.
> She was to play a vital role in my life. (*BPR*, 126)

While the first paragraph quoted above records in the fashion of a traditional novel the largely irrelevant details of a physical environment, Dougal's list provides the clichéd responses typical of characters in popular fiction – in fact, responses that Dougal is collecting in order to incorporate them into a thoroughly fictional 'autobiography' that he is writing for a former music hall star. Side by side we have two entirely conventional, not to say hackneyed, versions of how you write a novel, one focused on the 'realisation' of the physical location of the action, and the other on the (commonplace) psychological responses of its characters. Spark's text foregrounds itself as a parody of the kind of novel which assumes that the rendering of the 'real' – the reality effects of a world filled with manufactured objects and an equally standardised set of emotions – is what novels are supposed to provide. One at least of the characters in this situation is, however, a sophisticated reader who is not taken in by the mere surface of a text:

> 'Read us it again, Trev,' Leslie said. 'It sounds like English Dictation. Perhaps he's a teacher as well.'
>
> Trevor ignored him. He tapped the notebook and addressed Collie.
>
> 'Code,' he said. 'It's worth lolly.' (*BPR*, 127)

Trevor, mirror image to the reader of the novel, recognises that the meaning of the text is not 'overt' (as the reversal of his name implies) but has to be decoded in order to unlock its concealed significance: 'It's a code. Autumn means something else. Everything means something else. Everything means something' (*PBR*, 127). The scene ironically plays with the fact that 'every thing' that appears in a novel does so because it 'means something' (except that the objects of this room actually mean very little), and in which 'every thing' has to be understood in such a way that it 'means something else' (except that in this case the phrases are actually so trite that they mean rather less than more). This scene not only undermines Aristotelian notions of mimesis but also more modern symbolist notions of the novel's construction of higher-order levels of significance which can only be understood if one has access to the appropriate 'code' (as in the bird symbolism of James Joyce's *Portrait of the Artist*, or the classical parallels in his *Ulysses*). Spark's parody effectively satirises the traditional Aristotelian purposes of writing (as representation) and the modern symbolic tradition of reading (as decoding: note that one of the characters in this novel has the surname 'Morse'), making us conscious not of the action of the novel we are reading, as though we were spectators of a drama, but of the medium through which that action is constructed. For Aristotle, of course, mimesis had two dimensions, one of which was representation in the sense in which a painter might 'represent' objects in the world (or a novelist might 'paint' a scene) and the other of which was mimicry – the performance through which actors 'imitate agents'.[15] In Chapter Four of *The Ballad of Peckham Rye*, Dougal Douglas, who is also already performing the role of himself as Douglas Dougal, thrusts himself into the midst of a dancefloor, 'bearing before him the lid of a dust-bin' and, like Eleanor in *The Comforters*, demonstrates the power of mimesis as mimicry:

> he placed the lid upside down on the floor, sat cross-legged inside it, and was a man in a rocking boat rowing for his life [. . .] Next, Dougal sat on his haunches and banged a message out on a ton-tom. He sprang up and with the lid on his head was a Chinese coolie eating melancholy rice. He was an ardent cyclist, crouched over handlebars and pedalling uphill with the lid between his knees. He was an old woman with an umbrella; he stood on the upturned edges of the lid and speared fish from his rocking canoe; he was the man at the wheel of a racing car [. . .] (*BPR*, 78–80)

On the dancefloor, Dougal transforms himself into many characters, but what he does as a dancer he is also doing in 'real life' in the plot of *The Ballad of Peckham Rye*, as he metamorphoses into different characters depending on who or what he is dealing with: at his second interview with Mr Druce, 'Dougal changed his shape and became a professor' (*BPR*, 14) and then 'leaned forward and became a television interviewer' (*BPR*, 16); later, teasing out Mr Druce's marital situation, he is 'like an exhausted medium of the spiritualist persuasion' (*BPR*, 91). Dougal explains his mediumistic capacities on the basis of having 'Highland blood' and being 'fey' (*BPR*, 91), and demonstrates his shape-changing abilities to Merle Coverdale by posing on a grave 'like an angel' and then like an 'angel-devil, with his hump shoulder and his gleaming smile, and his fingers of each hand widespread against the sky' (*BPR*, 36). Dougal is an anti-mimetic principle within the novel, insinuating art and artifice into reality, turning the categories of Aristotle's account of tragedy into the everyday context of Peckham: thus Aristotle's analysis of the tragic hero as suffering from a 'fatal flaw' (*hamartia*), Dougal democratises, applying it not only to himself – his 'fatal flaw' is his aversion to other people's illnesses – but to everyone in the community: 'we all have a fatal flaw' (*BPR*, 34). Others of Aristotle's key terms are similarly parodied in *The Comforters* when the emotions that Aristotle describes as typical of tragedy are found to be inadequate when applied to Mrs Hogg, whose earlier life before her meeting with Caroline at St Philumena's is summarised as 'tragic':

> Her pale red-gold hair, round pale-blue eyes, her piglet 'flesh-coloured' face: Georgina Hogg had certain attractions at the time of her marriage. Throughout the 'tragic' years which followed (for when misfortune occurs to slightly absurd or mean-minded people it is indeed tragic for them – it falls with a thud which they don't expect, it does not excite the pity and fear of the onlooker, it excites revulsion more likely, so that the piece of bad luck which happened to Georgina Hogg was not truly tragic, only pathetic) [. . .] (*C*, 152)

Tragedy is not the medium by which Mrs Hogg can be understood, any more than it can provide a satisfactory account of the conclusion of *The Driver's Seat*:

> '[. . .] I was hoping to start a new life.' He sees already the gleaming buttons of the policemen's uniforms, hears the cold and confiding, the hot and the barking voices, sees already the holsters and epaulets and all those trappings devised to protect them from the indecent exposure of fear and pity, pity and fear. (*DS*, 160)

The categories of Aristotle's account of art are no longer adequate to the rendering of the modern world.

Drawing on the anti-mimetic tactics of Scottish precursors such as Hogg, Stevenson and Barrie, Spark's early novels not only set out to subvert the traditions of mimesis but also to overthrow the whole weight of the tradition of the English novel as it was conceived in the 1950s, largely under the influence of F. R. Leavis. This was a task undertaken by her second novel, *Robinson*. If critics have generally agreed that this is a problematic novel – 'too mechanical and even geometrical in conception and structure to be satisfactory',[16] as Norman Page puts it – their discomfort may reflect how radically it challenges the traditions of the novel in English in which most of those critics specialised. In *Robinson*, the central character, January Marlow, is trapped, after a plane crash, on a strange island in the Atlantic, owned by a reclusive lapsed Catholic called Robinson, who lives alone on the island except for a boy whom he has taken into his care: so identified is Robinson with the island that it, too, is called Robinson. Only two other men survive the plane crash, Tom Wells and Jimmie Waterford, but when Robinson disappears each of the survivors suspects the others of having murdered him. January Marlow's unusual name sets an ambiguous context for Spark's narrative: her Christian name invokes the Roman god of doors, 'Janus', who looks in two directions, which may imply that January, a recent convert to Catholicism, is still uncertain whether she is entering or leaving the Church. Her surname, Marlow, however, might also suggest the narrator of Conrad's *Heart of Darkness* (1899), and thus imply that her meeting with Robinson is in some ways parallel to Marlow's meeting with Kurtz, the civiliser turned savage in the African jungle. Robinson, however, is very different from Kurtz: he has not used the powers of civilisation to rule over savagery, but has secluded himself on his island to escape both the Catholic Church – 'he left the church on account of what he considered its superstitious character' (*R*, 79) – and the conflicts of the modern world – he 'fought with the Republicans in Spain, but suffered a revulsion and deserted after six months' (*R*, 79–80). He has retreated not into savagery but into spiritual isolation. Conrad's story had its own precursor, however, in Robert Louis Stevenson's *The Ebb-Tide* (1894), co-written with Lloyd Osborne, which is the story of three drifters in the South Seas who steal a boat and end up in a lagoon on an island ruled over by

Attwater, a fanatical Christian who has become a godlike figure on his island. Spark's three survivors of the air crash and Stevenson's three drifters are equally unwelcome intruders on the domain of the islands' charismatic 'owners', and threaten the retreat they have made from the world. The three crash survivors on the island of Robinson represent three claims on his identity that Robinson is impelled to resist: the demands of his family inheritance, as represented by Jimmie Waterford and the businesses that Robinson owns and that Jimmie wishes authority to run back in the mainstream of the world; the illusions of fake religion, as represented by Tom Wells's occult 'charms' and his newspaper, *Your Future*; and the religious femininity – Robinson has a profound hatred of 'Mariolatry' – represented by January and her rosary beads. Like Attwater, Robinson holds the guns, but unlike Attwater he will not use them, faking his own death in order to retreat further into isolation. That retreat, however, is itself a fulfilment of Attwater's predestinarian conception of the universe, for on his return Robinson implies 'that he had foreseen all the consequences of his action to the last detail, and that he more or less held the wires that made us move' (*R*, 175).

Robinson, as a man isolated (with one companion) on an island, cannot help but invoke Daniel Defoe's *Robinson Crusoe* (1719),[17] but the significance of Defoe's novel was the basis of an argument about the nature of the novel put forward in Ian Watt's *The Rise of the Novel*, which appeared in 1957,[18] the same year in which *The Comforters* was published. For Watt, the novel in English is rooted in the work of Defoe, and its founding statement is *Robinson Crusoe*, a work which establishes the novel as the genre of 'formal realism' (*RN*, 32), in which language is 'much more referential [. . .] than in other literary forms' (*RN*, 31), and in which 'the character is to be regarded as though he were a particular person and not a type' (*RN*, 20). This new literary form is shaped by the forces of an economic individualism directed away from the past and towards the future – 'it posits a whole society mainly governed by the idea of every individual's intrinsic independence [. . .] from that multifarious allegiance to past modes of thought and action denoted by the word "tradition"' (*RN*, 62); that economic individualism derives from Protestantism – 'if there is one element which all forms of Protestantism have in common it is the replacement of the rule of the Church as the mediator between man and God by another view of religion in which it is the individual who is entrusted with the primary responsibility for his own spiritual direction' (*RN*, 77). The formal origins of the novel are in the 'the autobiographical memoir which was the most immediate and widespread literary expression of the introspective tendency of Puritanism' (*RN*, 78). Thus the 'works of Defoe are the supreme illustration in the novel of the connexion between the democratic individualism of Puritanism and the objective representation of the world of everyday reality and all those who inhabit it' (*RN*, 83) and, equally, of the 'tendency to secularization which was rooted in material progress' (*RN*, 86). The new economic individualism represented in Crusoe judged material success as a sign of God's confirmation that one belonged to the elect, so that Crusoe's island 'offers the fullest opportunity for him to realize three associated tendencies of modern civilization – absolute economic, social and intellectual freedom for the individual' (*RN*, 89).

If Watt's analysis is correct about the meaning of the novel *as a form*, it is a form which can be of no value to a writer who has just denied the inheritance of the Reformation to embrace the 'tradition' of Catholicism: Watt, for instance, cites Georg Lukács on the fact that the novel 'is the epic of a world forsaken by God' (*RN*, 87). Nor, indeed, can the novel in this form be of any value to a woman writer, since the tradition which Watt outlines is insistently male – 'Studies in Defoe, Richardson, Fielding' is his subtitle – and women in Defoe's fiction, we are told, 'have only one important role to play, and that is economic' (*RN*, 71). If this is the nature of the medium that is the novel, it is a medium impossible to a female writer inspired by Catholicism: idling in Robinson's library, January 'cast around for a novel' and happened to open an eighteenth-century edition of *Tom Jones* at the page in which Sophia's 'agonies [. . .] rather augmented than impaired her beauty; for her tears added brightness to her eyes, and her breasts rose higher with her sighs' (*R*, 160), a male construction of the female heroine as sexual object very different from Spark's analysis of Emily Brontë as a writer whose personality 'was more than human; she was some strange rugged monolithic mystic'.[19] January's lighting on the *Tom Jones* passage is her creator's gesture of defiance to a tradition which would find no place for women authors like Brontë, or indeed like Spark.

The realist tradition of which *Robinson Crusoe* is the foundation assumes a certainty about the novel's ability to describe reality – 'the objective representation of the world of everyday reality' – and to categorise its characters in terms of their being 'primarily responsible for determining [their] own economic, social, political and religious roles' (*RN*, 63). It is this tradition which Spark's novel aims to overthrow: in opposition to notions of isolated individuals, it presents us with a deliquescent conception of character, of individual identity as constantly mobile and never reducible to a single 'cause', because identity forms and reforms in the course of people's interaction with others. When Robinson returns after his supposed death, he insists that 'motives are seldom simple' (*R*, 176), and though January rejects this as a specious refusal to justify his actions it is, nonetheless, a truth about the characters in *Robinson* – they are shaped by motives where simple cause and effect has ceased to operate. In Watt's version of *Robinson Crusoe* all effects are reduced to economic causes:

> The hypostasis of the economic motive logically entails the devaluation of other modes of thought, feeling and action: the various forms of traditional group relationship, the family, the guild, the village, the sense of nationality – all are weakened, and so, too, are the competing claims of non-economic individual achievement and enjoyment, ranging from spiritual salvation to the pleasures of recreation. (*RN*, 66)

This is the world in which relationships require to be formalised in a legal 'contract': 'Crusoe, we notice, acts like a good Lockean – when others arrive on the island he forces them to accept his dominion with written contracts acknowledging his absolute power' (*RN*, 66). On Robinson, Tom Wells is the representative both of the economic exploitation of the world of individualism – he uses his newspaper to encourage readers to communicate with him as though he were a friend, subsequently 'extorting money from men and women who had, in their innocence, confided their most cherished secrets, the deepest anguish of their souls, to Wells' (*R*, 184) – and also the representative of a world in which the only relations are contractual relations:

> 'We'll burn the evidence to-night,' he said, 'and we shall sign the statement to-morrow.'
>
> 'What statement?'
>
> 'The one I'm going to prepare. I just wanted to know whether you preferred suicide or an accident.' (*R*, 147)

For Wells, reality has to be reshaped to meet the terms of his 'contract', a contract designed to maximise the economic value of his current situation. Wells is representative of the economic individualism which, for Watt, is homologous with the novel itself and which reshapes 'reality' to the requirements of a legal fiction: January has to 'sign the statement' (*R*, 148) agreeing to Wells's version of events; if not, as Jimmie tells her, 'He has prepared to accuse you, that you have stabbed with the knife' (*R*, 149), in order 'to gain for me [Jimmie] the fortune' (*R*, 150). But this is a world which Spark rejects and which *Robinson* is designed to challenge, for if the formal origins of the novel are as Watt describes them, and lie in 'the autobiographical memoir which was the most immediate and widespread literary expression of the introspective tendency of Puritanism', then Spark goes back to those origins to rewrite her own version of 'the autobiographical memoir', not as the expression of the 'the introspective tendency of Puritanism' but as the *retro*spective tendency of a reversion to Catholicism, a retrospective tendency which seeks to accommodate the past to the present rather than accommodate the present to the future; January, for instance, finds herself repeating her grandmother's welcome to the new moon:

> It was on this occasion I experienced that desire to worship the moon, and I thought, how remarkable, since I was a Christian: I thought of my grandmother bowing in the roadway, 'New Moon, New Moon, be good to me.' (*R*, 48)

Robinson invokes and erases the tradition of the English novel which would find no place for a female, Scottish, Jewish, Catholic, novelist who is drawn to pagan ceremonies.

The formal principle used to disrupt realism in both *The Comforters* and in *Robinson* is the ambiguous role of the central character who seems to be both inside the narrative and, at the same time, outside it. In Caroline's case in *The Comforters*, the 'Typing Ghost' gives her access to an authorial consciousness apparently beyond the frame and outside of the temporality of the narrative, one which incorporates into the narration the kinds of statements which are usually part of the novel's paratextual preliminaries: 'At this point in the narrative it might be as well to state that the characters in this novel are all fictitious, and do not refer to any living persons whatsoever' (*C*, 76).

Equally, when Caroline is confined to hospital in the second part of the novel, we are informed that,

> It is not easy to dispense with Caroline Rose. At this point in the tale she is confined in a hospital bed, and no experience of hers ought to be allowed to intrude. Unfortunately she slept restlessly [. . .] When her leg was not too distracting, Caroline among the sleepers turned her mind to the art of the novel, wondering and cogitating those long hours, and exerting an undue, unreckoned, influence on the narrative from which she is supposed to be absent for a time. (*C*, 150)

Removed from the action of the narrative, Caroline, as the representative of the higher-order voice of the narrator, continues to shape the action from which she has, apparently, been removed. The status of the events of *Robinson* is equally ambiguous, for the events of the narrative are recounted by January as her recollection of the events on the island, but though we are told they are based on a diary she kept at the time we are given almost no details of what is in the diary, so that we have no evidence of the relation of her recollections to the reality of the events. And since the island itself has subsequently disappeared in a volcanic eruption, the very place of the action only exists in her memory – or her imagination. On the island she fears that 'Robinson and his household were a dead woman's dream' (*R*, 34); in the first weeks after the crash she was suffering from concussion, and, later, after Robinson's disappearance, was 'in a state similar to my first week on the island, concussion, stupor' (*R*, 111), a state made more uncertain by moods which 'are not stable at the best of times' (*R*, 48) and which, on the island, 'were like a pendulum' (*R*, 125). What the novel presents is not the 'facts' which she claims her journal to have recorded but the *instability* of January's perceptions and of her responses to her situation, an instability in which past and present mingle with each other in a continual disruption of a 'realist' narrative. Thus she is haunted by her hatred of her brother-in-law Ian Brodie, a Catholic who, like Robinson, despises Mariolatry:

> Ian Brodie used to return from the Continent having gone out of his way to feed his fury by witnessing all the religious processions and festivals.

> 'Awful old crones hobbling along after the statues, clinking their rosaries, mumbling their Hail Marys, as if their lives depended on it. And the sickening thing, young people, people in their prime, caught up in the mob hysteria. That sort of thing corrupts the Faith. (*R*, 93–4)

Brodie has been, for January, 'a stumbling block' to her faith – 'for years I was put off the Catholic Church because he was a member, and a carping exponent, of it' (*R*, 81) – but he is also, like Robinson, a threat to her independence of action: 'He was always inexhaustible in trying to catch me in an illicit love affair, but he never succeeded; and whether this was because I never, in fact, had a lover, or whether I had, but effectively concealed the fact, you may be sure Ian Brodie is still guessing' (*R*, 84), just as Robinson is desperate to detect 'any possibility of a love affair between Jimmie and me' (*R*, 83). That fusion (or confusion) of past and present means that January is not just a retrospective narrator of her own earlier life – she is the retrospective narrator of an earlier life which may or may not have happened as she recalls it. The reality evaporates in the narration, producing a generic instability in which the pattern of the events are constantly reshaped according to different literary conventions: thus they turn from tragedy – 'That he should have met his end at the hands of one of his beneficiaries seemed to me the essence of tragedy' (*R*, 137) – to farce – 'Your reason for arranging this farce – it was to separate Jimmie and me' (*R*, 175) – and then, in retrospect, after January's return home, they 'are transformed, there is undoubtedly a sea-change, so that the island resembles a locality of childhood, both dangerous and lyrical' (*R*, 186). Both inside and outside the narrative, January is at one and the same time a character in the time-scheme of the narrative and a narrative voice with access to a supra-human, transcendent perspective on the events that are being related.

Such narrator-characters are in a very similar situation to one that Kierkegaard describes himself as suffering from in a journal entry in 1836:

> Every time I want to say something someone else says it at the very same moment. It is just as though I were a double-thinker and my other I always forestalled me, or else while I stand and talk everyone

> believes it is someone else, so that I might quite well ask the question that Soldin the book-seller asked his wife: is it I who am speaking? – Or the echo – yes, Echo, you master of irony who parody all that is most noble and profound on earth. (*J*, '90', 36)

Caroline's voices are like that Echo – 'the author', she tells Laurence, 'obviously exists in a different dimension from ours' (*C*, 104) – but that interaction between a higher order and the world represented in the text parallels one of Kierkegaard's most striking philosophical innovations – the fact that many of his major works were published not under his own name but under pseudonyms who treat Kierkegaard's life and thought as a subject for their narration and analysis – Johannes *de silentio* in the case of *Fear and Trembling*, Constantine Constantius in *Repetition*, and several embedded authors in the various sections of *Either/Or* which have been assembled by Victor Eremita:

> As is known, my work consists of two parts: one is pseudonymous, and one is signed with my name. These pseudonyms are poetically created characters, held together poetically so that what they say is in character with their poetic individuality. Sometimes I have said in a preface, signed with my name, exactly how I understood what the pseudonym said. (*J*, '1238', 453–4)

Pseudonymous authorship allowed Kierkegaard to be both outside and inside his own works, the characters and their fictional author forming a conceptual whole which concealed the identity of the real author. Kierkegaard was well aware of the possible complications of this method of authorship, since,

> It is obvious that anyone who wanted some fun, as they say, need only lump a lot of quotations hurly-burly together, now from the *Seducer*, now from Johannes Climacus, again from me, print them altogether as though they were all my words, point out the contradictions between them and so produce an impression of such confusion and dismemberment, as though the author were a sort of lunatic. (*J*, '1238', 454)

Kierkegaard's pseudonymous texts require a double reading, in which the events and the opinions expressed have to be related to the personality of their pseudonymous author and then, indirectly, to their actual author. This dispersed authorship is intended, by Kierkegaard, to prevent his becoming a didact, uttering apparently ultimate truths, but rather to be a pathfinder who will help his readers realise the limitations of their own aesthetic or ethical values. Comedy is central to such a displacement of the author, since it allows a character on a lower level of religious awareness to be viewed from a higher vantage point, one from which the character's efforts can been seen as comically fulfilling only aesthetic or ethical values and revealing how inadequate those efforts are as a route towards the religious. Comedy is the medium through which the aesthetic and the ethical can be both accepted – even the religious person has to live most of the time in an aesthetic and an ethical environment – but also, with whatever difficulty, transcended. It is an interaction between the different levels of fiction and reality which is enacted in the final sentences of *The Comforters*: Laurence, having read Caroline's notes for her novel, writes to her to tell her 'You misrepresent all of us', and to declare that 'I dislike being a character in your novel' (*C*, 223). He decides, however, not to send his letter, and 'tore it up into small pieces, scattering them over the Heath where the wind bore them away' (*C*, 223); in defiance of his actions as 'a-character-in-a-novel', however, his letter is retrieved and recreated on another level of the ontology of the novel:

> He saw the bits of paper come to rest, some on scrubby ground, some among the deep marsh weeds, and one piece on a thorn-bush; and he did not then foresee his later wonder, with a curious rejoicing, how the letter had got into the book. (*C*, 224)

The scraps of paper replicate the seeds sown in Christ's Parable of the Sower,[20] but the piece that is stuck on a thorn bush recalls Kierkegaard's own identification of himself with the Apostle Paul's declaration that he had a 'thorn in the flesh':[21] for Kierkegaard, of course, it was his betrayal of Regine and his refusal to go through with the marriage that produced the 'sad discord with its attendant suffering (which without doubt would have driven most of those with sense enough to understand it to suicide) I have always looked upon as my thorn in the flesh, my limit and my cross' (*J*, '600', 170). But, as with Caroline and Laurence, an art that translates personal suffering into something on 'a different dimension from ours' (*C*, 104) transfigures the existence it may seem to have abandoned.

Notes

1. See Annie Cohen-Solal, *Sartre: A Life* (London: Heinemann, 1985) for an account of the circumstances and the impact of the lecture.
2. Jean-Paul Sartre, 'The Humanism of Existentialism', in *Jean-Paul Sartre: Essays in Existentialism*, ed. Wade Baskin and trans. Bernard Frechtman (New York: Citadel Publishing, 1990; 1947), 41.
3. Sartre, 'The Humanism of Existentialism', 55.
4. Jean-Paul Sartre, *What is Literature?*, trans. Bernard Frechtman (New York: The Philosophical Library, 1949; 1947).
5. Quoted Philip Thody, *Jean-Paul Sartre: A Literary and Political Study* (London: Hamish Hamilton, 1960), 42.
6. Jean-Paul Sartre, *The Age of Reason*, trans. Eric Sutton (Harmondsworth: Penguin, 1961; 1947), 300.
7. Glenda Norquay (ed.), *R. L. Stevenson on Fiction: An Anthology of Literary and Critical Essays* (Edinburgh: Edinburgh University Press, 1999), 85.
8. Gabriel Marcel, *The Philosophy of Existence*, trans. Manya Harari (London: Harvill Press, 1948), 64–5.
9. Ibid. 62–3.
10. Gabriel Marcel, *The Mystery of Being*, vol. 1, *Reflection and Mystery*, trans. G. S. Fraser (London: Harvill Press, 1950), 46.
11. Marcel, *The Mystery of Being*, 33–4.
12. James Hogg, *The Private Memoirs and Confessions of a Justified Sinner*, ed. John Carey (Oxford: Oxford University Press, 1969), 254.
13. Erich Auerbach, *Mimesis: The Representation of Reality in Western Literature*, trans. Willard R. Trask (Princeton: Princeton University Press, 1953; 1946).
14. 'the air of reality (solidity of specification) seems to me to be the supreme virtue of a novel', Henry James, 'The Art of Fiction', in *Henry James: The Future of the Novel: Essays on the Arts of Fiction*, ed. Leon Edel (New York: Vintage Books, 1956), 14.
15. *Aristotle/Horace/Longinus: Classical Literary Criticism*, trans. T. S. Dorsch (Harmondsworth: Penguin, 1965), 32: 'The imitative medium of dancers' rhythm alone, unsupported by music, for it is by the manner in which they arrange the rhythms of their movements that they represent men's characters and feelings and actions.'
16. Norman Page, *Muriel Spark* (London: Macmillan, 1990), 19, paraphrasing Peter Kemp.
17. The relationship between *Robinson* and Defoe's *Robinson Crusoe* is central to the argument of Joseph Hynes's *The Art of the Real: Muriel Spark's Novels* (Rutherford: Fairleigh Dickinson University Press, 1988), and to his attempt to distinguish between the conventions of

realism and the kind of fiction Spark is exploring, which 'combines realism with romantic psychology in aid of a larger reality' (33).

18. Ian Watt, *The Rise of the Novel* (Harmondsworth: Penguin, 1963; 1957).
19. Muriel Spark and Derek Stanford, *Emily Brontë: Her Life and Work* (London: Peter Owen Limited), 88. This was published in 1960, two years after *Robinson*, but Spark had been working on Brontë since editing her letters in 1953 and her book with Stanford had been commissioned in that year; see Martin Stannard, *Muriel Spark: The Biography* (London: Weidenfeld & Nicolson, 2009), 136.
20. Matthew 13:1–23, Mark 4:1–20 and Luke 8:4–15.
21. 2 Corinthians 12:7; see Kierkegaard, *Journals*, '661', 206.

Chapter 3

Kierkegaard: The Limits of the Aesthetic

In his biography of Kierkegaard, Walter Lowrie examines Kierkegaard's pseudonymous works in a chapter entitled 'Away from the Aesthetical'. Lowrie acknowledges the irony of this, since the pseudonymous works are themselves, by definition, aesthetical but, he argues, those aesthetic works 'are not an exaltation of the aesthetic stage, but a movement away from it, a fond farewell, and represent the first decisive step in his education in Christianity'.[1] The aesthetic works represent both a rejection of the aesthetic and, at the same time, an analysis both of just how profound were its attractions and how necessary it remains to the wholeness of Christian experience. The point of Kierkegaard's movement away from the aesthetic is not a rejection of the aesthetic as such, but a rejection of a way of life in which the aesthetic – our immediate, sensual experience of the world – is the only basis for our existence. The mass of humanity live – and die – in the aesthetic: Kierkegaard's writings are both an exposition of why this is so and, at the same time, a call for the rejection of the aesthetic as the principal determinant of our lives. This inner conflict produces the typical dialectical structure of his pseudonymous works, for they are both expressions *of* the aesthetic and challenges *to* the aesthetic – they are, in the title of the first of those pseudonymous works, a confrontation with the *Either/Or*, in which the aesthetic comes to consciousness of its own limitations, of its need to find an 'or' by which it can transcend itself and to realise a different order of existence and a higher set of values.

The second section of the first part of *Either/Or* opens with an analysis of 'The Immediate Erotic Stages', in which the central figure is Mozart's Don Giovanni, who represents, for Kierkegaard – or, at least for the fictional author of 'the Papers of A', as this section is described – desire at its most abstract:

> If, for instance, Don Juan's love were qualified other than as sensual, if he were a seducer in an intellectual sense, something which would later become the object of reflection, then it would have been a radical fault in the play for the heroine of the seduction which dramatically engages our attention, to be only a little peasant girl. Then the aesthetic would require that Don Juan should have been set a more difficult task. To Don Juan, however, these differences mean nothing [. . .] To Don Juan every girl is woman in general, every love affair an everyday story. Zerlina is young and pretty, and she is a woman; this is the uncommon which she has in common with hundreds of others; but it is not the uncommon that Don Juan desires, but the common, and this she has in common with every woman. (*E/O*, I, 78–9)

The nature and meaning of seduction as practised by Don Giovanni is taken up in the final section of the first volume of *Either/Or*, entitled 'The Seducer's Diary', which presents us with a series of diary entries and letters that chart the development of a relationship between a man and a younger woman, a relationship which is undertaken, on his part, not for love or fulfilment or, indeed, as a fulfilment of Don Giovanni's constant need to add to the numbers he has seduced, but for the aesthetic pleasure of the seduction itself. The diarist has turned seduction into an art form, or, at the very least, into something that generates the pleasures of art:

> I am an aesthete, an eroticist, who has understood the nature and meaning of love, who believes in love and knows it from the ground up, and only makes the private reservation that no love affair should last more than six months at most, and that every erotic relationship should cease as soon as one has had the ultimate enjoyment. (*E/O*, I, 305)

Living by the imagination – 'his life had been an attempt to realize the task of living poetically' (*E/O*, I, 252) – he seeks to transform reality until it corresponds with his own desires:

> What am I doing? Do I fool her? Not at all; that would not help me. Am I stealing her heart? By no means; I really prefer that the girl

> I love should retain her heart. Then what am I doing? I am creating for myself a heart in the likeness of her own. An artist paints his beloved, that gives him pleasure; a sculptor fashions his. I do this too, but in a spiritual sense. She does not know that I possess this picture, and therein lies my real deception. Mysteriously have I secured it, and in this sense I have stolen her heart [. . .] (*E/O*, I, 323)

The Seducer reworks both himself and the target of his seduction so that they will become, aesthetically, mirror images that produce no resistance on her part precisely because, as the Seducer acknowledges, he has 'known how to drug her aesthetically' (*E/O*, I, 368). Their eventual union is, by this invented mutuality, apparently inevitable, until the deceit with which it has been built up is revealed: 'Generally I can assure any girl who entrusts herself to me, a perfect aesthetic conduct: only it ends with her being deceived; but this is consistent with my aesthetics, for either the girl deceives the man, or the man deceives the girl' (*E/O*, I, 315). The aesthetic is the medium of a deceit which, when its end is achieved, dissolves and disappears: 'Now all resistance is impossible, and only as long as that is present is it beautiful to love; when it is ended there is only weakness and habit. I do not wish to be reminded of my relation to her; she has lost the fragrance [. . .]' (*E/O*, I, 371). The deceit dissipates along with the promised relationship. The Seducer of 'The Seducer's Diary' is the opposite of Don Giovanni, who 'requires no preparation, no plan, no time; for he is always prepared' (*E/O*, I, 82), whereas the Seducer's aim is a long drawn-out affair, whose meticulous planning is part of its aesthetic pleasure; the end, however, is the same, the abandonment of the seduced and the revelation that she has been tempted by an imagined future which will never exist, and a past relationship to which there can be no return because it was never real.

The 'The Seducer's Diary' is presented as an edited text, and the editor compares the Seducer's life to a theatre stage, where,

> Back of the world in which we live, in the remote distance, lies another world which bears about the same relation to the one in which we live, as the scene one sometimes sees in the theatre back of the actual scene, bears to that. Through a thin gauze we see, as it were, a world of gauze, lighter, more ethereal, qualitatively different from the actual world. Many people who appear bodily in the actual world do not belong in it, but in that other. (*E/O*, I, 253)

The Seducer is one who lives between reality and the hallucinatory background of an alternative, 'ethereal' world: 'As soon as reality lost its significance as a stimulus, he was disarmed, and this constituted the evil in him' (*E/O*, I, 253). Evil is the outcome of the increasing displacement of reality by the imagination to produce a space where the aesthetic – the theatre stage – is reduplicated – the stage behind the stage – until all contact with reality is lost: 'reality was submerged in the poetic' (*E/O*, I, 253). The Seducer is a man in thrall to the pleasures of the aesthetic, but the seductiveness of the aesthetic is not merely sensual: the aesthetic seduces by its apparent invitation to a sense of the supernatural and the infinite, for in the aesthetic it is 'as if the very moment demanded and was prepared to view the extraordinary'; it is 'like an eye that surveys itself, so that her glance travels beyond that which appears immediately before it, and sees the marvellous' (*E/O*, I, 332). The aesthetic is the means of living on a double stage, where the real is displaced by a beckoning infinity. Kierkegaard's Seducer knows that he must tempt his prey not just with sensuality but with the promise of the infinite:

> Her soul must be set in motion, agitated in every possible direction; not, however, piecemeal and by sudden gusts, but totally. She must discover the infinite, experience what it is that lies nearest to man. This must she discover, not by the way of thought, which for her is the wrong way, but in imagination, which is the real mode of communication between her and me; for what is but a part with man, is the whole with woman. (*E/O*, I, 325)

The aesthetic is, in effect, an invitation to overleap the limits of the real but to overleap them not into a Christian eternity, an eternity of judgement, but into a pseudo-eternity of the imagination:

> Not by the toilsome labour of thought should she work toward the infinite, for woman is not born for intellectual work, but she should grasp it through imagination and the easy way of the heart. The infinite is just as naturally part of a young girl as is the conception she holds that all love must be happy. A young girl has above all, wherever she turns, the infinite about her, and the transition is a leap, but, it is well to note, a feminine not a masculine leap. (*E/O*, I, 325)

In this aesthetic infinitude, there are no real choices: as Judge Wilhelm insists in the second part of *Either/Or*:

> Your choice is an aesthetic choice, but an aesthetic choice is no choice. The act of choosing is essentially a proper and stringent expression of the ethical. Whenever in a stricter sense there is a question of an either/or one can always be sure that the ethical is involved. The only absolute either/or is the aesthetic choice between good and evil, but that is also absolutely ethical. The aesthetic choice is either entirely immediate, or it loses itself in the multifarious. (*E/O*, II, 141)

In the realm of the aesthetic choices decline into the substitution of one aesthetic possibility for another – the substitution of one act of seduction for another. In the end, however, such refusals of ethical choice will come to a point where evil will reveal itself as the ultimate end of a commitment to the aesthetic, and where the ethical cannot be evaded. The aesthetic will, inevitably, bring itself to a choice which enforces the need for the ethical, an ethical in which the aesthetic will be revealed as necessarily complicit with evil, in which the evil of the aesthetic will be revealed.

Kierkegaard's analysis of the art of seduction in 'The Seducer's Diary' is a theme taken up by Spark in her fourth novel, *The Bachelors* (1960), in which Patrick Seton is an ageing version of Kierkegaard's Seducer, who is about to go on trial for having seduced his landlady, Frieda Flower, into handing over to him her life's savings while, at the same time, he is also trying to deal with the pregnancy of a much younger woman, Alice, whom he has seduced into a relationship on the basis of his aesthetic qualities: 'He recites poetry so beautifully. He's a sort of real artist' (*B*, 20), she tells her friend Elsie. Patrick's aesthetic nature has given him the ability to step beyond reality into that alternative world of the imagination that Kierkegaard describes as looking 'like a world of gauze, lighter, qualitatively different from the actual world' (*E/O*, I, 253). Symptomatic of his ability to step across that boundary is the fact that he makes his living as 'medium', giving people access to their dead who continue to exist in an ethereal otherworld. The medium gives to his audience the pleasure of the pseudo-eternity of the aesthetic, and it is by such an aesthetic infinitude that the characters of *The Bachelors* are tempted: Freda Flower believes Patrick has access to 'the Beyond', while Ewart Thornton fears 'Patrick was definitely in touch with things out there in the Unseen' (*B*, 199); the spiritualist group for whom Patrick performs is named 'the Wider Infinity', and allows its organiser, Marlene Cooper, to believe that she is in communication both with her dead husband Harry and her former lover Carl who, very differently from their lives in time, can placidly share companionship in their 'land of perpetual summer' (*B*, 27). Equally, Patrick is, for Alice, confirmation of her religious intuitions, so that she insists to Elsie that she prays

> '[. . .] day and night. I go into churches and pray if the doors are open, and I pray that Patrick will be saved from prison.'
>
> 'I wouldn't build on it,' Elsie said.
>
> 'I am building on it. I pray for Patrick, and that's the test. If Patrick doesn't get off, I don't believe in God.' (*B*, 205)

Alice's desire that Patrick be 'saved' from the law rather than saved by religion reveals her misplaced valuation of both law and religion, while, for Elsie, a working relationship with Father Socket provides an aesthetic sense of the infinite: 'After all,' she thinks, 'Alice had Patrick; and it was nice for a girl to have someone on the spiritual side of life. Men like Father Socket lifted one up whereas young men so often pulled one down' (*B*, 131). After she has finished typing up Socket's texts 'on the subjects of the Cabbala, Theosophy, Witchcraft, Spiritualism, and Bacon wrote Shakespeare' (*B*, 129), he reads her 'a bit of what he's just written of his spiritual autobiography' (*B*, 129–30). Both Socket and Patrick encourage the belief that poetry will open the way to the infinite but as Kierkegaard's pseudonymous author puts it in *Either/Or*:

> The poetic ideal is always a sickly ideal, for the true ideal is always the real. So when the spirit is not allowed to soar up into the eternal world of spirit it remains midway and rejoices in the pictures reflected in the clouds and weeps that they are so transitory. A poet existence is, therefore, as such, an unhappy existence, it is higher than finiteness and yet not infiniteness. (*E/O*, II, 177)

The characters of *The Bachelors* are continually 'midway' towards a 'beyond' and an 'unseen' which they hope will allow them to encounter the infinite, but never being more than 'midway' means that they will never reach their desired destination: in their disputes about who has the most insight or the best telepathic powers they are always going to fall back into the finite, as Patrick and Socket do when they use their séances as the medium by which they can gain information that allows them to blackmail some of the attendees. On the basis of a single meeting and a single communication from Gloria who 'had died as the result of an illegal operation in the summer of 1932' (*B*, 103), Patrick is able to extort money and drugs from his doctor. The aesthetic may gesture towards the infinite but it redounds in an all too material exploitation of the finite: as with Kierkegaard's Seducer, the aesthetic is the medium by which evil seduces the world.

Patrick's abilities as a medium are what make him interesting, both sexually and morally: 'If you just saw him in the street without knowing he was a medium,' Alice's friend Elsie insists, 'you'd think he was a little half-pint job'; Alice, however, is entirely convinced by the aesthetic: 'But I do know him. He means everything to me. He loves poetry and beauty' (*B*, 21). Patrick has indeed always lived in the medium of the aesthetic – and as a medium for the aesthetic – so that even the theatre is a disruption of the world of his imaginings:

> He is a dreamy child: a dreamer of dreams, they say with pride, as he wanders back from walks in the botanical gardens, or looks up from his book. *Mary Rose* by J. M. Barrie is Patrick's favourite, and he is taken to the theatre to see it acted, and is sharply shocked by the sight of the real actresses and actors with painted faces performing outwardly on the open platform this tender romance about the girl who was stolen by the fairies on a Hebridean island. (*B*, 171)

The stage is not enough of an aesthetic illusion for Patrick: the ethereal stage beyond the stage is where his imagination is at home, a place into which the ethical cannot intrude:

> As a young man he memorizes the early poems of W. B. Yeats and will never forget them. Now, on his first enchanted visit to the Western Isles he first encounters an unfortunate occurrence, having sat up reciting to an American lady far into the night and the next morning being accused of having taken money from her purse. He is thinking of her, in his poetic innocence, as a kindred soul to whom money does not matter, but now she carries on as if money mattered. (*B*, 171–2)

Patrick's 'poetic innocence' allows him not only to resist responsibility for his own actions but even to erase the memory of them:

> He remembered most of all his childhood, and could possibly have brought to mind the latent image of being taken with his class round an art gallery by his art teacher, a woman. She is endeavouring to explain impressionist art by bidding them look at the palm of their hands for a moment, and nowhere else. 'All round your hand you are aware of objects – you see them, but not distinctly. What you see round the palm of your hand is an impression.' Patrick's memory had become this type of impression. (*B*, 171)

Patrick is a person entirely seduced by the aesthetic, who then uses the aesthetic as his means of seduction. He can do so successfully, however, only because he lives in a world that is itself immersed in the aesthetic. Kierkegaard's Seducer works towards the fulfilment of his aesthetic purpose by a series of indirections and one of his most successful ploys is to pretend to be a confirmed bachelor, who shows more interest in the aunt of the girl he wants to seduce than the girl herself:

> I have presented the perfect picture of a confirmed bachelor. All I talk about is sitting at my ease, being comfortably lodged, having a competent servant, friends of good standing whom I can rely upon as intimates [. . .] One can laugh at a bachelor, even have sympathy for him, but a young man, who has any spirit at all, shocks a young girl by such conduct; the entire significance of sex, its beauty, and its poetry, is destroyed. (*E/O*, I, 291)

By posing as a bachelor he is both revealing his real nature – he has no intention of marrying – but also forces the young girl to realise how much she will lose if 'the significance of her sex, its beauty and poetry' should be ignored, thereby making her more concerned to draw his attention and making it easier for him to manipulate her towards acceptance of his refusal 'to distinguish poetry and reality from one other' (*E/O*, I, 253). The bachelors of Spark's novel live in and for the aesthetic, and resist 'the ethical' which 'is just as tiresome in philosophy as in life', because, 'under the heaven of the aesthetic everything is light, beautiful, transitory; when the ethical comes along, then everything becomes harsh, angular, infinitely boring' (*E/O*, I, 305). In order to maintain the order of the aesthetic, however, Spark's bachelors have to ensure that the women with whom they are involved can never be so aesthetically interesting that their relationships draw them into an ethical commitment. Thus when Martin Bowles is visiting Isobel Billows, whose financial affairs he oversees but whom he sometimes considers marrying, she is visited by Walter Prett, an art critic whom Isobel had failed to invite to her recent cocktail party; angered by Martin's contempt and Isobel's attempt at apology, Walter takes a tea-tray and smashes Isobel's favourite crockery in the fireplace. Promoter of the value of the aesthetic, Walter nonetheless deprives Isobel of her aesthetic possessions, a physical loss which is then compounded by her diminishment in Martin's eyes:

> Martin looked at his watch and at her plump behind as she knelt over the broken pieces, and wanted to kick it. For he felt suddenly that he was to her only the man who handled her property and shares, and that she slept with him only to ensure his loyalty and save herself the trouble of investigating the property deals. (*B*, 153–4)

Maintenance of their life in the aesthetic depends, for the bachelors, on ensuring that the aesthetic is strictly rationed in order to prevent it seducing the seducer towards the ethical. Patrick's seduction of Alice, and his delay in saying when they will get married, is founded on his account that he is waiting for the completion of his divorce from a previous marriage, a marriage which turns out to be entirely fictitious; Martin Bowles will not give in to his feelings for Isobel because he finds living with his mother and his old nurse more comfortable; Ronald Bridges is an epileptic who breaks up with his girlfriend because he is afraid she will mother him; Ewart Thornton is happy to maintain telephone relationships with women from whom he can always escape by claiming he has schoolwork to mark; Matthew Finch eats onions to try to make himself unpalatable when tempted by sex; and Father Socket and his friend Mike Garland are homosexuals who employ women to perform as live aesthetic objects in unlicensed clubs where films about nudity are shown. In the second volume of *Either/Or*, Judge Wilhelm, arguing for 'The Aesthetic Validity of Marriage', declares, 'I do not know where anything is said in the Scriptures about a special blessing upon bachelors' (*E/O*, II, 42). Matthew Finch, of Irish Catholic descent, also insists 'there's no justification for being a bachelor and that's the truth, let's face it. It's everyone's duty to be fruitful and multiply according to his calling either spiritual or temporal, as the case may be' (*B*, 71); but when asked by Ronald, 'Do you want to marry at all?', Matthew has to admit, 'I can't say I do' (*B*, 80). Ronald himself turns down the opportunity to sleep with Elsie who then confesses her failure to find a satisfactory relationship with any of the men with whom she has had sex: 'It's much better for men not to come at all if they're always going to go away and leave me alone. I'm not lonely before they come. I'm only lonely when they go away' (*B*, 180). *The Bachelors* explores a world where the dialectic of Kierkegaard's either/or has become a neither/nor – neither the Seducer's wholehearted commitment to the fleeting world of the aesthetic nor the Judge's assertion of the permanent virtues of the ethical. The 'bachelors' live in their half-hearted aesthetic as a deliberate suspension of decisions about their future, and therefore as a deliberate postponement of their confrontation with the ethical.

For Patrick, however, the looming realities of his trial for defrauding Freda Flower and of the arrival of Alice's baby put his future aesthetic bachelorhood in jeopardy:

> It is so much easier to get away from a girl in any other part of the country than in London. In the provinces one only has to go to London and disappear. But once you have a girl in your life in London she knows all your associates, you have established yourself, she knows some of your affairs; she knows where to find you; and it is impossible to disappear from Alice without disappearing from the centre of things, the spiritualist movement – Marlene – his Circle – 'My bread and butter.' (*B*, 173)

An aesthetic existence is, for Patrick, also his 'bread and butter', and the pseudo-infinity of the aesthetic always has to be made to pay material dividends, material dividends that are threatened by Alice and her baby. Challenged by Elsie about Alice's being hungry, which might be a sign that her insulin injections are not being properly managed, Patrick responds,

> 'She's hungry because she brought up her lunch,' said Patrick defensively.
>
> Elsie looked at him suspiciously. 'I hope you do give her the injection regularly,' she said. 'She needs taking care of.'
>
> It was then Patrick's mind turned a corner. (*B*, 20)

Patrick does not come to an ethical decision about his and Alice's future: instead, 'his mind turned a corner', as he suddenly senses – like the reader of a poem discovering an ambiguity on which its meaning turns – the double implication of 'She needs taking care of'. The conflict between Alice and his 'bread and butter' means that Alice 'must be dealt with, and her unbelievable baby', but her death will simply be a different encounter with the infinite: 'He loved her. Always would. Even unto her passing over. The spirit giveth life' (*B*, 57). So Patrick switches from the aesthetic appreciation of Alice alive to the equally aesthetic appreciation of her dead: looking at her on her bed, in a posture which he recognises because it 'made her so like the other women, crumpled up on the bed after their fury' (*B*, 174), he experiences

> an acute throb of anticipatory pleasure at the mental vision of Alice, crumpled up – in the same position as she now was on the bed – on the mountainside in Austria [. . .] Crumpled up on the mountainside in Austria, Alice, overloaded with insulin, far from help, beyond the reach of a doctor, beyond help – far from the intrusive knowledge of his friends and enemies in London, outside the scope of his bread and butter, free from her heavy body, beyond good and evil. She has agreed to it, not in so many words, but . . . (*B*, 174–5)

In the realm of the aesthetic there is neither good nor evil: one aesthetic response turns into another with no ethical implication. Thus Alice's coming death will be, for Patrick, her release into spirituality, her final 'leap' into the infinite with which he has seduced her, just as for Kierkegaard's Seducer the aim is to get the girl 'falling into my arms as it were by natural necessity'; though he strives to bring her to the point 'where she gravitates towards me, it will still not be like the falling of a heavy body, but as spirit seeking spirit' (*E/O*, I, 299). Equally, when confronted by the lipsticked Mike Garland in Father Socket's home, Elsie

> ate a slice of walnut cake very quickly because she was so very upset inside at the sight of Mike in his highly sexual attire. She clutched her handbag all the closer, and was damned if she would part with the letter now that Father Socket had let her down so badly. Be damned to his paternal solicitude for dear Patrick. She should have known

> before, indeed she had really, inside, known all along that the Master was homosexual as Alice had said. She could have put up with it, even preferred it, if he had no sex at all, was above sex, but if there was one thing she detested . . . (*B*, 136)

Elsie 'discovers' what she had always already 'known all along' but failed to acknowledge, and her response is an aesthetic revulsion rather than an ethical judgement; similarly, when Ronald Bridges comes to her flat to try to recover Patrick Seton's forged letter, she offers to return it in the morning if he will sleep with her. Trapped in the aesthetic she is always en route but can never find a final purpose or even a resting point:

> 'They don't want intelligence. They don't come if there's no sex. I'm a sexy type, I get excited about it. And that's what they like. But it only leaves me lonely.'
>
> 'Don't you enjoy it at the time?'
>
> 'No. But I can't do without it, and these men know it. They fumble about with their french letters or they tear open their horrible little packets of contraceptives like kids with sweets, or they expect me to have a rubber stop-gap all ready fitted. All the time I want to be in love with the man and conceive his child, but I keep thinking of the birth-control and something inside me turns in its grave. You can't enjoy sex in that frame of mind.' (*B*, 181)

The aesthetic is self-defeating: it makes no choices but engages in evasive substitutions that result in the repetition of the same pleasures and the same failures.

Patrick's supposed access to an 'infinite' is set by Spark in opposition to Ronald Bridges' epilepsy, which has not only barred his route to the priesthood but underlines that he lives in world that is both fallen and still falling. The drugs that Ronald uses to control his epileptic fits, Patrick uses to stimulate his trances; in his fits, Ronald's heels beat upon the floor or the pavement; in his trances, Patrick's 'feet kicked with sharp clicks of the heels on the parquet wooden floor' (*B*, 35), and when Ronald collapses after giving evidence in Patrick's trial, 'His eyes turned upward, and the drum-like kicking of his heels began on the polished wooden floor' (*B*, 221), leading the judge to ask, given the previous evidence about Patrick's behaviour when he 'goes under', 'Is this man a medium?' (*B*, 221). For his acquaintances, Ronald is indeed a kind of medium, since his illness seems to draw out from those around him 'some ancient superstition about his epilepsy: "the falling sickness", "the sacred disease", "the evil spirit". Ronald felt he was regarded by his friends as a sacred cow or a wise monkey' (*B*, 67). Asked what he thinks goes on in Patrick's mind when he looks back at his past, Ronald replies by describing his own symptoms:

> 'when he considers his past life he suffers from a rush of blood to the head, giddiness and bells in the ears. And therefore he does not consider his life at all.' And having thus described his own symptoms when a fit was approaching, Ronald fell silent. (*B*, 67)

Ronald and Patrick are thus yoked together as alternative versions of how it is possible to live in a fallen world – Patrick's is the evasion offered by an aesthetic infinitude while, as Ronald tells Tim, 'There are only two religions, the spiritualist and the Catholic' (*B*, 190). In the aftermath of his fits, Ronald experiences a kind of inverted spiritualism in which he is visited by the living as though they were demonic spirits:

> Ronald went home to bed. He slept heavily and woke at midnight, and went out to walk off his demons.
>
> Martin Bowles, Patrick Seton, Socket.
>
> And the others as well, rousing him up: fruitless souls, crumbling tinder, like his own self which did not bear thinking of. But it is all demonology, he thought, and he brought them all to witness, in his old style, one by one before the courts of his mind. Tim Raymond, Ewart Thornton, Walter Prett, Matthew Finch – will I, won't I marry her? – Eccie, and himself kicking under the witness box, himself, now, incensed; and all the rest of them. He sent these figures away like demons of the air until he could think of them again with indifference or amusement or wonder. (*B*, 240)

The living with whom Ronald must interact in his daily life thus become the demons of an apparent afterlife for which he can find no consolation, but in this he is living out what Kierkegaard described in a journal entry in 1850:

> In contradistinction to the Middle Ages and those periods with all their discussion of possession, of particular men giving themselves to evil, I should like to write a book:
>
> *On diabolic possession in modern times*

> and show how mankind *en masse* gives itself up to evil, how nowadays it happens *en masse*. That is why people flock together, in order that natural and animal hysteria should get hold of them, in order to feel themselves stimulated, enflamed [. . .] (*J*, '1063', 377)

The modern world is a demonic world, haunted by false infinities, making the aesthetic the justification for the banality of the vices that Ronald recognises in his friends: listening to Martin Bowles questioning Patrick about the money he received from Freda, Ronald silently cross-questions his friend about the hypocrisy of his own relationships: 'Ronald sat with the demonic aftermath of his fit working within him [. . .] And you deny, thought Ronald, that you are swindling Isobel Billows?' (*B*, 225). After one of his epileptic attacks, Ronald

> resolved to go to Confession, less to rid himself of the past night's thoughts – since his priest made a distinction between sins of thought and these convulsive dances and dialogues of the mind – than to receive, in absolution, a friendly gesture of recognition from the maker of heaven and earth, vigilant manipulator of the Falling Sickness. (*B*, 121–2)

His God is the God of his medical condition – 'vigilant manipulator of the Falling Sickness' – not the God by whom one is to be judged, before whom one must become an individual. The novel cannot transcend its own involvement in the aesthetic to release the possibility of a truly religious consciousness: what it can do is to reveal the evil of the aesthetic when unrestrained by religious belief. While silently Ronald entertains this realisation of the banality of the evil by which he is surrounded, Patrick is looking up at Alice on the balcony, seeing not the future which she is willing him to preserve but

> visualizing, with fretful eagerness, Alice as she should lie on the mountainside, crumpled up, overdosed with insulin; the liberation of Alice's spirit was so imminent, it was like a sunny radiance to distract his understanding from the proceedings of the court. (*B*, 209)

With increasing intensity, Patrick commits himself to the art of death as the only possible conclusion to his exploitation of the aesthetic, while Ronald seeks ways of redeeming the world of the aesthetic into which he has fallen: continually preparing to manage his inevitable fallings, Ronald may not be in touch with the infinite in the way that he had hoped to be when he planned to enter the priesthood, but neither is he tempted to live only in the aesthetic and in the aesthete's version of the infinite. He may not have reached the ultimate goal of religious individuality, or even the goal of a consistent ethics, but in the world of the aesthetic he is, as he tells Elsie, 'a stranger. That's why I can't sleep with you' (*B*, 180). The novel dramatises a world in which the aesthetic reigns and from which there can be no escape because the novel is, itself, a portion of and infused by the values of the aesthetic. *The Bachelors* is a novel seeking to warn about the aesthetic through the medium of the aesthetic, and thus replicates the irony of Kierkegaard's pseudonymous writings, in which the contortions of the narrative structure are designed to reveal that Kierkegaard is a poet-philosopher who must work through the medium of the aesthetic but who must, at the same time, warn against the consequences of allowing the aesthetic to become the dominating element in our perception of the world. Without the aesthetic, we have no way of responding to the daily pleasures of life, but unregulated by the ethical and the religious the aesthetic opens the way to the tyranny of evil.

Kierkegaard's fear of the power of the aesthetic is central to Spark's conception of the novel: if Ronald Bridges is a possible but unreliable bridge between the aesthetic and the ethical or the religious, the novel itself is such a bridge – a medium which cannot evade its participation in the aesthetic but which, at the same time, must reveal through that medium its resistance to the aesthetic which makes it possible. Just as the negations of Kierkegaard's narrative structures are designed both to invoke and defy the aesthetic which is his medium, so Spark's novels are ambiguously poised between the aesthetic, which is their medium, while at the same time making themselves strangers to that world – which is perhaps why, in her next novel, *The Prime of Miss Jean Brodie* (1961), the central consciousness through which Miss Brodie's life is presented is that of Sandy Stranger. Sandy is, like Patrick Seton, someone who lives in the aesthetic, continually displacing the life around her with fictional narratives: 'Sandy, who had been reading *Kidnapped*, was having a conversation with the hero, Alan Breck, and was glad to be with Mary MacGregor because it was not necessary to talk to Mary' (*PJB*, 24). Sandy's imaginary world takes over from the real world so that she 'was walking unevenly, in little spurts forward and little halts, as Alan Breck began to sing to her his ditty before she took to the heather to deliver the message that was going to save Alan's life' (*PJB*, 35). Alan Breck will later be displaced by Sandy's imaginary encounter with the ballet dancer Pavlova, who declares that Sandy is 'an artist and will carry on the torch' (*PJB*, 82), and then by Sergeant Anne Grey, Sandy's invented name for the policewoman who was investigating Jenny's encounter with 'a man joyfully exposing himself beside the Water of Leith' (*PJB*, 86). Sandy imagines herself as 'Anne Grey's right-hand woman in the Force, and they were dedicated to eliminate sex from Edinburgh and its environs' (*PJB*, 89). These aesthetic displacements of reality are prologues to Sandy and Jenny's realisation that Miss Brodie is doing exactly the same thing when her 'old love story' about the fiancé who died in the war is

> newly embroidered, under the elm, with curious threads: it appeared that while on leave from the war, her late fiancé had frequently taken her out sailing in a fishing boat and that they had spent some of their merriest times among the rocks and pebbles of a small seaport. 'Sometimes Hugh would sing, he had a rich tenor voice. At other times he fell silent and would set up his easel and paint. He was very talented at both arts, but I think the painter was the real Hugh.' (*PJB*, 93–4)

Hugh takes on the characteristics of the male teachers – one a music teacher, the other a teacher of art – who are vying for Miss Brodie's attention in the Marcia Blaine School: Hugh is resurrected to a new identity just as Sandy and Jenny have resurrected him in their story 'The Mountain Eyrie', in which Hugh's death turns out to be a false report and in which he returns to Edinburgh only to be told by Miss Mackay, the headmistress, 'that Miss Brodie did not desire to see him, she loved another' (*PJB*, 20). It is Sandy's own imaginative embroidering of reality that makes her so sensitive to Miss Brodie's equivalent recreations, even though Sandy uses her own imaginings to resist capitulating to Miss Brodie's fictions:

> Miss Brodie was reciting poetry to the class at a quarter to four, to raise their minds before they went home [. . .]:
>
> Down she came and found a boat
> Beneath the willow left afloat,
> And round about the prow she wrote
> *The Lady of Shalott.*
>
> 'By what means did your ladyship write these words,' Sandy inquired in her mind with her lips tight shut.
>
> 'There was a pot of white paint and a brush which happened to be standing on the grassy verge,' replied the Lady of Shalott graciously. 'It was left there no doubt by some heedless member of the unemployed.' (*PJB*, 24)

It is Sandy's capacity for resistant imagination that makes her both an object of Miss Brodie's scorn – 'One day, Sandy, you will go too far.' [. . .] 'I have my eye upon you, Sandy. I observe a frivolous nature. I fear you will never belong to life's élite or, as one might say, the crème de la crème' (*PJB*, 27) – but at the same time makes Sandy Miss Brodie's representative among the girls of her 'set':

> The Lady of Shalott placed a white hand on Sandy's shoulder and gazed at her for a space. 'That one so young and beautiful should be so ill-fated in love!' she said in low sad tones. (*PJB*, 24)

The message is delivered to Sandy but it applies more forcefully to Brodie herself. Sandy is the medium by which Brodie's imagination is channelled as well as resisted; so that when Monica reports having seen Miss Brodie kiss Teddy Lloyd, the art teacher, Sandy performs the event for the appreciation of her classmates:

> She seemed satisfied with her experimental re-enactment but it so delighted her friends that she repeated it. Miss Brodie came up from behind her on her fourth performance which had reached a state of extreme flourish.
>
> 'What are you doing, Sandy?' said Miss Brodie.
>
> 'Only playing,' said Sandy, photographing this new Miss Brodie with her little eyes. (*PJB*, 62)

Sandy imaginatively transforms herself into a surrogate for Jean Brodie and, aesthetically, performs the changed reality that she now recognises and records in Brodie's personality.

Jean Brodie and Sandy Stranger are, from one perspective, opposed to one another, especially after Sandy 'betrays' her former teacher and has her sacked from her post, but in fact they are both proponents of the aesthetic. Sandy as much as Jean Brodie is a product of her teacher's 'prime', which grows and develops as the girls do: "These are the years of my prime. You are benefiting by my prime', Jean Brodie declares, but it is a prime, the narrator informs us, 'whose nature was growing under their eyes, as the girls themselves were under formation. It extended, this prime of Miss Brodie's, still in the making when the girls were well on in their teens' (*PJB*, 55). Sandy may be both fascinated by Miss Brodie's 'method of making patterns with facts' and, at the same time, desperate 'to prove Miss Brodie guilty of misconduct' (*PJB*, 94), but Sandy herself is a product of Miss Brodie's aesthetic education, which is based on 'an excessive lack of guilt':

> The side-effects of this condition were exhilarating to her special girls in that they in some way partook of the general absolution she had assumed to herself. [. . .] All the time they were under her influence she and her actions were outside the context of right and wrong. (*PJB*, 113)

Being entirely aesthetic, however, the growth of Brodie's prime is not towards the ethical but merely to the substitution of one aesthetic experience for another:

> The term started vigorously as usual. Miss Brodie stood bronzed before her class and said, 'I have spent most of my summer holidays in Italy once more, and a week in London, and I have brought back a great many pictures which we can pin on the wall. Here is a Cimabue. Here is a larger formation of Mussolini's fascisti, it is better view of them than that of last year's picture. (*PJB*, 55)

This change which is no change is reflected in Miss Brodie's avid desire for stories about Teddy Lloyd – 'Miss Brodie could not hear enough versions of the same story if it involved Teddy Lloyd' (*PJB*, 121–2) – and in Lloyd's paintings of the girls which turn them all into versions of Jean Brodie. In the aesthetic, all change is similitude, all difference a repetition. Brodie's attraction to her pupils is precisely her promotion of the aesthetic as a justification of her own personal preferences:

> 'Who is the greatest Italian painter?'
> 'Leonardo da Vinci, Miss Brodie.'
> 'That is incorrect. The answer is Giotto, he is my favourite.' (*PJB*, 9–10)

In the aesthetic, the world presents itself as a reflection of, rather than a challenge to, the values of the self, so that the self is suspended from real change, and, like Lloyd's portraits, reveals the essential unity between the desires of the self and the world which it inhabits. Secure in the fortress of the aesthetic, Miss Brodie is unmoved by the contempt of her fellow teachers or the head teacher's threat to have her sacked. She has taken up the position outlined by Kierkegaard's Judge Wilhelm who describes a person who thinks he has chosen his own identity as believing he can say, 'Now I possess myself, I require nothing more, and to all the changes of the world I oppose the proud thought: I am the man I am' (*E/O*, II, 194). Such a commitment to the aesthetic, however, involves a false conception of the individual's relationship to eternity:

> The temporal vanishes before his eyes. At the first instant this fills him with indescribable bliss and gives him a sense of absolute security. If then he begins to gaze upon this bliss, the temporal advances its claim. This is scorned. What the temporal can give, the more or the less which now presents itself, is so very unimportant in comparison with what he eternally possesses. Everything comes with him to a standstill, he has, as it were reached eternity before the time. (*E/O*, I, 194)

Jean Brodie's endlessly extending 'prime' is a false eternity, a lure to young people without the experience to measure its real significance. Her commitment to the aesthetic makes of her 'prime' a secular eternity that turns the present into a repetition of the past – each year she has a new set that defies the ethos of the school – and, at the same time, an anticipation of an unchanged future: 'These years are still the years of my prime. It is important to recognize the years of one's prime, always remember that' (*PJB*, 8). Miss Brodie has made her life into the simulacrum of a work of art, able to defy time and to rise above good and evil. Even the unexpected marriage of

Gordon Lowther to Miss Lockhart, depriving Miss Brodie of her weekend love-nest in Cramond, only reinforces her sense of her aesthetic significance:

> 'I am his Muse,' said Miss Brodie, referring to Teddy Lloyd, 'But I have renounced his love in order to dedicate my prime to the young girls in my care. I am his Muse but Rose shall take my place.' (*PJB*, 120)

The apparently ethical claim of 'renunciation' leads only to the reassertion of the aesthetic, and also to the demonic desire to impose her aesthetic values on those she teaches. Brodie's pupils may be growing and changing but, as far as Jean Brodie is concerned, they are changing only to become the characters who are already foreknown to her as projections of herself and her ambitions:

> '[. . .] all my ambitions are for you and Rose. You have got insight, perhaps not quite spiritual, but you're a deep one, and Rose has got instinct, Rose has got instinct.'
>
> 'I ought to know, because my prime has brought me instinct and insight, both.' (*PJB*, 140)

Brodie has become a surrogate author, denying the freedom of her pupils by seeking to direct and shape their future lives in conformity with her own wishes. It may seem like an act of freedom when Sandy disrupts Jean Brodie's plot to have Rose, 'famous for sex' (*PJB*, 47), fulfil Miss Brodie's own desire to be Teddy Lloyd's lover – 'Miss Brodie put her arm round Rose's shoulder and thanked Mr Lloyd for his help, as if she and Rose were one' (*PJB*, 91) – but Sandy's displacement of Rose simply fulfils by a different route Miss Brodie's desire that Teddy Lloyd should enter into a relationship with one of her 'crème de la crème'. It is a purely aesthetic outcome which does not disrupt Miss Brodie's belief in the rightness of the part she is playing:

> 'And after all, Sandy,' she said, 'you are destined to be the great lover, although I would not have thought it. Truth is stranger than fiction.' (*PJB*, 165)

The truth, however, that is stranger than fiction is that it is Sandy who is transformed by the relationship with Teddy Lloyd, since

> By the end of the year it happened that she had quite lost interest in his mind, from which she extracted, among other things, his religion as a pith from the husk. Her mind was full of his religion as a night sky is full of things visible and invisible. She left the man, took his religion and became a nun in the course of time. (*PJB*, 165)

With her adoption of Catholicism, the aesthetic is displaced by the ethical: 'She was more fuming now, with Christian morals, than John Knox' (*PJB*, 167). As Judge Wilhelm writes to his aesthetic friend,

> Young people who have no notion of how dearly experience is bought, nor any presentiment of the unspeakable wealth which it is, may easily let themselves be carried away by the same whirlwind; they may perhaps be affected by your talk as by a fresh breeze which lures them out upon the infinite ocean to which you point them; and you yourself may become almost uncontrollably intoxicated by the thought of that infinity which is your element which, like the ocean, conceals everything which lies upon its changeless floor. Should not you, who are already an experienced navigator in these waters, know how to tell of disasters and distress at sea? (*E/O*, II, 70)

The death of Joyce Emily on her way to fight for Franco at Miss Brodie's instigation is the 'disaster and distress' which reveals, for Sandy, the ethical perspective in which Miss Brodie's promotion of the aesthetic leads not to the revelation of a world infused with beauty but to an art of evil. An aesthetic commitment to fascism does not only have aesthetic consequences, for the aesthetic is the medium by which the art of evil can reshape the world.

The relationship between Jean Brodie and Sandy Stranger is a dialectical one, in which each redefines the other as the relationship develops, and in this it resembles the dialectical structures by which Kierkegaard shaped his pseudonymous works – the aesthetics of the Seducer in the first part of *Either/Or* balanced against the ethical views of Judge Wilhelm in the second. But there is a second dimension to the dialectics of Kierkegaard's works, which is the relationship between the characters and the supposed author or editor of the work in which they appear and the relationship of those author-editors to the 'real' author, Kierkegaard himself – of the relationship between an aesthetic Kierkegaard and the theological Kierkegaard who publishes books under his own name. In Spark's novel there is a similarly complex relationship between the characters and the author who makes her presence continually felt by her adoption of precisely those novelistic strategies which Sartre had deplored – revealing the future in the midst of the action, commenting on the nature and moral beliefs of her characters. The dialectic between the characters, between Brodie and Sandy, is thus translated into a dialectic between the characters and the author's choices in the mode of their presentation. The form of the novel points to the metaphysical presence of its creator, both Godlike in her omniscience but also, like her characters, steeped in the aesthetic: the novel itself becomes both a presentation of and an enactment of the art of evil. The dialectical structure of the novel requires, however, that the recognition of the art of evil cannot be a final resting place for the narrative. Sandy, in the role of Sister Helena of the Transfiguration, is the author of what has become a famous book of psychology, *The Transfiguration of the Commonplace*, whose title evokes not only the biblical account of Jesus' transfiguration in the eyes of his disciples but a key term in Kierkegaard's philosophical vocabulary, in which transfiguration is what is accomplished through the individual's relationship to God:

> *Aug 20.* According to the teaching of Christianity man is not to be merged into God by way of a sort of pantheistic disappearance, or by the obliteration of all his individual traits in the divine ocean, but through a heightened consciousness. 'Man shall give an account of every idle word he has spoken,' and although grace washes away sin, the union with God proceeds through personality, transfigured by that whole process. (*J*, '220', 63)

Jean Brodie's anticipated narratives of the lives of her pupils, like Teddy Lloyd's portraits, transfigure the 'Brodie set' into aesthetic simulacra of Brodie herself: they are the false transfiguration by which a human being claims a personal eternity that prevents the recognition of the true transfiguration brought about by religion. Sister Helena has been sufficiently imbued with the aesthetic that she can, apparently, only resist it by being caged within the nunnery, 'clutching the bars of the grille' (*PJB*, 127), but her book implies a possible transfiguration of our ordinary reality which would correspond with Kierkegaard's account of transfiguration, and of the relationship thereafter of the aesthetic, the ethical and the religious. When we choose belief and a personal relationship with God, we also choose acceptance of ourselves as who we have been, though with a new conception of how our past relates to the future we have chosen. In so doing, we also accept our necessary participation in the various levels of human existence:

> The personality, through choosing itself, chooses itself ethically and excludes the aesthetic absolutely; but since it is, after all, he himself the person chooses, and through choosing himself does not become another nature but remains himself, the whole of the aesthetic returns in its relativity. (*E/O*, 491)

The aesthetic can be reincorporated as a value in our lives once we have overthrown it as the determinant of those lives by submitting to the ultimate demands of religion. From the position of an achieved religious perspective, the aesthetic is allowed to return because it can now be rightly valued in relation both to the universal requirements of ethics and the truth of religion. Unchecked by religion, a life lived by commitment to the aesthetic leads inevitably to what the ethical will identify as evil, but without the aesthetic the ethical, and after it, the religious, will be nothing more than a repressive negation of the possibilities of human life: the danger is that a poet, like all who live in the aesthetic, is, 'from the religious point of view a deceiver' (*J*, '907', 307), but from the security of religious commitment 'the aesthetic returns, and you shall see that only then is life beautiful, and that only in this way can a person succeed in saving his soul and gaining the whole world, in using the world and not abusing it' (*E/O*, 492). Thus Sister Helena can re-accept the Jean Brodie against whom Sandy had fumed as one who had indeed taught *The Transfiguration of the Commonplace*:

> 'What we the main influences of your school days, Sister Helena? Were they literary or political or personal? Was it Calvinism?'
>
> Sandy said: 'There was a Miss Jean Brodie in her prime.' (*PJB*, 171)

Sandy's acknowledgement of 'Jean Brodie in her prime' reveals how, to one who has chosen religion, 'the whole of the aesthetic returns in its relativity', redeemed from the evil to which it once led.

Spark's narrator tells us decisively that 'It is not to be supposed that Miss Brodie was unique at this point in her prime; or that (since such things are relative) that she was in any way off her head' (*PJB*, 52), contrasting her with others in Edinburgh consigned to spinsterhood as a consequence of the First World War. Nor, however, was she unique in finding that the aesthetic responded positively to fascism's projection of itself through art, from Mussolini's adoption of 'futurism' to the Nuremberg rallies of Hitler. Many of the most significant modernist artists of the interwar period expressed at one time or another their sympathy for a totalitarian regime which would give art and the artist a special place in modern society. Significantly, however, Miss Brodie's prime is also the time when she begins the study of comparative religion and begins to expatiate to her pupils on the relation of other religions to Christianity:

> The whole question was, during the winter terms, being laid open by Miss Brodie who, at the same time as adhering to the strict Church of Scotland habits of her youth, and keeping the Sabbath, was now, in her prime, attending evening classes in comparative religion at the University. (*PJB*, 36)

'Comparative religion' is a discipline castigated by Walter Lowrie in his biography of Kierkegaard: Lowrie points out that the term had not yet been invented in Kierkegaard's time, but nonetheless opposes Kierkegaard absolutely to the foundational implications of 'comparative religion':

> One cannot reasonably complain that it is now called the comparative study of religion – although perhaps it is ominous that this name may be taken to imply that the task is to compare rather than to distinguish, or at least that the differences discoverable between the various religions, including Christianity, must be regarded as quantitative rather than qualitative. But another name commonly in use is more ominous, and at the same time so absurd that I hardly know whether to laugh or weep over – it is called the study of 'comparative religion'. It is unfortunately true that a great deal of religion is only

> too comparative, conceived even by its votaries to be only comparatively true, or 'true up to a certain point', to use the phrase which S. K. [Søren Kierkegaard] anathematizes.[2]

The failure of 'comparative religion', according to Lowrie, is its failure to recognise what Kierkegaard argues in *Concluding Unscientific Postscript* about the difference between what he denominates Religion A, which would include all pagan forms of religious worship as well as all of the major religions of the world, and Religion B, which has only one representative – Christianity itself, a singular religion among all other religions. The difference between Religions A and B is that B is the only one in which God enters history: 'The doctrine of the Incarnation stamps Christianity as an historical religion in a sense peculiar to it. It deals with eternity *in* time, challenging time, conflicting with time, and looking forward eschatologically to the termination of time.'[3] If Christian faith depends on the recognition of the presence of 'eternity in time', many of Spark's novels focus on the ways in which this perception can be corrupted to produce a seeming eternity *of* time – a condition in which time is no longer the medium through which the eternal makes itself manifest but in which time is translated into a pseudo-eternity. The imagination is the faculty by which this transformation is achieved, reversing the relation of the aesthetic to the ethical by devolving the eternity promised by religion into the aesthetic, and thus by-passing the ethical. Jean Brodie's prime is a secular eternity, defying the time in which it develops and is, necessarily, an art of evil, founded on the evil that art produces when it seeks to make itself a surrogate for the eternity which is the fulfilment of religion.

It is a theme Spark took up again in *The Girls of Slender Means* (1963), which begins by recalling a particular period of history – 'Long ago in 1945' (*GSM*, 1) – and then insistently marking the passage of time in that year from the celebration of 'the victory in the war with Germany' (*GSM*, 14) at its opening in May 1945 to the victory over Japan in the August of that year. The language of time in the novel, however, hovers between past and present and between the present and eternity: 'It was July 1945, three weeks before the general election' (*GSM*, 62), we are told at the beginning of Chapter 4, but then the narrative perspective shifts to provide a closer inspection of a character about whose life and death we have already been informed: 'We come now to Nicholas Farringdon in his thirty-third year' (*GSM*, 52). It is a phrasing which allows 'now' to point both to a present in which Nicholas is a certain age but also to the present of the reading of text, a 'now' which defies a definite location in historical time, and which creates a dialectic between the characters in the novel and the 'we' who share with an author a location outside the time in which those characters move. In the midst of the rush of events of 1945, Nicholas, sometime anarchist and aspiring writer, encounters the girls who live in a hostel known as the May of Teck Club: his view of them is shaped by Jane Wright, who works for a publisher and sees herself as belonging to 'the world of books' (*GSM*, 42), and who 'told him things, in her clever way of intuition, which fitted his ideal of the place' (*GSM*, 106). She, in turn, passes on things that she learns about Nicholas from her work in publishing, and 'the scraps of his history that came to her [. . .] gave him an irresistible heroism in her mind, and, through her, in the eyes of the top-floor girls' (*GSM*, 64). Nicholas and Jane live in a dialectical relationship that supports their mutual construction of an aesthetic conception of the world, allowing Nicholas to view the May of Teck Club in terms of 'an aesthetic and ethical conception of it, a lovely frozen image' (*GSM*, 108) that transfigures it into a pseudo-eternity. It is a world dominated by 'love and money' in which 'love came first, and subsidiary to it was money for the upkeep of looks and purchase of clothing at the official black-market price of eight coupons for a pound' (*GSM*, 27); symbol of this economy of the aesthetic is a Schiaparelli taffeta evening dress given to one of the girls 'by a fabulously rich aunt, after one wearing. This marvellous dress, which caused a stir wherever it went, was shared by all the top floor on special occasions, excluding Jane whom it did not fit' (*GSM*, 39). The culture of the aesthetic also shapes their attitudes to their relationships, which can be changed as easily as a change of dress:

> The weeks had passed and since in the May of Teck Club they were weeks of youth in the ethos of war, they were capable of accommodating quick happenings and reversals, rapid formations of intimate friendships, and a range of lost and discovered loves that in later life and in peace would take years to happen, grow, and fade. (*GSM*, 120)

Even Nicholas, whose anarchism justifies a somewhat dissolute lifestyle, 'was shocked at heart by the rapid turnover of their week-by-week emotions' (*GSM*, 121). A symbol of this escape into the aesthetic is a bathroom window by which those slender enough can get out on to the roof to sunbathe, and through which Selina Redwood, having been abandoned by an American lover when he discovers his wife is shortly to arrive in London, will secretly exit to spend her nights with Nicholas.

The first thing 'we' have learned about Nicholas, however, from a telephone conversation between Jane and one of the girls who had been in the May of Teck Club, is the fact that, years later, he has 'been martyred' (*GSM*, 5) as a missionary Brother in Haiti. Jane, who is trying to put together an article about Nicholas based on their wartime acquaintance, is told by one of her informants that 'the man was making a complete nuisance of himself preaching against the local superstitions. He had several warnings and apparently he got what he asked for' (*GSM*, 149). To Jane's acquaintances, living like her in a world of post-war secularism, the choice of becoming a missionary in Haiti – by then infamous for the conflict between the local voodoo cults and the Catholic Church: 'They're getting rid of a lot of Catholic priests' (*GSM*, 86) – is conceivable only as some kind of individual illness – 'Something must have infected his brain' (*GSM*, 149) – while the notion of 'martyrdom' itself becomes nothing but a 'story' (*GSM*, 5) put about by the Catholic Church and which will, in due course, be understood as a purely political event. Thus, in her next conversation Jane notes simply that 'he's been killed in a local rising' (*GSM*, 17). But the possibility – perhaps, indeed, the necessity – of martyrdom was a key element in Kierkegaard's account of the demands of Christianity on those who would live truly as Christians and not just as passive members of a Christian institution. Kierkegaard insists that,

> according to the New Testament, to be Christian properly means . . . to be sacrificed. The Apostle rushes forth to protest, testifying that one sacrifice was made once for all and that no further sacrifice is needed – and to make sure that this preaching is well understood he is . . . sacrificed. Thereupon thousands and thousands of martyrs are sacrificed to confirm the preaching that no other sacrifice is needed; the New Testament itself predicts that every true Christian will be sacrificed in one way or another.[4]

Walter Lowrie suggests that martyrdom was necessary to Kierkegaard because 'he could think of no other imitation of Christ but the imitation of His suffering and death'.[5] The true Christian must re-experience in his own life Christ's torments upon the cross: 'A religious movement must be served religiously – otherwise it is a sham. Consequently, the emancipation must come about through martyrdom, whether bloody or bloodless' (*J*, '1184', 428). The return of martyrdom is what is needed to transform – or transfigure – the modern era: 'What the age needs is not a genius – it has had geniuses enough, but a martyr, who in order to teach men to obey would himself be obedient unto death' (*J*, '714', 224).

Farringdon, however, is not the only possible martyr in *The Girls of Slender Means* – the other is Joanna Childe, a teacher of elocution whose recitations provide an aesthetic accompaniment to the social life of the May of Teck Club: 'The vibrations of Joanna's elocution voice from her room and from the recreation room where she frequently rehearsed, were felt to add tone and style to the establishment when boyfriends called' (*GSM*, 7). Joanna has taken to poetry as a substitute for her planned life as a curate's wife, because 'all her ideas of honour and love came from the poets' (*GSM*, 21), and she had taken from Shakespeare's sonnet, 'Love is not love', the lesson that 'once you admit that you can change the object of a strongly-held affection, you undermine the whole structure of love and marriage' (*GSM*, 22). Joanna, being unfulfilled in love and refusing to seek another lover, 'had decided to enter maimed into the Kingdom of Heaven' (*GSM*, 25) but replaced the 'sensation of the curate' with 'the sensation of poetry' (*GSM*, 25). Poetry is Joanna's pseudo-eternity, the repetition of the same poems seeming to defeat, in their regular return, the passage of time – 'Once more,' said Joanna's voice, 'Ah! Sun-flower! weary of time' (*GSM*, 69). Joanna's refusal of any further relationships with men is a kind of martyrdom, which elevates her in Nicholas's estimation: to him, her language, charged with religious implications, makes her seem like one 'proclaiming these words so sexually and matriarchally as if in the ecstatic act of suckling a divine child' (*GSM*, 110). Joanna provides Nicholas with a perception of womanhood as having entered into a relationship with the divine, and he tries to capture and make permanent the effect of her readings by recording her rendition of Hopkins's *The Wreck of the Deutschland*, that celebration of the Catholic martyrdom of nuns drowned at sea:

> Thou mastering me
> God! Giver of breath and bread;
> World's strand, sway of the sea;
> Lord of the living and dead
> Thou hast bound bones and veins in me, fastened me flesh
> And after it almost unmade [. . .]

The 'bones', 'veins' and 'flesh' of these lines become an ironic commentary on Joanna's physique, which is too large to make it possible for her to escape through the window on the upper floor used by 'the girls of slender means':

> it was known all through the club that thirty-six and a quarter inches was the maximum for hips that squeeze themselves through it, but as the exit had to be effected sideways with a manoeuvring of the shoulders, much depended on the size of the bones, and on the texture of the individual flesh and muscles. (*GSM*, 157)

On top of the building made unstable by the explosion of the bomb in the garden, Nicholas has a double perception of the relationship of art to eternity: the first is Selina's re-entry into the burning building and reappearance carrying the Schiaparelli dress – 'the coat-hanger dangled from the dress like a headless neck and shoulders' (*GSM*, 160) – a revelation at which 'he involuntarily signed himself with cross' (*GSM*, 161). When Nicholas later tracks her down, she 'couldn't stop screaming' (*GSM*, 178), which he attributes to the fact that he 'must have brought all the horrors back to her mind' (*GSM*, 179), but to which Jane replies, 'It was hell' (*GSM*, 139), a sentence whose potential ambiguity reveals what Nicholas – or, indeed, Selina – foresees as the conclusion of her art of evil. Nicholas's second revelation is of Joanna, trapped in the burning building, and no longer reciting poetry but reverting to the Anglican texts of her childhood: 'she herself stood as one hypnotized into the strange utterances of Day 27 in the Anglican order' (*GSM*, 162):

> Yes, the Lord hath done great things for us already, whereof we rejoice.
> Turn our captivity, O Lord: as the rivers in the south.
> They that sow in tears: shall reap in joy.
>
> (*GSM*, 163)

Joanna finds the voice of her Christian faith in the moment when, as the last in the queue of those waiting to escape, she is about to be consumed by the collapse of the house. It is a moment of revelation that Nicholas tries to share later with her clergyman father until he 'perceived that the man had never seen the reality of his daughter' (*GSM*, 170), and that the father feared that such a story might reveal that she 'had gone over to Rome at the last, or somehow died in bad taste' (*GSM*, 171). Joanna's father is like the clergy whom Kierkegaard describes as wishing 'to emancipate the church by secular and worldly means (thus saving themselves from martyrdom', and who have 'introduced a conception of tolerance entirely consonant with that of the world (where tolerance = indifference) and that is the most terrible offence against Christianity' (*J*, '1184', 428). For Joanna's father, to listen to a recording of the intensity of Joanna's recitation of Hopkins's poem –

> The frown of his face
> Before me, the hurtle of hell
> Behind, where, where was a, where was a place?
>
> (*GSM*, 171)

– would not bring forth to her father the reality of her 'sense of Hell' (*GSM*, 171) as a portion of the Christian account of eternity but reveal only the morbid effect of 'the influence of London' (*GSM*, 172). Nicholas's ultimate martyrdom is not the product of one moment of revelation in the London of 1945, but of three: the revelation of the pseudo-eternity which justifies Selina's evil and therefore impels his decision to commit to Christianity; Joanna's father's inability to understand the implications of the Christianity of which he is supposed to be a representative, which justifies Nicholas's adoption of Roman Catholicism; and the revelation of the Christian relationship between time and eternity which makes Joanna, for Nicholas, a martyr of the faith which he will seek to proclaim. Through the false relation between time and eternity revealed by Selina's appropriation of the Schiaparelli dress – an appropriation by which she seeks to make the future replicate the past as a defiance of time and the events of time – the true meaning of time's relation to eternity comes to be imaged in Joanna's death, and which might be summed up in Kierkegaard's concept of 'the Instant', a notion which was developed most fully in Kierkegaard's late writings but which was given prominence in both E. L. Allen's and Walter Lowrie's accounts of Kierkegaard from the 1930s:

> Such an instant has a peculiar character. It is short, indeed, and temporal, as every instant is, fleeting as every instant is, gone like all instants, the following instant, and yet it is decisive, and yet it is full of eternity. Such an instant must have a special name, let us call it *the fullness of time*.[6]

The Instant reverses the traditional conception of time and eternity: 'the Instant is not properly an atom of time, but an atom of eternity' and thereby replicates 'the paradox that God became man. It is then the decisive Instant of faith.'[7] The Instant is that moment when faith asserts itself as an act of will, a leap, a risk and, in the end, an escape from the false eternity of the aesthetic into the recognition of the Christian meaning of eternity. As Allen puts it, 'Human nature is a paradox, the meeting ground of opposites. The union of finite and infinite is at once the deepest mystery of our being and the most urgent of our present tasks.'[8] As a result, when we risk ourselves for faith, we can declare 'I shall be another man, for something out of eternity itself will have become incarnate in me!'[9] The vocabulary of time in *The Girls of Slender Means* dramatises that intersection of time with eternity: 'We are in the summer of 1945' (*GSM*, 108) turns the past into an immediate present but also suggests a time which 'is full of eternity'. Spark's text, like Joanna's recitations, is a celebration of how time might be redeemed by eternity if it could, however paradoxically, overthrow the pseudo-eternity of the aesthetic, even if the main body of characters in the novel, those whom Jane calls for recollections of Nicholas Farringdon, show no signs of living in a world that is interested either in martyrdom or in a Christian eternity.

The *Girls of Slender Means* thus enacts, through its poetic quotations, its grammatical dislocations of temporality and its recuperation of what, in the perspective of history, is only one of many incidental deaths, a sense of eternity's paradoxical entry into the world of time. The novel calls into the desacralised post-war world in which Jane plies her trade as a journalist a wartime event which tells an alternative story about humanity's relationship to eternity. That desacralised world of post-war Europe is also the setting for Spark's *The Public*

Image (1968), which charts the careers of three minor actors and writers – Annabel and Frederick Christopher and Frederick's friend Billy O'Brien – whose lives are transformed when Annabel is suddenly discovered to have an unexpected screen presence: 'Her eyes were not large, but on the screen they came out so by some mystery' (*PI*, 13). The 'mystery' leads to an Italian film career in which she comes to be known, after her most famous character, as the 'English Lady-Tiger', a soubriquet which imprints her on public consciousness, much to the annoyance of her husband Frederick, who 'was continually overcome by a dazzled exasperation at her capacity for achieving the most impressive effects by the most superficial means' (*PI*, 25). She is, on screen, the 'transfiguration of the commonplace'. Believing himself to be a superior talent – he has a script accepted for a film in which she appears – Frederick decides that 'No one but he could know how shallow she really was' (*PI*, 26). Nonetheless he finds himself having to play out in public the image of their marriage on which her career is based: 'their personal lives became from a few weeks' exposure on the covers and within the pages of the world's popular magazines, a trailing extension of the film' (*PI*, 34). Their lives are reshaped in public as an aesthetic extension of her film identity, trapping them in a narrative from which both would like to escape but which both, for economic reasons, continue to maintain.

In *Either/Or*, Kierkegaard's Judge Wilhelm complains of his contemporaries that they would like to turn marriage into a contract:

> It is also evident that such marriages as are contracted for a definite time are of no avail, since they involve the same difficulties as those which are contracted for a whole life, and at the same time are so far from bestowing the required strength for living that on the contrary they enervate the inner power of married life, relax the energy of the will, and diminish the blessing and confidence which marriage possesses. (*E/O*, II, 23)

Annabel and Frederick's marriage has become a contract – a contract not just between themselves but between themselves and the expectations of the public. It is, however, a contract which Annabel effectively controls, a control demonstrated by her acquisition of a flat in Rome:

> For one who was unaccustomed to organize anything, and who was constitutionally haphazard, she was astonished at what had in fact

> come about by her own effort, so that it had been possible for her to take on the flat, have it cleaned and painted, decide on the essential minimum furniture necessary to move in with her husband and baby. (*PI*, 8)

By taking control of choosing what is to become their home, Annabel effectively demonstrates Frederick's dependence on her, a dependence which she assumes will continue because she finances their lives and does not interfere in his sexual liaisons; he has, in any case, 'settled into a routine of deciding to break with Annabel' which is then undone by his decision 'to wait until they had left these gossipy circles' (*PI*, 45). Frederick, however, is too weak actually to break their relationship and escapes by committing suicide, a suicide for which he symbolically chooses a place of martyrdom – the excavations in Rome 'where they have placed the martyrdom of St Paul' (*PI*, 86) and where he and Annabel have previously visited 'the house where two Roman officers had lived, converts to Christianity' and which was 'the place of their martyrdom' (*PI*, 87). There is no evidence of Christian commitment in Frederick's life but his choice of a place of Christian martyrdom implies that he has also died a martyr's death, martyr to the illusions of the 'public image' in which he has been entrapped.

Frederick's suicide is thus a deliberate challenge to the public perception of his and Annabel's relationship, and Annabel's initial response is to re-establish the aesthetic which has governed their lives. Having returned from identifying Frederick's body at the hospital, she constructs a press conference surrounded by her supportive neighbours, almost all of whom are unknown to her since she has only just moved into her apartment. Their presence, however, not only gives authority to her insistence that Frederick's death could not have been suicide – 'I will never believe it was suicide. Never' (*PI*, 72) – but re-establishes the value of the aesthetic as the environment in which she lives: the gathering of the neighbours looks 'like some vast portrayal of a family and household by Holbein' (*PI*, 72). She has not, however, gauged the extent to which Frederick has become committed to the art of evil: not only has he committed suicide but he has carefully crafted a series of suicide notes which attribute his decision to do so to his wife's life of orgiastic hedonism that has deceived the public and destroyed their marriage. To his mother, who has in fact been dead for three years, he writes, 'I die with the Holy Martyrs in the hope of attaining peace' (*PI*, 86). He also tells her that 'even as I go to my death Annabel has organised a wild and horrible party in a new flat she has taken on for the purpose' (*PI*, 86), a party which Frederick himself has organised, so that his death and her partying amid drink and drugs would inevitably and causally be linked in the public mind as an aesthetic outrage. Frederick's friend, Billy O'Brien, claims to have saved Annabel from the consequences of these suicide notes by retrieving them before they are discovered by the police, but as she listens to their contents Annabel realises the true determination of her adversary: 'Annabel sat up in bed, alert now, and no longer bewildered. She sat up to hear the rest, fully strained towards the professional nature of the enemy, desiring only to know the full extent and scope of his potential force' (*PI*, 83). What she still has to discover, however, is the intensity of the enemy that is Billy O'Brien, whose apparent altruism is a disguise for future blackmail.

The Public Image reworks Kierkegaard's 'The Seducer's Diary' from the point of view of the seduced: where Kierkegaard's focus is on the act of seduction and the fictions by which the Seducer ensnares his victim, Spark's focus is on the woman seduced by fictions, one who has not been abandoned by her seducer but who has been tempted into what Judge Wilhelm describes as the 'aesthetic validity of marriage', a marriage, however, from which her husband, like a domestic Don Giovanni, escapes into endless acts of seduction. From being a bit-part player in low-budget movies Annabel has become a film star, but only to become a bit-part player in her own life, its narrative shaped by men who all want to be the 'author' of her future: Annabel is thus struggling to extricate herself from multiple layers of fiction that seek to define and control her identity – the film industry whose characterisation of her has had to be replicated in her private life; her husband's plot to reveal how false that characterisation has been; the director, Luigi's, fears that she will no longer be able to star in his movies because her image will now be in conflict with the parts he expects her to play; and O'Brien's effort to manipulate the public and private versions of her identity to his own benefit. Frederick, a failed artist in life, uses art to exert control over the life in time which he has abandoned: he achieves a kind of eternity – or, at least, a kind of longevity – by making his fiction the evil medium in which Annabel must live.

The novel thus dramatises a struggle to control the future by competing fictions – Frederick's accounts of Annabel's orgiastic lifestyle and Annabel's version of their fulfilling marriage – both of which cannot be true. Annabel can, therefore, either submit to Frederick's fiction or resist it, not by the declaration of the truth – because 'truth' is precisely what cannot be established – but by a more effective counter-fiction. Spark's plot is focused on Annabel's construction of this counter-fiction, so that Annabel, having been in her acting career a performer in other people's plots, becomes the author of her own version of reality, in which Frederick has indeed been a martyr, but a martyr not to her sexual profligacy but to his own. Realising that the girl found unconscious in her bathroom on the day following Frederick's death had actually attempted suicide because of her love for Frederick, Annabel uncovers a new plotline for her defence:

> 'She'd said she was in love with Frederick.'
>
> This gave Annabel to let the script fall out of her hand on to the floor. She stopped slumping and stared at Luigi with her tawny eyes.
>
> 'No wonder Frederick was driven to suicide with all these women chasing him!' She spoke like the jab of a needle, and watched to see if her words had gone in. (*PI*, 143)

The 'script' which she lets fall may, literally, be that of her next movie, but metaphorically it is the script by which her life with Frederick is to be narrated. In her version, Frederick is a 'martyr' to a society liberated from the mores of 'The Aesthetic Validity of Marriage', the target of the unrestrained passions of those who have, in Kierkegaard's terms, adopted Don Giovanni as their moral mentor. Annabel's response is to act out her forgiveness of those who have been seduced – 'I forgive those who killed him' (*PI*, 160) – while at the same time making Frederick a victim of rather than the perpetrator of his seductions. Annabel takes control of Frederick's narrative and reshapes it into a moral tale for the age, with herself as the forgiving heroine who accepts the weaknesses of those around her. She finally disrupts the controlling narratives in which she is entangled by handing Frederick's letters to the judge, telling him her husband 'was insane' (*PI*, 189) and telling her lawyer she had done this because, 'I want to be free like my baby' (*PI*, 190). She has walked out of others' fictions into a self which is free of its past, and walks out of Spark's fiction into being 'both free and unfree' (*PI*, 190), carrying with her Frederick's characterisation of her as an empty shell but reshaping that image into one of endless depths – 'the echo and harking image of former and former seas' (*PI*, 192). Annabel is released from the evils of the art of fiction, including Spark's own artful fiction. She flies off beyond the reach of any narrative that would limit her freedom to shape her own future: she becomes the free human being who, despite Sartre's attempt to make fiction depend on such freedom, cannot exist within a novel. She has become an existential heroine only by escaping from the world of art and, therefore, from the art of evil.

This group of Spark's novels are each an exploration of the ways in which their characters are trapped in the aesthetic: they are shut out from fulfilment, whether personal or religious, by their deluded acceptance of the aesthetic's false version of eternity. They seek escape not by making a leap into the alternative reality of the religious but by substituting one aesthetic distraction for another. They are seduced by a demonic world whose rejection of Christianity is announced by Annabel's surname in *The Public Image* – Christopher. She, like the other characters of these novels, lives in a world in which the era of 'Christ' is 'over', even if Christ's 'offer' is still available to those who go in search of it. The way to Christ in such a world is not by the revelation of the good but by the recognition of the art of evil by which the world of the aesthetic is governed. Spark's novels both reveal and revel in the aesthetic but only in order to underline the need to escape the evil which the aesthetic cannot help but invoke.

Notes

1. Walter Lowrie, *Kierkegaard* (London: Oxford University Press, 1938), 232.
2. Ibid. 326.
3. Ibid. 323.
4. Quoted in Ibid. 542.
5. Ibid. 459.
6. Ibid. 312.
7. Ibid. 312.
8. E. L. Allen, *Kierkegaard: His Life and Thought* (London: Stanley Nott, 1935), 144.
9. Ibid. 145.

Chapter 4

Negating Sartre

The false eternities of the Kierkegaardian aesthetic which produce the art of evil in Spark's early novels might seem to be recapitulated in *The Hothouse by the East River* (1973). Paul Hazlett and his wife Elsa live in their apartment in New York in the late 1960s or early 1970s in imaginative defiance of historical time, for they were both killed in England by a German bomb in 1944. Paul had, during the war, made several visits to the United States as an advisor to the British government on the Balkans, and returned bringing 'wonders' (*HBER*, 147) for his wife from the material riches of a country that had not been devastated by war: 'She takes out the presents, all unobtainable in England or rationed – a box of Dupont stockings, a box of Lanvin soap, a bottle of Chanel No. 5 scent, a white frilly blouse . . . She packs her treasures away' (*HBER*, 148). The 'presents' are, in effect, present symbols of the future, of the life that Paul and Elsa anticipate they will live when, after the war, they 'settle in America' (*HBER*, 147). Their desire for such a future is so intense that, despite their deaths, Paul's imagination wills them back into existence as richly endowed inhabitants of post-war New York, where Elsa can decide, on a whim, to 'buy a present' for herself (*HBER*, 95) – the gift of time as well as a material good. The lives that they might have lived in time had their railway carriage not taken a direct hit from a V2 they live out as their version of eternity, the eternity of a continuous present – Spark uses the present tense for her narration – defined entirely by the values of the aesthetic – choosing shoes is the first important decision we encounter in the novel. Material wealth provides them with an apparently endless freedom but it is, precisely, a freedom without end, having neither a point of conclusion nor an ultimate purpose: their lives are endless, both beyond time and without final justification.

This false eternity, however, contains an ontological paradox, for Paul and Elsa have a son and a daughter, born and bred in New York and indulging in its materialistic lifestyle. The children of ghosts, their material presence defies the logic of reality, for they are, apparently, alive in a historical moment which they cannot logically or biologically inhabit. Their paradoxical status is advertised in their names – Pierre and Katerina – which are linguistically at odds both with their parents' English backgrounds and their anglophone American environment. The oddity of Pierre's francophone name is underlined by the fact that he aims to be the producer of a new stage version of J. M. Barrie's *Peter Pan*, a character whose names not only assert the anglophone version of 'Pierre' but gesture to a confusion of Christian and pagan traditions, invoking both the founder of the Christian church – St Peter – and the pagan god – Pan – traditionally associated with the overthrow of order and the indulgence in sensuality. Pierre's version of *Peter Pan* will, however, defy Barrie's celebration of eternal childhood by having all the characters played by old people. Instead of the world of the eternally young, Pierre's *Peter Pan* will reveal an eternity which is simply a prolongation of the world of time, reflecting the reality of his parents' lives: they inhabit the New York of the 1960s which they did not live to see but where, nonetheless, they live out their afterlives, as though eternity was not different from the world of time but simply its continuation into a future which they had, in time, imagined for themselves. Peter Pan's home is, of course, 'The Never Land',[1] and despite the pressing reality of urban New York it is such a 'neverland' that Paul, Elsa and their family inhabit in *The Hothouse by the East River*: 'What is now?' Paul thinks, 'Now is never, never' (*HBER*, 59). They have escaped from time not to encounter eternity but only to live over again in time, producing a paradoxical ontology in which they both *are* – for they exist in the New York of the 1960s – and *are not*, having been dead since the 1940s.

The ontological uncertainty of Paul and Elsa's existence is not simply a device by which Spark reveals the hell which victory in the Second World War has produced in a secular America which has replaced religion with psychiatry as an explanation of humanity's ills, it is also a very precise analogue of Sartre's atheistic existentialism with its insistence on the 'nothingness' which allows human beings, through their power of negation, to liberate themselves from their pasts, both personal and cultural. For Sartre, his kind of existentialism insists that 'if God does not exist, there is at least one being in whom existence precedes essence, a being who exists before he can be defined by any concept, and that this being is man';[2] as a consequence man's 'being' is his lack of being, his 'nothingness':

> Man exists, turns up, appears on the scene, and, only afterwards, defines himself. If man, as the existentialist conceives him, is indefinable, it is because at first he is nothing. Only afterward will he be something, and he himself will have made what he will be.[3]

As migrants in New York, Paul and Elsa Paul are the symbols of a present and a culture which has dispensed with its past but has no future towards which its action can be directed. The nothingness which is the source of human freedom is also, in a different sense, the condition in which human life is continuously lived – it is a life of material excess with nothingness at its core. Nothingness as the foundation of the world is a revelation that has apparently come to Elsa in *The Hothouse by the East River*: as she stares obsessively out of her window on to the East River her husband conjectures that 'She is looking for something out there. The sun has gone down. Yes, she is looking for it again. Silently Paul says to himself: "It's not there." And again, "There's nothing there"' (*HBER*, 11). 'Nothing' is all that is there: as Sartre puts it, 'nothingness haunts being' (*B&N*, 16) and Elsa has discovered herself as, in Sartre's terms, '"face to face" with nothingness' (*B&N*, 17). The 'sun' has gone down, but this is not simply a fact about the physical universe in which Paul and Elsa exist: the sun has gone down because the Son has not risen and she looks to the East in despair because she cannot see what is asserted in Matthew 24, 'For as the lightning cometh out of the east, and shineth even unto the west; so shall also the coming of the Son of man be.' Her eternity is not the eternity promised by Christianity but an eternity in which the past projects itself as a continuous present founded only on nothingness.

That Sartre's atheistic existentialism is the target of Spark's satire in *The Hothouse by the East River* is underlined by the fact that Sartre initiates his discussion of metaphysical 'nothingness' by the quotidian event of looking for, and failing to find, his friend Pierre in a café:

> But now Pierre is not here. This does not mean that I discover his absence in some precise spot in the establishment. In fact, Pierre is absent from the whole café, his absence fixes the café in its evanescence;

> the café remains ground, it persists in offering itself as an undifferentiated totality to my only marginal attention; it slips into the background; its pursues its nihilation [. . .]. I myself expected to see Pierre, and my expectation has caused the absence of Pierre to happen as a real event concerning this café. (*B&N*, 10)

Pierre can be absent only because he is expected to be present: if he were present there would be no absence but, equally, if he had not been expected, there would also have been no absence: it is his absent presence and his present absence which reveals the nature of negation and, therefore, of being's dependence on nothingness. The absent presence of Pierre in *Being and Nothingness* is mirrored in Pierre's status in *The Hothouse by the East River*, absently present in a world of which he cannot possibly be a citizen. Pierre – both Sartre's and Spark's – is the exemplary figure of humanity's capacity for negation, a negation which does not only set him free from the past but which intervenes in his relations with those with whom he interacts. Sartre tells us,

> When Pierre looks at me, I know of course that he is looking at me. His eyes, things in the world, are fixed on my body, a thing in the world – that is the objective fact of which I can say: it is. But it is also a fact *in the world*. The meaning of this look is not a fact in the world, and this is what makes me uncomfortable. (*B&N*, 61–2)

The 'meaning' behind the interactions of human beings are always inscrutable, because, if human beings are founded on nothingness, they have the potential to make their future radically different from their past; Sartre's discomfort at being looked at by Pierre arises from the sense that the person one thinks one is talking to might already be on the edge of an escape into an alternative future. Spark's Pierre talks to his father not because of their relationship of father and son, but because he is paid by Elsa to maintain the illusion of friendship, using his meetings with his father as opportunities to blackmail him into providing financial support for his theatrical project. The personal relationship is 'uncomfortable' because it is in fact exploitative: Pierre's existence confirms for Paul the reality of his life in New York, his parents' existence provides, for Pierre, the material resources for his aesthetic lifestyle. Pierre's geriatric version of *Peter Pan*, however, reveals that their lives continue to be determined by the time from which they are actually absent, a time which reveals their existential nothingness, a deathly and ironic alternative to the nothingness proposed by Sartre as the very basis of human existence.

The Hothouse by the East River effectively adopts a Sartrean perspective on the world in order to satirise it: the friend Pierre, whose arrivals and departures punctuate Sartre's account of the philosophy of nothingness, is, in Spark's version, precisely that – nothing, neither friend (because he remains 'essentially' unknowable), nor son (because Elsa and Paul's Pierre could not have been born), nor the Peter of a childhood remembered in Barrie's play as eternal, nor the symbol of the rock upon which the Church was built. Spark has created a plot which takes literally the 'nothingness' on which Sartre's account of freedom is based but reveals that for her characters 'nothingness' can neither be an escape from the past of the kind that Sartre thinks possible, nor the basis of the freedom to choose a new future. The nothingness that Sartre proposes as the foundation of human freedom becomes the echo chamber of a dead past and an unlived future. If the purpose of man is, from being 'nothing' to 'be something, and he himself will have made himself what he will be', Elsa challenges what her son has made of himself by throwing ripe tomatoes at the actors on the first night of Pierre's version of *Peter Pan*. When intercepted by the police, she declares 'I'm the mother of the author' (*HBER*, 93), a statement which has multiple possible applications, all false: she is not the mother of the real author, J. M. Barrie, nor is she the mother of the author of the book in which Barrie's play is travestied, for that is Muriel Spark; she cannot really be the mother of Pierre because she did not survive the Second World War. This self-defeating assertion nonetheless points to an underlying truth – a man is not 'nothing', he is the creation of a mother, her shadow follows him even when, as in Elsa's case, it falls the wrong way. *The Hothouse by the East River* takes the terms of Sartre's philosophy and his relationship with his friend Pierre to satirise the notion that you can make something out of nothing – for only God can do that. Sartre's existentialism is an effort to transfer to man the capacities which belong only to God. The failure to be able to build atheistic existentialism into a philosophy of what it is to exist as human being is revealed when Elsa and Paul return to their apartment block, the cause of so many annoyances in the early part of the novel, only to discovered that it is already half-demolished: they are homeless – 'Elsa stands in the morning light reading the billboard. It announces the new block of apartments to be built on the site of the old' (*HBER*, 140) – allowing them at last to escape from their nothingness.

The Hothouse by the East River is not unique in Spark's oeuvre, for many of Spark's novels play satirically on the implications of 'atheistic existentialism': when Ronald Bridges in *The Bachelors* describes himself as 'a stranger' (*B*, 183) and when Sandy in *The Prime of Miss Jean Brodie* is given the surname 'Stranger', both implicitly invoke and, by their religious convictions, oppose the most influential 'existentialist' novel of the 1940s, Albert Camus's *L'Étranger*, translated into English by Stuart Gilbert and published as *The Outsider* in the United Kingdom, but appearing in the United States under the more literal version of its title as *The Stranger*. In style, Camus's novel anticipates what will become characteristic of Spark's novels – a short, intense narrative (*The Outsider* in English is divided in two parts with only six chapters in the first section and five in the second, amounting to less than 120 pages in total) which refuses to provide causal explanations for its characters' actions. The lack of explanation for those actions effectively dramatises the 'nothingness' out of which human decisions emerge, but in *L'Étranger* the nothingness that is the source of human freedom is also a trap – atheistic existentialism presents human beings as the heroic creators of a future which they have chosen for themselves, but in the end consigns them to another nothingness, a death about which they have no choice and which offers no prospect of continuing existence. Both Ronald and Sandy are outsiders and strangers in their societies, but what makes them strangers is precisely their refusal of the secular and implicitly atheistic world of modernity. Their belief in Christianity is, from a rational point of view, absurd, but it is precisely the recognition of the absurd, as in Kierkegaard, that is the basis of their belief: every act is an act of faith and every faith is equally an act for which there can be no justification. If Kierkegaard – and Ronald Bridges and Sandy Stranger – take absurdity as the basis for faith – 'I choose faith', as Kierkegaard insists (*J*, '820', 364) – then Camus's Meursault is resigned to absurdity itself: confronted by the chaplain who has come to get him to confess his sins, Meursault realises,

> Nothing, nothing mattered and I knew very well why. He too knew why. From the depths of my future, throughout the whole of this absurd life I'd been leading, I'd felt a vague breath drifting towards me across all the years still to come, and on its way this breath had evened out everything that was being proposed to me in the equally unreal years I was living through.[4]

The chaplain exemplifies what it is to follow a pre-existing set of values and, therefore, never to have to confront the absurd: in the confines of Meursault's cell, on the other hand, the chaplain 'didn't have much choice. He either had to stand up or sit down',[5] and yet he has no basis for choosing either stance:

> He seemed so certain of everything, didn't he? And yet none of his certainties was worth one hair of a woman's head. He couldn't even be sure he was alive because he was living like a dead man. I might seem to be empty handed. But I was sure of myself, sure of everything, surer than he was, sure of my life and sure of the death that was coming to me.[6]

The chaplain is an example of what Sartre describes as 'bad faith' – the belief that you have made a choice when you have, in fact, only conformed to the social expectations of your environment. What distinguishes Meursault from the chaplain is that Meursault has not simply lived according to the values of his society – he has chosen the life that he has led, whatever the consequences of that choice turn out to be. Meursault may be a creature of nothingness and, therefore, of freedom but he is also locked in the prison cell of time: the prison cell in which he is actually confined at the end of the novel, awaiting execution, is 'right at the top of the town', and from there Meursault recounts how 'One day when I was clinging to the bars, with my face straining towards the light, a warder came in and told me that I had a visitor.'[7] The freedom on which Meursault has based his life comes down to a prison cell from which the only exit is death, his visitor the representative of a social world from which, by his refusal to acknowledge his mother's death and his subsequent killing of an Arab, he has forever alienated himself. The image of Meursault clinging to the bars of his prison cell is repeated in Spark's image of Sandy – the 'stranger' – as she deals with her own visitors from the outside world:

> She clutched the bars of the grille as if she wanted to escape from the dim parlour beyond, for she was not composed like the other nuns who sat, when they received their rare visitors, well back in the darkness . . . she clutched the bars and received the choice visitors, the psychologists and the Catholic seekers, and the higher journalist ladies and the academics who wanted to question her about her odd psychological treatise [. . .] (*PJB*, 43)

Meursault clings to the bars to see the outside world from which he will shortly depart; Sandy clutches 'the bars of the grille' to meet the outside world that has come to converse with her; Meursault accepts the death that will come when he goes to the guillotine, while Sandy, by her choice of becoming a nun, seems to make Miss Brodie's final exit from the world a prefiguration of Sandy's own exit from that world: 'This was her last year in the world and in another sense it was Sandy's' (*PJB*, 72).

A Christian existentialism and an atheistic existentialism are, in Kierkegaard's terms, equally acts of faith: one a faith in God and in eternity, the other a faith in the future that one chooses, or that one has already chosen, in a world unredeemed by religion. For Kierkegaard, the paradox of freedom is that you cannot simply rest on the surety that you have freedom of choice – you actually have to make a choice, and, by making that choice, accept that you have given up some of the options that existed before that choice was made. The freedom is in the act of choosing, and not in the 'freedom-of-choice' that makes such choosing possible: 'By directing his mind towards "freedom of choice" instead of choosing he loses both freedom and freedom of choice' (*J*, '1051', 372). The freedom to choose must be exercised and, paradoxically, as soon as it is exercised it necessarily limits the choices thereafter available:

> The most tremendous thing which has been granted to man is: the choice, freedom. And if you desire to save it and preserve it there is only one way: in the very same second unconditionally and in complete resignation to give it back to God, and yourself with it. If the sight of what is granted to you tempts you, and if you give way to the

> temptation and look with egoistic upon the freedom of choice, then you lose your freedom. And your punishment is: to go on in a kind of confusion priding yourself on having – freedom of choice, but woe upon you, that is your judgment: You have freedom of choice, you say, and still you have not chosen God. (*J*, '1051', 372)

Freedom of choice requires that a choice be made, even if that choice results in the individual necessarily foregoing some of the choices which might otherwise have been available: to choose is necessarily to limit the freedom which made your choice possible, but without the act of choosing 'freedom-of-choice' is meaningless. Atheistic existentialism insists on the choice; Christian existentialism on the choice of Christ. Sandy and Meursault travel in opposite directions: one towards the Kierkegaardian leap to faith in the face of absurdity, the other into an acceptance that the indifference of the world is so much like himself that it is 'fraternal' in its absurdity.[8]

By ironically adopting the perspective of an atheistic existentialism which assures one of one's freedom only by denying the choice of God, Spark produces fictions which are often haunted by the absence rather than the presence of God. Dougal Douglas in *The Ballad of Peckham Rye*, for instance, may be a leftover devil from an earlier set of religious beliefs but he inhabits a world where only the old mad woman, Nelly Mahone, 'who had lapsed from her native religion on religious grounds' (*BPR*, 11), proclaims the word of God. Dougal's belief that, having been born as a version of the devil with horns on his head, he has 'the ability to drive devils out of people' (*BPR*, 142) does not commit him to any kind of Christian eternity – indeed, having learned of the 'time and motion' expert from Cambridge who 'did marvels in the factory' by working out 'the simplest pattern of movement involving the least loss of energy and time' (*BPR*, 15), Dougal envisages himself as the choreographer of temporal efficiency:

> 'I have a dream at nights,' Dougal said, pouring the wine, 'of girls in factories doing a dance with only the movements of their breasts, bottoms, and arms as they sort, stack, pack, check, cone-wind, gum, uptwist, assemble, seam, and set. I see the Devil in the guise of a chap from Cambridge who does motion-study, and he's the choreographer. He sings a song that goes, 'We study in detail the movements requisite for any given task and we work out the simplest pattern of movement involving the least loss of energy and time.' (*BPR*, 64–5)

The diabolic 'choreographer' of time, Dougal tells Humphrey, 'is a projection of me' (*BPR*, 65): Dougal's choreographic dream is designed not to release people from the dictates of time, but to make them – like Pierre's version of *Peter Pan* – playfully content within its constraints. Similarly, Dougal appears to offer every character whose life he interrupts the possibility of an escape from the past – from, as in the case of Merle Coverdale and Mr Druce, 'living a lie' (*BPR*, 88) – but, as with his 'human research' into the 'inner lives' (*BPR*, 17) of the factory workers, Dougal's interventions only intensify the problems they are supposedly designed to solve – 'Mr Druce said with embarrassment, "I feel I should just mention the fact that absenteeism has increased in the six weeks you've been with us"' (*BPR*, 64). Dougal encourages everyone to play at being free from the constraints of their existing conditions and past lives – his advice is 'Take Monday off [. . .] Take Tuesday off as well. Have a holiday' (*BPR*, 43) – but the freedom he offers is illusory: in the end, they will have to return to their lives in time, their 'holiday' unredeemed by the revelation in it of any 'Holy Day'. The stylistic irony of Dougal's attempted exploration of the workers' 'inner lives' is that *The Ballad of Peckham Rye* is one of Spark's most relentlessly *external* novels, giving us no access to the interiority of her characters' experiences, as though the metaphysical 'nothing' that existentialism posits as necessary to human freedom might amount to no more than an emptiness, an absence, a spiritual absenteeism. Dougal employs the language of existentialism – 'Are you a free woman or a slave?' he asks Merle Coverdale (*BPR*, 36) – echoing a passage from *Being and Nothingness*, in which Sartre asserts that 'Man cannot be sometimes slave and sometimes free; he is wholly and forever free or he is not free at all' (*B&N*, 441). This assertion appears in a section to which Gabriel Marcel draws particular attention:

> This passage from *L'Être et le Néant* seems to me one of the most significant and explicit in all Sartre's work. I do not believe that in the whole history of human thought, grace, even in its most secularised forms, has ever been denied with such audacity or such impudence. Having taken this step, Sartre naturally finds himself under the necessity to establish that every human action, even when it appears to be determined, is in reality free – that is to say, the result of choice.[9]

Dougal insists that Merle, like a Sartrean existentialist, is free simply to choose an alternative future:

> 'Get another job and refuse to see him any more. It's easy.'
> 'Oh everything's easy for you. You're free.'
> 'Aren't you free?' Dougal said.
> 'Yes, as far as the law goes.'
> 'Well, stop seeing Druce.'
> 'After six years, going on seven, Dougal, I'm tied in a sort of way [. . .]' (*BPR*, 137)

Marcel would argue, however, that human beings are not mere metaphysical nothings, free to remake themselves in every moment, for this misrepresents both metaphysically and socially the ways in which human beings discover themselves:

> My existence as a living being preceded the discovery of myself as a living being. One might even say that, by a fatal necessity, I pre-exist myself. But this forces us to take up a position diametrically opposed to that, for instance, of Sartre, in that sentence of his that has been so often quoted: 'Man's motto is to be a maker and, as a maker, to make himself and to be nothing but the self he had made for himself.' Everything that we have been saying up to this very moment forces us to take our stand against any such affirmation. 'It would be impossible to deny in a more aggressive fashion the existence of any sort of natural world, of anything that is inherited by us, or, more profoundly, of reality itself, that reality which is conferred upon us or in which we participate, and which gives us a greater impetus, the deeper we penetrate into it.'[10]

Merle's inheritance in life may not amount to much – 'I've had a rotten life' she insists (*BPR*, 136) – but what she has attained, however trivial in the eyes of others, is fundamental to her sense of her self:

> '[. . .] And what sort of job would I get at thirty-eight?'
> 'You would have to come down,' Dougal said.
> 'After being head of the pool,' she said, 'I couldn't. I've got to think of my pride. And there's the upkeep of my flat. Mr Druce puts a bit towards it.' (*BPR*, 137)

Merle's independence – her own flat – is tied up with her dependence – her relationship with Druce – just as Druce himself, as Dougal intuits, is dependent financially on the wife for whom he has no regard (*BPR*, 91) and which makes his relationship with Merle both possible and necessary. They are characters who may have very little but that little is not the nothing that Sartrean existentialism requires if man is 'to make himself and to be nothing but the self he had made for himself'.

Dougal not only promotes the notion of freedom to the other characters in *The Ballad of Peckham Rye*, but acts as though he were a diabolic version of Sartrean existentialism, able to remake his identity moment by moment and free at any time to choose a different future for himself: 'At the second interview, Mr Druce paced the floor while Dougal sat like a monkey-puzzle tree [. . .] Dougal changed his shape and became a professor [. . .] Dougal leaned forward and became a television interviewer' (*BPR*, 14–15). When Dougal takes a job with a competing company without giving up his first job it is as though he has not only escaped from the temporal constraints by which other workers' lives are governed but has demonstrated the nothingness on which his metaphysical freedom is based, since by this means he is 'drawing two pays for nothing' (*BPR*, 170). Those beside whom Dougal works are defined by their jobs: they have given up their freedom and become creatures identified by their function within the system of industrial production – 'Dawn Waghorn, cone-winder, Annette Wren, trainee-seamer, Elaine Kent, process-controller, Odette Hill up-twister; Raymond Lowther, packer, Lucille Potter, gummer' (*BPR*, 11) – but Dougal is defined by nothing, as he substitutes one identity for another in the multiplicity of plots in which he involves himself. In *The Mystery of Being*, Gabriel Marcel uses an actor on a stage as a metaphor for the relationship of the individual to the life by which he is surrounded:

> When I ask myself whether my life has a point, it does seem that I am imagining a kind of significance, or relevance, which my life would go on having whether or not I wanted it to; I am, or so it seems to me, more or less explicitly relating my question to the idea of a play in which I have to take part; I am asking myself about the possible theme of the performance in which I have been induced to participate. From this point of view I might compare my situation with that of an actor who has been given his own cues and lines, but who has not had the

> play as a whole read to him and has not even been told briefly what it is about. He has merely been told: at such and such a cue, you will make your entrance, you will speak the following lines, accompanying your lines with this piece of business, then you will make your exit. The actor has to suppose that his lines and his business, which in themselves seem to him almost pointless have their point in relation to the total pattern of the play. Thus if life as a whole has a point – or as we would say here, not to break the metaphor, a plot or theme – then in some sense my own life has a plot or theme, too.[11]

The actor assumes that there is a relationship between his own role and the totality of the play of which he has no grasp. From the perspective of atheistic existentialism there is, however, no such totality to which we can appeal: 'Keeping to the theatrical comparisons', Marcel continues,

> we might say that in fact I am not told in advance what lines and business are to be; I have to go right out there and improvise. But where the actor of the *commedia dell'arte* had to improvise on the rough outline of a story given to him in advance, I am given no such rough outline. It is just as if – or so it seems at first glance – the producer of the play had carelessly omitted to provide me with just the information I needed to carry out the task that had been entrusted to me in a proper fashion. Given all this, might I not be led into calling the very existence of the producer into question? Or, to put the point more precisely, would I not have solid grounds for asserting that, whether or not there really is a producer, everything is run just as if there wasn't one? This comes down once more to saying that there is no rough outline, no plot, or, to go back to the phrase we started with, that my life has no point. From this perspective, I will naturally be led to ask whether I myself, against the grain as it were of this general pointlessness, can by my own efforts give my life a point: can I myself confer a kind of significance on it? This is, in its atheistic form, the position of contemporary existentialism.[12]

Dougal is an existential devil without a God: there is no – or is no longer – any pre-existing plot in which he has a part. Dougal plays at making choices out his nothingness but what his hectic multiplication of identities and relationships reveals is that Dougal is a performer in an endlessly rewritten script of his own devising – 'endlessly' implying, as in the case of Paul and Elsa in *The Hothouse by the East River*, a life without end or purpose – in Marcel's terms, 'without point'. A devil without a God is a creature who has become redundant in the world, and the negation on which existentialism depends produces the same outcome: existentialism may claim that it projects a heroic conception of mankind as the only free creature in an otherwise determined universe, but it is also, in Marcel's sense, the invocation of a pointless existence, or an existence to which each of us tries to give meaning in defiance of our knowledge of its ultimate pointlessness. Dougal, as a diabolic version of existentialism, uses his capacity for negation not to commit himself to any particular meaning for existence but simply to substitute one performance for another, one nothing for an alternative nothing. For Dougal, the world is a stage for his performances: he plays at being a 'being-in-time' – or, rather, many beings in time – but that playful diversity is a substitute for the eternity from which, as minor devil, he has always been shut out. His 'fatal flaw' – he cannot abide other people's sicknesses, which is what leads to Jinny's rejection of him – reveals his fundamental horror at the body's life in time. For Dougal, sickness is a symptom of the weakness of the body as the medium of our life in time and also of its fatal destination. He does not mind impersonating a corpse to divert his landlady, Miss Frierne, from the news of the death of the person who was probably her brother –

> Presently he placed a kitchen chair to face the chair on which he sat. He put up his feet on it and said, 'Ever seen a corpse?' He lolled his head back, closed his eyes and opened his mouth so that the bottom jaw was sunken and rigid.
>
> 'You're callous, that's what you are,' Miss Frierne said.
>
> Then she screamed with hysterical laughter. (*BPR*, 72–3)

– but when he discovers Miss Frierne herself in a state of collapse and near to death after a stroke, Dougal packs his bags and leaves instantly. Dougal's life in time is a series of escape routes from his 'fatal flaw' and from the fatality which is the only destination of human beings in a godless world. He is the fictional embodiment of a character envisaged by Kierkegaard in *Fear and Trembling* as the necessary adjunct to an age which thinks it has reached the highest, despite the fact that 'no age has fallen so much victim to the comic than ours':

> Indeed it is hard to grasp why it hasn't already given birth, by a *generatio æquivoca* [spontaneous generation], to its hero, the demon

> who would remorselessly produce the dreadful spectacle of making the whole age laugh and making it forget that it was laughing at itself. (*F&T*, 156)

Dougal as the demon of laughter reveals to the modern age a 'horrifying play' of the nothingness on which it is built, but which it is incapable of recognising as the mirror image of itself.

Sartre's insistence on the fact that human beings must be 'nothing' if they are to be free – 'All my "modes of being" manifest freedom equally since they are all ways of being my own nothingness' (*B&N*, 445) – means that there can be no prior 'cause' for human actions or decisions, raising a host of questions about the nature of causality,[13] and how human beings relate to the causalities which govern the world of things: the nothingness of the human interrupts the causal relations between events in the world, or redirects them in ways that, to any onlooker, may appear entirely arbitrary. Problems of causality punctuate the action of *The Ballad of Peckham Rye*, from Dougal's apparently supernatural intuitions into the motives of other characters which appear to come from access to an authorial level of omniscience about the world in which he operates – 'I'm fey. I've got Highland blood' (*BPR*, 67) – to his displacement of attention from real to imagined causes:

> 'Goodness, look at that,' Dougal said.
> She looked upward to where he was pointing.
> 'What?' she said.
> 'Up there,' Dougal said; 'trees in the sky.'
> 'What are you talking about? I don't see anything.'
> 'Look properly,' Dougal said, 'up there. And don't look away because Mr Druce is watching us from behind the pavilion' (*BPR*, 138)

Dougal improvises a surreal alternative to the actual cause of his actions – the appearance of Mr Druce – and we encounter many such displacements between causes and their effects throughout the novel. So, when Dougal goes to take up the challenge to fight with Trevor Lomas, he 'heard a sound as of women screaming':

> Between two distant lamp-posts, in their vague oblique light, a group was gathered. Dougal discerned Humphrey and Trevor with a strange youth called Collie who was without a coat and whose shirt

> was unbuttoned, exposing his chest to the night air. These figures were apparently molesting three further figures who turned out to be Dixie, Elaine, and Beauty, who were screaming. Soon it appeared that the men were not molesting but restraining them. Dixie had a long-strapped shoulder bag with which she was attempting to lay about her, largely in the direction of Elaine. Elaine, who was at present in the grip of Trevor, managed to dig Beauty's leg with her steel stiletto heel. (*BPR*, 59)

The cause of this affray switches from 'molesting' to 'restraining', but then the action is suddenly reframed in a different way:

> In a few seconds everyone except Dougal was singing, performing the twisting jive, merging the motions of the fight into those of a frantic dance. Dougal saw Humphrey's face as his neck swooped upwards. It was frightened. Dixie's expression was, with a decided effort, bright. So was Elaine's. A one-sided smile on the face of the strange boy, and the fact that, as he bent and twisted in the jive, he buttoned up his shirt, made Dougal look round outside the group for the cause of this effect. He saw it immediately. Two policemen were quite close to them now. (*BPR*, 60–1)

The 'cause of the effect' is the introduction of a new set of actors into the scene, whose perceptions of the event have to be manipulated by giving the actions an apparently different intention: the fight becomes a dance. One nothing replaces another. That it is the police who produce this transfiguration is ironic, since it is the business of the police to trace the causes of crimes, an end which is only possible if effects are the consistent outcomes of identifiable causes. Dougal further undermines the order of cause and effect by pretending that his 'human research' is carried out on behalf of the police as an investigation into 'youthful terrorism' (*BPR*, 160), and 'certain irregularities in the industrial life of Peckham' (*BPR*, 160). By adopting the role of the police, Dougal is able to threaten, through Nelly Mahone, reprisals on Trevor for the theft of Dougal's manuscript: 'if he returns my notebooks to me there will nothing further said. We policemen have got to keep our records and our secret codes, you realize' (*BPR*, 162). Dougal, who is, in effect, the subverter of causality in Peckham, becomes its fictional enforcer on the promise of saying – or, perhaps more accurately, of being – nothing, threatening action by a police force to which he does not belong to recover a manuscript which contains no information about any real world, secret or otherwise.

When Merle Coverdale declares that she has had a 'rotten life', Dougal's answer has two parts to it – 'And it isn't over yet' and 'There might be worse ahead' (*BPR*, 136) – which prompts Merle to admit that 'Sometimes I think I'll swallow a bottle of aspirins' (*BPR* 139). If death is indeed the only way out of her situation with Mr Druce, Merle, who notes that he squeezed her neck 'tight the other day [. . .] for fun, but I got a fright' (*BPR*, 140), seems almost to invoke her own murder as the only resolution of the narrative in which she is trapped. It is a possibility which Spark was to present again in *The Driver's Seat* (1970) in the character of Lise, whose life as an office worker – 'she has five girls under her and two men. Over her are two women and five men' (*DS*, 12) – is an even more spartan version of Merle's, since the flat in which she lives is not only designed in an 'austere taste' (*DS*, 19), but is kept by Lise 'as clean-lined and clear to return to after her work as if it were uninhabited' (*DS*, 20). Lise's is an 'uninhabited' life: for Sartre, the 'nothingness' of the human provides the opportunity for human beings to make themselves:

> We mean that man first exists, that is, that man first of all is the being who hurls himself toward a future and who is conscious of imagining himself as being in the future. Man is at the start a plan which is aware of itself, rather than a patch of moss, a piece of garbage, or a cauliflower; nothing exists prior to his plan; there is nothing in heaven; man will be what he will have planned to be.[14]

In the case of Merle and of Lise, as though ironically underlining Sartre's implicit masculinism, there is, however, no such plan and no such future, because for them there is no future that is not simply a repetition of the past – Lise 'finished laughing and started crying all in a flood' and her 'little fat superior, conveyed to her that she had done again what she had not done for five years' (*DS*, 13). Merle and Lise live as though they were already dead, for if, as Sartre argues, 'death is never that which gives life its meanings; it is, on the contrary, that which removes all meaning from life' (*B&N*, 539), then Merle and Lise already exist in a condition which has removed 'all meaning from life', in part because they have already accepted the Sartrean premise that 'there is nothing in heaven': they have no cause, in the sense of a project or aim, so existence to them is simply the continuous experience of their nothingness.

To the freedom of the Sartrean 'nothing', however, there are two threatening boundaries. The first is the Other who threatens my subjectivity by viewing me as simply an object in the world – 'by means of the upsurge of the Other there appear certain determinations which I am without having chosen them' (*B&N*, 523); the second is death, which ultimately negates the projects which have defined a particular human existent: 'death is never that which gives life its meanings; it is, on the contrary, that which on principle removes all meaning from life' (*B&N*, 539). The two are ironically related by virtue of the fact that the threat of the Other to a living presence is transformed by the Other's death, producing a situation in which only the memories of the living can offer any continuing significance to an extinguished life: 'The unique characteristic of a dead life is that it is a life of which the Other makes himself the guardian' (*B&N*, 541). When the missing friend Pierre becomes fatally and finally absent he is no longer able to assert the meaning of his own life:

> these various explanations of the meaning of Pierre's life – when it was Pierre himself who effected them in his own life – resulted in changing the meaning and the orientation; for every description of one's own life when it is attempted by the for-itself is a project of the self beyond this life. And as the altering project is by the same token bound to life which it alters, it is Pierre's own life which metamorphoses its meaning by continually temporalizing itself. Now that his life is dead, only the *memory of the Other* can prevent Pierre's life from shriveling up in its plenitude in-itself by cutting all its moorings with the present. (*B&N*, 541)

The relationship of the self to the Other and to death within the universe as defined by existentialism is central to the structure of *The Driver's Seat*. Lise's initially absurd behaviour seems to defy any reasonable explanation: the novel opens with her discarding a dress she was about to buy because the salesgirl informs her that 'the material doesn't stain': 'The customer, a young woman, is suddenly tearing at the fastener at the neck, pulling at the zip of the dress. She is saying, "Get this thing off me. Off me, at once"' (*DS*, 9). A dress which does not stain is free of the accidents by which life is beset – 'If you spill like a bit of ice-cream or a drop of coffee, like, down the front of this dress it won't hold the stain' (*DS*, 7) – and therefore of the traces of the causes of those accidents. It is, like the existential conception of the nothingness of self, undetermined by the causes which shape the physical world, but Lise is in search of a dress which will record its passage through time: the dress she seeks is 'the necessary dress' (*DS*, 12), a phrasing which turns what is a matter of choice, and, therefore, a sign of her freedom, into a matter of necessity, a determinism which she is now about to construct. The 'necessary dress' turns out to be one of violently contrasting colours which, when combined with a coat of red and white stripes, produces an ensemble of which, despite the protestations of the salesgirl, Lise declares, 'Those colours of the dress and the coat are absolutely right for me' (*DS*, 15–16). Their 'rightness', however, is not their aesthetic harmony but the fact that their lack of harmony turns Lise into an unforgettable object in the eyes of the Other; she has stepped out of her nothingness to become an object in the world:

> She stops abruptly at the top of the escalator and looks back, then smiles as if she sees and hears what she had expected. The salesgirl, thinking her customer is already on the escalator out of sight, out of hearing, has turned to another black-frocked salesgirl, 'All those incredible colours together!' she is saying. 'Those incredible colours. She said they were perfectly natural. Natural! Here in the North, she said . . .' Her voice stops as she sees that Lise is looking and hearing. (*DS*, 17)

From a life in which she has been nothing, an absence, an 'uninhabited' self, Lise has transformed herself by her clothes into an object to be noticed and to be remembered: the concierge of her apartment asks, 'Are you going to join a circus?', but Lise's aim is more metaphysical, it is to complete her transformation from a person, a nothingness, into an object – no longer a 'becoming' but, like Sartre's now fatally absent Pierre, one who exists only in and through the memory of the Other. One route to this would be the one considered by Merle – a bottle of aspirins and suicide – but Sartre insists that suicide fails to offer any kind of completion for an individual life because the act of suicide is self-contradictory: all human acts are directed at changing the future but suicide is the negation of the future:

> Since it is an act of my life, indeed, it itself requires a meaning which only the future can give to it; but as it is the last act of my life, it is denied this future. Thus it remains totally undetermined. If I escape death or I 'misfire,' shall I not judge later that my suicide was cowardice? But since those solutions can only be my own projects, they can appear only if I live. Suicide is an absurdity which causes my life to be submerged in the absurd. (*B&N*, 540)

Suicide is inadequate as an event by which a life acquires its finality, since it is a finality which fails to determine the meaning of the life thus brought to its conclusion. Sartre insists on excluding death from consciousness – death can be no part of consciousness because it is the denial of consciousness – and thereby makes death irrelevant to the projection of freedom:

> Thus death haunts me at the very heart of each of my projects as their inevitable reverse side. But precisely because this 'reverse' is to be assumed not as my possibility but as the possibility that there are for me no longer any possibilities, it does not penetrate me. The freedom which is *my freedom* remains total and infinite. Death is not an obstacle to my projects, it is only a destiny of these projects elsewhere. And this is not because death does not limit my freedom but because freedom never encounters this limit. I am not 'free to die,' but I am a free mortal. Since death escapes my projects because it is unrealizable, I myself escape death in my very project. (*B&N*, 547–8)

This punning 'escape' from death is simply its deferral to a moment when its occurrence cannot be known by the self: the 'nothingness' of the free human being can never, according to Sartre, encounter the nothingness of death, because death, when it happens, has already turned the For-itself into an In-itself. It is precisely this that *The Driver's Seat* refuses to accept, by making death itself the project towards which the For-itself is aimed. Sartre lays stress on the fact that human life consists of intentions and actions but that it is also 'made up not only of waitings but of waitings which themselves wait for waitings' (*B&N*, 539): Lise refuses to wait, driving to encounter her death not as something beyond her own existence but as the only goal of her life's actions. Lise takes control of the only thing left to her, her death, in order to be certain that she will encounter it as *her* death and, therefore, retrospectively to give meaning to her life. Lise, who failed to leave the envelope with her car keys with the concierge, is now in the driving seat of causality: she is causing the Other to take note of her, to remember her presence, to acknowledge her existence, so that in the future there will be a narrative to be retraced, as in the case of the woman from Johannesburg who

> will come forward and repeat all she remembers and all she does not remember, and all the details she imagines to be true and those that are true, in her conversation with Lise when she sees in the papers that the police are trying to trace who Lise is, and whom, if anyone, she met on her trip [. . .]. (*DS*, 32–3)

Lise is constructing her life not as a Sartrean project aimed at the future but as the construction of a past which will be recoverable after her death, despite the fact that there is nothing to be found in the story of her life. Sartre mocks those who say 'I did not ask to be born' (*B&N*, 555–6) as a way of denying their responsibility for the world they live in, but Lise insists precisely on the absurdity that comes from having been born: '"Look at my clothes," Lise says. "My new clothes. It's best never to be born. I wish my mother and father had practised birth-control. I wish that pill had been invented at the time. I feel sick, I feel terrible"' (*DS*, 112). Her only way of overcoming the absurdity of having been born is to become the author of the detective novel that will begin with her own death – 'She will be found tomorrow morning dead from multiple stab-wounds' (*DS*, 37) – and for which she has sown the clues by which future readers of her life will be able to trace the meaning – or meaninglessness – of her death. No Sartrean project aimed at the future – 'I myself escape death in my very project' (*B&N*, 548) – intervenes to protect us from death: Lise, by her name, is the readable, the *lisible* in Roland Barthes' account of the nature of textuality, but Lise can make herself readable only by making her life a route map to her death.

The contradiction between a supposedly inalienable Sartrean freedom, with which we are endowed at birth, and the determining necessity of death, is realised in *The Driver's Seat* by a present-tense narration which implies that the future is, as yet, undetermined – 'Meanwhile the only other person in the hall, a youngish man in a dark suit, stands before the desk with a brief-case and a tartan hold-all by his side' (*DS*, 149) – and a future tense in which the events of time have come already to be governed by an irresistible necessity: 'The morning will dawn, and by the evening the police will place in front of him the map marked with an X at the point where the Pavilion is located' (*DS*, 155–6). Chance – 'It was only by chance that I met her' (*DS*, 156), her killer tells the police – becomes necessity; he was the one she had chosen to be her killer because he was as necessary to her plot as her 'necessary dress'. Lise's plot completes itself because she, like a Sartrean existentialist, has willed it do so, but in denial of Sartrean existentialism what she has willed is her own negation; not the negation of the world by the self but the negation of the self by itself. Asked if she will 'feel a presence' when she encounters the person for whom she is searching, Lise replies, 'The lack of an absence, that's what it is. I know I'll find it' (*DS*, 105). By her death, Lise will finally have transformed her life into the 'lack of an absence' and will have done so, like Dougal tutoring Humphrey to say 'no' in *The Ballad of Peckham Rye*, by schooling her killer in his role: 'She says, "I'm going to lie down here. Then you tie my hands with my scarf; I'll put one wrist over the other, it's the proper way. Then you'll tie my ankles together with your necktie. Then you strike"' (*DS*, 157). Life is turned into the art of drama and art turns into death: Lise is the director of her own production of the art of death.

Notes

1. J. M. Barrie, *The Plays of J. M. Barrie*, ed. A. E. Wilson (London: Hodder & Stoughton, 1942), 523.
2. Jean-Paul Sartre, 'The Humanism of Existentialism', in *Jean-Paul Sartre: Essays in Existentialism*, ed. Wade Baskin and trans. Bernard Frechtman (New York: Citadel Publishing, 1990), 35.
3. Ibid. 36.
4. Albert Camus, *The Outsider*, trans. Joseph Laredo (London: Penguin, 1982; 1942), 115.
5. Ibid. 113.
6. Ibid. 115.
7. Ibid. 72.
8. Ibid. 117.
9. Gabriel Marcel, *The Philosophy of Existence*, trans. Manya Harari (London: Harvill Press, 1948), 58.

10. Gabriel Marcel, *The Mystery of Being*, vol. 1, *Reflection and Mystery*, trans. G. S. Fraser (London: Harvill Press, 1950), 174–5; the final quotation is from his own essay, *Techniques de dégradation* in a collection of essays on Evil (Paris: Plon, 1948).
11. Marcel, *The Mystery of Being*, 173.
12. Marcel, *The Mystery of Being*, 173–4.
13. These dominate Part Four of *Being and Nothingness*, 'Having, Doing and Being'.
14. Sartre, 'The Humanism of Existentialism', 36.

Chapter 5

Repetition

In Spark's *The Only Problem* (1984), Harvey Gotham is so offended by his wife Effie's stealing of a bar of chocolate from a motorway service station and by her attempted justification of it as an act of defiance against 'the multinationals and monopolies' because they 'are capitalising on us' (*TOP*, 15), that he not only walks out on the holiday they are then sharing with his wife's sister, Ruth, Ruth's husband Edward and their young friend Nathan, but walks out altogether on his marriage. Having put wife, family and friends behind him, he goes into isolation in the French countryside to work on a monograph on the Book of Job, the book of the Bible which, for Harvey, presents at its most intense what he considers to be the 'only problem' – that 'a benevolent Creator, one whose charming and delicious light descended and spread over the world, and being powerful everywhere, could condone the unspeakable sufferings of the world' (*TOP*, 19). Harvey, like Job before his afflictions, is a rich man but nonetheless chooses to live in solitude and in apparent poverty in order to come to terms with Job's capacity for accepting suffering as long as its cause is God: 'the Lord gave, and the Lord hath taken away; blessed be the name of the Lord'.[1]

Harvey's retreat from marriage into the study of Job repeats a narrative that is presented in Kierkegaard's *Repetition* (1843), in which the pseudonymous author, Constantine Constantius, tells of his relationship with a 'Young Man' (we are never given his name) who flees the love affair by which his life has apparently been consumed in order to hide himself away in an isolated location where he meditates on the significance of the Book of Job. Constantius's story is itself clearly another reworking of Kierkegaard's own flight from his engagement to Regine Olsen, but in this case the explanation for the breaking off of the relationship is that through love the Young Man has discovered his true vocation, poetry, which makes the love itself redundant:

> There was awakened in him a poetical productivity upon a scale which I had never thought possible. Then I easily comprehended the situation. The young girl was not his love, she was the occasion of awakening the primitive poetic talent within him and making him a poet. Therefore he could love only her, could never forget her, never wish to love anyone else; and yet he was forever only longing for her. She was drawn into his very nature as a part of it, the remembrance of her was ever fresh. She had meant much to him, she had made him a poet, and thereby she had signed her own death warrant. (*Rep*, 15)

The Young Man's contradictory relationship to his lover is repeated in Harvey's relationship to his wife: he tells his lawyer,

> 'I don't want to divorce Effie, I don't want a divorce.'
> 'Are you still in love with Effie?'
> 'Yes.'
> 'Then you are an unhappy man. Why did you leave her?'
> 'Because I couldn't stand her sociological clap-trap. If she wanted to do some good in the world she had plenty of opportunity.' (*TOP*, 124)

He wants Effie but an Effie who has 'grown out of' what Harvey considers to be a view of life by which he is 'intellectually insulted' (*TOP*, 125): he wants her not as she was in time but as she might be, or might have been, in another time, at a different stage of life. She has made him a writer of theological works who cannot take her seriously and thereby – and in her case quite literally – 'signed her own death warrant'.

Constantius interprets his young friend's abandonment of his lover as a symptom of the very nature of romantic love which, Constantius argues, is actually founded on the pleasure of 'recollection':

> He was in love, deeply and sincerely in love; that was evident, and yet at once, on one of the first days of his engagement, he was capable of recollecting his love. Substantially he was through with the whole relationship. Before he begins he has taken such a terrible stride that he has leapt over the whole of life. (*Rep*, 12)

The emotion which drives the Young Man's love exists in two different time frames: from the perspective of an immediate present it is directed towards the future and to the fulfilment of his lover but from the imagined perspective of a more distant future his love is already over: 'He longs for the girl, he has to restrain himself by force from hanging around her the whole day, and yet at the very first instant he has become an old man with respect to the whole relationship' (*Rep*, 12). To Constantius, recollection of this kind is intimately related to the very nature of 'romantic love' – 'This potentiated act of recollection is the eternal expression of love at the beginning' (*Rep*, 13) – because it allows love to be seen as completed and finished and, therefore, translated from the dubieties of time into the certainty of the eternal: 'this act of recollection is precisely the counter-current of eternity flowing back into the present' (*Rep*, 14). If such recollection comes to predominate in the experience of love, however, it is as though 'one's life is over at the first instant' (*Rep*, 13) – life is already viewed only from the perspective of the death that will necessarily fix the lovers in a past long since finalised. The force of recollection thus overwhelms the life yet to be lived, and Constantius urges that such an exhaustion of the future has to be resisted: 'there must be vitality enough to kill this death and transform it into life' (*Rep*, 14). Recollection, too, is Job's problem – he will not be comforted for his losses and continues to recollect and assert his own innocence – just as it is Harvey's problem: 'I miss Effie, I miss her a lot, Harvey told himself' (*TOP*, 61).

From his analysis of the Young Man's experiences, Constantius decides that not only has recollection to be resisted but it has to be replaced with a different principle, that of *repetition*. Repetition, he suggests, anticipates a future that is like the past but understands that that which is repeated is also, in the moment of its repetition, made different: 'what is repeated has been, otherwise it could not be repeated; but precisely the fact that it has been gives repetition the character of novelty' (*Rep*, 19). Recollection, Kierkegaard suggests through Constantius, was the traditional conception of human knowledge as developed by the ancient Greeks – 'they taught that all knowledge is a recollection' (*Rep*, 8). But repetition, Constantius suggests, will play an equivalent role in modern philosophy,[2] for recollection is effectively an evacuation of the value of life while repetition is the promise of its fulfilment:

> he who does not comprehend that life is a repetition and that this is the beauty of life, has condemned himself and deserves nothing better than what is sure to befall him – namely, to perish. For hope is an alluring fruit which does not satisfy, recollection is a miserable pittance which does not satisfy, but repetition is the daily bread which satisfies with benediction. (*Rep*, 5)

Repetition is the fundamental fact of a life in time and, according to Judge Wilhelm in *Either/Or*, the fundamental basis of the virtue of marriage:

> You, who have so many observations will certainly grant that I am right in making the general observation that men are divided into two great classes: those who predominantly live in hope; and those who predominantly live in recollection. Both have a wrong relation to time. The healthy individual lives at once both in hope and in recollection, and only thereby does life acquire true and substantial continuity. So, then, he has hope and does not will, like those who live off of recollection, to return backward in time. What, then, does recollection do for him? For, after all, some influence it surely must have. It sets a cross over the note of the instant – the further back recollection goes, and the more frequent the repetition, the more crosses there are. (*E/O*, II, 119)

It is repetition which makes recollection significant, something acknowledged, according to Judge Wilhelm, in our ordinary lives by the fact that marriages are celebrated as more valuable – 'first comes the silver wedding, then the golden wedding' (*E/O*, II, 119) – the more often the celebration is repeated. Constantius, being unmarried, has no access to this kind of cumulative experience – 'it has often occurred to me', Wilhelm ruminates, 'to wonder why, according to the universal usage and way of thinking, the state of single blessedness has no such brilliant prospects, that on the contrary, people rather turn it to ridicule when a bachelor celebrates a jubilee' (*E/O*, II, 120) – so that Constantius's assertion of the value of repetition is largely theoretical:

> Indeed, if there were no repetition, what then would life be? Who would wish to be a tablet on which time writes every instant a new inscription? Or to be a mere memorial of the past? Who could wish to

> let oneself be stirred by everything that is fleeting and new, and which ever newly delights the effeminate soul? If God himself had not willed repetition, the world would never have come into existence. (*Rep*, 6)

Because of its theoretical character in Constantius's life, he decides to test his new belief in the virtue of repetition by revisiting the city of Berlin, where he had previously spent some time, but discovers that, even if 'repetition is reality' (*Rep*, 6), encountering repetition is far from easy, since the Berlin he now experiences is not the same as the Berlin he remembers – everything is changed but changed for the worse: 'my mind was unfruitful, my troubled imagination was engaged in transmuting into the delights of Tantalus the memory of how richly the thoughts presented themselves on the former occasion, and this rank weed of memory strangled every thought at birth' (*Rep*, 37). By recalling the past only to make the present seem insignificant, repetition in his case defeats itself:

> When this experience had been repeated for several days I became so exasperated, so tired of repetition, that I resolved to make my way home again. My discovery was of no importance, and yet it was a strange one, for I discovered that there is no such thing as repetition, and I had convinced myself of this by trying in every possible way to get it repeated. (*Rep*, 71)

Constantius finds that repetition eludes him: it provides no accumulative value or, indeed, reveals itself only as 'the reverse of a repetition' (*Rep*, 37). The Young Man, however, in his isolation discovers the real virtue of repetition in his reading of Job:

> Speak, therefore, O Job of imperishable memory! Rehearse everything thou didst say, though mighty advocate who dost confront the highest tribunal, no more daunted than a roaring lion! There is pith in thy speech, in thy heart there is godly fear, even when thou dost complain, when thou wouldst justify thy despair against thy friends who rise up like robbers to assault thee with their speeches, and even when incited by thy friends thou dost tread their wisdom under foot and despise their defence of the Lord, accounting it the finite shrewdness of a veteran courtier or worldly-wise minister of state. Thee I have need of, a man who knows how to complain aloud, so that his complaint echoes in heaven [. . .] (*Rep*, 112)

Job is the spokesperson of repetition: his repeated refusals to accept that he must have done something wrong to have brought down on him all his losses and his sufferings turns stubbornness into heroism – he is the symbol of a humanity alienated from a God in whom he continues to believe and alienated, too, from a social world which cannot comprehend his faith. For both Constantius's Young Man and for Harvey Gotham, being with Job is a way of coming to terms with their individual suffering and the suffering of the world:

> My benefactor of imperishable memory, tormented Job, dare I join myself to your company, may I listen to thee? Do not repel me, I am not standing here as an imposter beside thy ash heap, my tears are not false, although all I am able to do is to weep with thee. [. . .] I have not been in possession of the world, have not had seven sons and three daughters, but he too may have lost all who possessed but little, he too may as it were have lost sons and daughters who lost his loved one, and he too was so to speak 'smitten with sore boils' who has lost honour and pride, and along with that the will to live and the meaning of life. (*Rep*, 113)

The sufferings of our individual lives are all repetitions of the sufferings of Job, no matter how different our particular circumstances, because, given the existence of a beneficent deity, all suffering is excessive. Job both demonstrates and requires repetition: 'Have you read Job? Read him, read him over and over again' (*Rep*, 121). When Harvey holds a press conference about his wife's possible terrorist activities, he turns it into an account of Job's dilemma:

> The very rapidity with which one calamity followed upon another, shattering Job's world, leaving him destitute, bereft and sick all in a short space of time, gave dramatic evidence that the cause was not natural, but supernatural. The supernatural, with power to act so strongly and disastrously, could only, in Job's mind, be God. (*TOP*, 109–10)

When challenged to answer questions from the press rather than give his interpretation of Job, Harvey insists, 'I'm giving you a seminar on *Job* without pay' (*TOP*, [418]): there is no answer that does not involve the problem of Job, a problem whose resolution is another kind of repetition – God returns to Job what he had lost; repetition becomes recovery. Similarly, in Kierkegaard's narrative, the Young

Man's life is transformed when he discovers that the lover whom he had abandoned has married someone else – 'I am again my old self, here I have the repetition. I understand everything' (*Rep*, 143) – with the result that the meaning of the story of Job is now repeated in his own experience:

> Did I not get everything doubly restored? Did I not get myself again, precisely in such a way that I must doubly feel its significance? And what is a repetition of earthly goods which are of no consequence to the spirit – what are they in comparison with such a repetition? Only his children Job did not receive again double, because a human life is not a thing that can be duplicated. In that case only spiritual repetition is possible, although in the temporal life it is never so perfect as in eternity, which is the true repetition. (*Rep*, 144)

Repetition invokes the return of the past but is directed towards the future and, in the end, towards eternity, the ultimate location of 'true repetition'.

In the relation between Constantius and the Young Man, as well as between both and their concealed author, Søren Kierkegaard, *Repetition* has the dialectical structure typical of all of Kierkegaard's works, with the result that the more the Young Man discovers the virtue of repetition the less can Constantius commit to it, dismissing his own previous assertion of its importance – 'It is lucky that the young man does not seek any enlightenment from me, for I have abandoned my theory, I am adrift' (*Rep*, 94) – and minimising the significance that the Young Man has found in the biblical story – 'Here he thinks he has found what he sought, and in this little circle of Job and the wife along with three friends the truth, as he thinks, seems more glorious and joyful and true than in a Greek symposium' (*Rep*, 94) – while insisting that the Young Man is trapped in the aesthetic: 'If he had had a deeper religious background, he would not have become a poet. Then everything would have acquired for him a religious significance' (*Rep*, 157). This dialectical structure is given formal enactment when the narrative switches from Constantius's account of his friend's life to the letters written by the Young Man in which, instead of being the subject of the narrator's evaluation, he turns the tables to consider the narrator's character:

> So you enthral me by an indescribable power, and this same power alarms me. So I admire you, and yet at times it seems to me as if you were deranged. Or is it not a sort of mental derangement to have subjected every passion, every emotion of the heart, every feeling, to this cold discipline of reflection? (*Rep*, 98)

Despite the apparent certainty he shows towards the Young Man, Constantius is revealed as a character in flux, one who could expound repetition but cannot live it: 'Repetition is too transcendent for me also. I can circumnavigate myself, but I cannot erect myself above myself' (*Rep*, 94).

The dialectic of Constantius's relationship with the Young Man is one that Spark combines in the character of Harvey in *The Only Problem*: he is, like Constantius, someone who seems to have 'subjected every passion, every movement of the heart' to a level of control that alienates him from the people around him –

> Edward said, 'I don't know if you realise how hateful you can be, Harvey. If it wasn't for your money you wouldn't speak like that.' For it struck him that, since Harvey had recently come into a vast share of a Canadian uncle's fortune, he ought not to carry on as if he were the moderately well-off Harvey of old. This treatment of Effie was brutal. (*TOP*, 25)

– but, like the Young Man, his obsessive struggle to come to terms with the meaning of Job reveals his commitment to finding an answer to 'the only problem', a religious perspective which will allow him not to 'take seriously the childish pranks of actuality' (*Rep*, 158), like the fact that the police believe his wife is also in hiding in France, where she has joined a terrorist organisation, seeking seriously to challenge the capitalism that she had childishly challenged by stealing a bar of chocolate. Despite his scholarly coldness and apparent lack of interest in other people, Harvey nonetheless insistently attracts the attention of those who are, initially, repulsed by his lack of passion: Edward cannot drag himself away from his conversations about Job; Ruth abandons her marriage to Edward to live with Harvey because 'He really is a most interesting man' (*TOP*, 50); through Ruth, Harvey is apparently able to recover and repeat the marriage he abandoned with Effie, even taking on responsibility for Effie's child for whom Ruth has become a surrogate mother. Having sought isolation Harvey finds himself surrounded by 'comforters' and by the need to acquire more property to make *them* comfortable: 'They think I'm such a bore that I have to bribe them to come and play the part of comforters' (*TOP*, 63). When he is arrested as a possible accomplice in his wife's terrorist activities, Harvey finds himself subject to the kind of interrogation that Job suffered and which Spark herself associated with the modern police state: 'They [the Comforters] resemble interrogators sent in one after the other to question a suspected prisoner and try to trip him up' (*GF*, 198). If Job's life is indeed a revelation of the significance of repetition, then so too is Harvey's, whose life comes increasingly to mirror that of the subject of his study: one of the reporters, come to question him about whether he supports his wife's terrorism, asks, 'Would you say that you yourself are in the position of Job, in so far as you are a suspicious character in the eyes of the world, yet feel yourself to be perfectly innocent?' (*TOP*, 109).

The interaction in Harvey's life of recollection – his memories of Effie – and repetition – Ruth's coming to live with him, as though giving him back his lost relationship with Effie – produces a dialectic of loss and recovery, of recovery followed by loss – Ruth subsequently abandons him to take the daughter back to her real father – which is a less dramatic but still a sustained version of the sufferings of Job. The ironies of the interaction of recollection and repetition are symbolised by a painting in the museum of the village of Epinal, a painting entitled *Job Visited by his Wife*, a painting which had first attracted Harvey to rent the nearby cottage in which he works on his account of Job. What is striking about the painting by seventeenth-century artist Georges de La Tour is that it is a 'repetition-in-advance', since Job's wife as presented by de La Tour bears a striking resemblance to both Effie and Ruth:

> In order to have a better look at Job's wife's face, Harvey put his head to one side. Right from the first he had been struck by her resemblance to Effie in profile. She was like Ruth, too, but more like Effie, especially about the upper part of her face. Oh, Effie, Effie, Effie. (*TOP*, 79)

The repetition opens the door to the pain of recollection. If Harvey now lives as a kind of repetition of Job, he wants to recover Effie as a version of Job's wife as she appears in de La Tour's mysterious painting:

> His face looks up at his wife, sensitive, imploring some favour, urging some cause. What is his wife trying to tell him as she bends her sweet face towards him? What does he beg, this stricken man, so serene in his faith, so accomplished in argument? (*TOP*, 77)

Though they are both repetitions of Job's wife, neither Effie nor Ruth can look to Harvey as Job's wife does to Job in de La Tour's painting. As Harvey comes more to resemble Job, the seventeenth-century painting comes increasingly to defy the traditional account of Job and his wife:

> Here, she is by no means the carrier of Satan's message. She comes to comfort Job, reduced as he is to a mental and physical wreck. 'You speak,' he tells her, 'as one of the foolish women;' that is to say he doesn't call her a foolish woman, he rather implies that she isn't speaking as her normal self. And he puts it to her, 'Shall we receive good at the hand of God, and shall we not receive evil?' That domestic 'we' is worth noticing, thought Harvey; he doesn't mean to abandon his wife, he has none of the hostility towards her that he has, later, for his friends. (*TOP*, 78–9)

Harvey's reading of the painting is also, of course, a reading of his failed relationship with Effie – there is no 'we' in their existence – and the mutuality which he has failed to find with her makes his love, like that of Constantius's Young Man, a matter of recollection and regret, a failure to achieve the fulfilment of repetition which Judge Wilhelm had praised in marriage. When he goes to Paris to identify his wife's body after she has been shot by the police, 'her head was bound up, turban-wise, so that she looked even more than ever like Job's wife' (*TOP*, 186): the repetition only adds to the loss that is involved in recollection but repetition will, in the end, be Harvey's apparent salvation since, like Job, he will recover his losses, adopting Effie's daughter and again living with Ruth, by whom he will have another daughter. Like Job, however, he is not necessarily 'satisfied with his plump reward', for 'his tragedy was that of the happy ending' (*TOP*, 185–6).

Spark's reworking of elements of *Repetition* in *The Only Problem* suggests not only an understanding of the paradox of repetition as Kierkegaard presents it – 'Repetition and recollection are the same movement, only in opposite directions, because what is recollected has been and is thus repeated backwards, whereas repetition properly so called is recollected forwards' (*Rep*, 3–4) – but also of the relation of the paradox of repetition to the paradox of faith, dependent as it is on the recollection and repetition of Christ's life as a temporal event which is yet the signal of the eternal and of the intersection between the two. Faith is the recollection of the entry of eternity into time which is repeated in every encounter of the faithful with God. *Repetition*, however, was not the only book that Kierkegaard published on 16 October 1843, for on the same day he also published *Fear and Trembling*, attributing it to Johannes *de silentio*, and repetition is not only its theme, but also its method, so that *Fear and Trembling* begins by repeating in different ways and from different perspectives the setting out of Abraham and Isaac to the place appointed for the sacrifice:

> It was early in the morning. Abraham arose betimes; he had the asses saddled, left his tent, and Isaac with him, but Sarah looked out of the window after them until they had passed down the valley and she could see them no more. They rode in silence for three days [. . .] (*F&T*, 10–11)

> It was early in the morning, Abraham arose betimes, he embraced Sarah, the bride of his old age, and Sarah kissed Isaac, who had taken away her reproach, who was her pride, her hope for all time. So they rode on in silence [. . .] (*F&T*, 12–13)

> It was early in the morning, Abraham arose betimes, he kissed Sarah, the young mother, and Sarah kissed Isaac, her delight, her joy at all times. And Abraham rode pensively along the way. (*F&T*, 13)

> It was early in the morning, everything was prepared for the journey in Abraham's house. He bade Sarah farewell, and Eleazar, the faithful servant, followed him along the way, until he turned back. They rode together in harmony, Abraham and Isaac, until they came to Mount Moriah. (*F&T*, 14)

The repeated effort to *imagine* what the setting out on such a journey might be for all those involved represents an effort to translate the timeless – the Word of God as recorded in the Bible, and God's intervention into the life of Abraham – into the existential experience of time, a time in which the meaning, purpose and end of the story is as yet uncertain. If repetition can be a prologue to eternity, because it is 'in eternity where there is true repetition' (*Rep*, 144), it can also be a reversal of that relationship, a reversal by which the apparently eternal is turned back into the multiple possibilities of time: 'It was early morning' is the repeated prologue to many different existential experiences of the same narrative events, and to the different possible meanings of Abraham's decision that he should sacrifice his son rather than defy God. To Kierkegaard, Abraham's actions are 'a paradox' unresolvable by reason, precisely because they defy the universality of the ethical, thereby placing Abraham above the law and making him dependent as an individual on his direct contact with God:

> For faith is this paradox, that the particular is higher than the universal – yet in such a way, be it observed, that the movement repeats itself, and that consequently the individual, after having been in the universal, now as the particular isolated himself as higher than the universal. If this be not faith, then Abraham is lost, then faith has never existed in the world. (*F&T*, 80–1)

Kierkegaard's language is tortuous because of the unthinkability of a faith that could put itself beyond the ethical, but in so doing Abraham actually demonstrates the nature of all faith:

> if it stands fast that Abraham is the representative of faith, and that faith is normally expressed in him whose life is not merely the most paradoxical that can be thought but so paradoxical that it cannot be thought at all. He acts by virtue of the absurd, for it is precisely absurd that the particular is higher than the universal. (*F&T*, 83)

It is in the encounter with the absurd, that moment when no reason is adequate to justify a decision, that faith exerts itself. To be 'faithful' – to be full of or full with faith – is to have passed beyond the bounds of reason into the 'absurd' but an absurd which is given justification by the intersection of the timeless with time, of the possibility that an event in time is also an event in eternity and that creatures who ought to be part of eternity must nonetheless exist in the world of time.

This potential double direction of repetition – moving beyond time or moving back through time – makes repetition a concept with complex implications depending on its direction of travel. In his journal, Kierkegaard adopts repetition as the context for a debasement of humanity's potential:

> The mass of people do not really *live*, they are mere repetitions, live in the security of the probable, and so they are not superstitious, that is to say that they do not notice that this belief of theirs in the probable, and their security within the probable is, in another sense, a tremendous superstition. (*J*, '1175', 425)

A life lived in repetition is like the lives of the workers in *The Ballad of Peckham Rye*, consisting of an endlessly repeated production line whose banal reduplication carries on into their lives outside the factory. When Dougal visits Dixie's home, her mother brings out her newspaper cuttings:

> 'Here we are again,' Dixie said.
> 'She always says that,' Mavis said.
> 'Well, Mum, you keep pulling them out; every new person that comes to the house, out they come.' (*BPR*, 37)

Mavis's repeated action is designed to reveal the great event of her life – her departure from Peckham as a 'GI bride' headed for the United States – but, the marriage having failed, what the cuttings now testify to is not the change that they prophesied but the life of repetition to which she returned in Peckham. So inured are the characters to repetition, and to a future that must be a secure reoccurrence of the past, that immediately after her wedding Dixie declares, 'I feel as if I've been twenty years married instead of two hours' (*BPR*, 143), as though to annul the change to which she has just committed herself. Like the Young Man in Kierkegaard's text, she has to see her present from a point in the future which reduces its challenge to her present experience. On the other hand, the notion of 'eternity' as the place of 'true repetition' (*Rep*, 75) is ironically presented in *The Hothouse by the East River*, in which the disruption of Paul and Elsa's life in New York begins with the appearance of someone whom Elsa takes to be Helmut Kiel, a prisoner of war with whom she had a relationship in in 1944. Kiel, like Paul and Elsa, is supposed to be dead but his reappearance, even though the man concerned claims to be called Mueller and not to have been born when Kiel died, initiates a series of repetitions of the lives they lived during the war: Elsa travels back to Europe with Mueller to establish, by sleeping with him, whether or not he is Kiel, and Paul propositions Mueller on the same basis:

> 'He tried to date me,' says the salesman. 'He wouldn't call me Mueller, he kept on calling me Kiel. He tried to date me for the evening but I told him I wasn't that way.'
>
> 'Pierre must have inherited the tendency from his father,' Elsa says.
>
> 'Your husband,' says the salesman in his correct accent, 'is under the impression that he and I had a sentimental encounter in the 1944, and he wishes to repeat the affair as an experiment, in order to establish my identity.' (*HBER*, 104)

Repetition here becomes revelatory of the past, since the nature of Elsa's and Paul's relations with Kiel have not been specified in the novel's various flashbacks to 1944, but repetition is also a pointer to the eternity towards which, eventually, they are moving, escaping from the times – both their lives during the war and their afterlife in New York – in which they have been trapped. Repetition points backward to reveal what the characters have refused to recollect about their past, but simultaneously points forward towards the full knowledge of the events of their lives which will be possible in the 'eternity where there is true repetition'. They have to escape their belief that they are still living in time, explaining their present by their past, and accept the necessity of their entry into the alternative repetition of eternity.

If, as Kierkegaard (or Constantius) suggests, repetition is to become the key concept in a modern understanding of knowledge, an expansion and extension of the Greeks' belief in the power of recollection, it is one that Spark makes peculiarly her own in the structure of her narratives. In *The Prime of Miss Jean Brodie*, for instance, the death of Mary MacGregor is first presented early in the novel, at the beginning of Chapter 2, when, in the novel's narrative time,

'Mary MacGregor was ten, there she was sitting blankly among Miss Brodie's pupils' (*PJB*, 15). Her death, which is foretold when Mary was ten, comes 'after the outbreak of the Second World War':

> She died while on leave in Cumberland in a fire in a hotel. Back and forth along the corridors ran Mary MacGregor, through the thickening smoke. She ran one way; then turning, the other way; and at either end the blast furnace of the fire met her. She heard no screams, for the road of the fire drowned the screams; she gave no scream, for the smoke was choking her. She ran into somebody on her third turn, stumbled and died. (*PJB*, 16)

It is a death which is in turn prefigured when Mary is terrified by magnesium flares in the science classroom and 'ran along a single lane between two benches, met with a white flame, and ran back to meet another brilliant tongue of fire' (*PJB*, 100), and it is finally recapitulated in the last pages of the novel when Sandy 'heard again from Miss Brodie at the time of Mary Macgregor's death, when the girl ran hither and thither in the hotel fire and was trapped by it' (*PJB*, 169). As many critical accounts have suggested, in narratological terms, these constitute examples of prolepsis and analepsis, the presentation of an event in advance of or later than its actual occurrence in the temporal sequence of a narrative, but from a Kierkegaardian perspective they represent dramatizations of the complexity of a repetition which can either be retrospective – like the return to Berlin of the narrator in *Repetition* in the hope of recapturing his previous experience – or prospective, an intimation of the 'true repetition' of eternity. The various recapitulations of Mary's life and death removes her from the flow of time, her ten-year-old self juxtaposed with the self who died in her twenties as if both were equally present in some other dimension than the forward direction of historical time. These scenes are not, in other words, simply elements in the novel's narratological tactics but revelations of how repetition can transfigure our understanding of events in time. Indeed, the possibility of the transcendence rather than just the disruption of time is inscribed in the word 'analepsis', since it is also in some parts of the Christian world a term for the feast of Christ's ascension into heaven. Mary Macgregor, the scapegoat of everyone's condemnation both in the Marcia Blane school and in the Brodie set, becomes the symbol of a resurrection from time into eternity – a possibility inscribed, of course, in her name as a repetition of the Mary who was the living vehicle for the appearance of the eternal in time. When Sandy discusses Mary's death with Jean Brodie in those final months before both, in their different ways, leave the world, Brodie interprets Mary's death as a punishment: 'If this is a judgement on poor Mary for betraying me, I am sure I would not have wished [. . .]' (*PJB*, 169). That an accidental death could reveal God's purpose in the world is the burden of what the Young Man in *Repetition* discovers through Job:

> Job! Job! Job! Job! Didst thou indeed utter nothing but these beautiful words: 'The Lord gave, and the Lord has taken away; blessed be the name of the Lord'? Didst thou say nothing more? In all they distress didst thou merely continue to repeat these words? Why wast thou silent for seven days and seven nights? What went on in thy soul? When the whole world fell to pieces above thy head and lay in potsherds around thee, didst thou at once possess this superhuman composure, didst thou at once have love's interpretation and the frank-heartedness of confidence and faith? (*Rep*, 110)

Faith defies the happenings of time: repetitions *in* time are transformed from indications of a temporality which, like the fire in which Mary is trapped, consumes existence and eradicates its future, to become instead a pre-figuration of eternity. Sandy's decision to become a nun follows rapidly on her conversation with Jean Brodie about Mary MacGregor and Brodie's insistence that Mary is the pupil most likely to have betrayed her: 'I think first of Mary Macgregor. Perhaps Mary has nursed a grievance, in her stupidity of mind, against me – she is such an exasperating young woman' (*PJB*, 168). Brodie's change of tense, turning Mary from a being in the past to one still continuing in the present – 'she *is* such an exasperating young woman' – may reflect the greater reality of the past to a Jean Brodie for whom the events of the present are no longer of significance, but it also implies the potential transcendence of time which Sandy will accept by her induction into the Catholic Church: Mary 'is' even when she is dead; her life, like her death, are repetitions in eternity and not simply narrative disruptions to the presentation of historical time; her name points to the transcendence which she herself was never able to envisage but which it became Sandy's responsibility to fulfil.

Similarly, only a few pages into *The Girls of Slender Means*, we encounter the following dispute:

> Anne trod out her cigarette contemptuously on the floor of the large entrance hall with its pink and grey Victorian tiles. This was pointed to by a thin middle-aged woman, one of the few older, if not exactly the earliest members. She said, 'One is not permitted to put cigarette-ends on the floor.' The words did not appear to impress themselves on the ears of the group, more than the ticking of the grandfather clock behind them. But Anne said, 'Isn't one permitted to spit on the floor even?' 'One certainly isn't,' said the spinster. 'Oh, I thought one was,' said Anne. (*GSM*, 9–10)

The minor contretemps illustrates the gulf in attitudes between the generations who reside in the May of Teck Club but also their resigned acceptance of each other's foibles; only two pages later, however, we are told:

> It was Greggie who had said to Anne by the notice-board:
>
> 'One isn't permitted to put cigarette-ends on the floor.'
>
> 'Isn't one permitted to spit on the floor, even?'
>
> 'No, one isn't.'
>
> 'Oh, I thought one was.'
>
> Greggie affected an indulgent sigh and pushed her way through the crowd of younger members. She went to the open door, set in a wide porch, to look out at the summer evening like a shopkeeper waiting for custom. Greggie always behaved as if she owned the club.
>
> The gong was about to sound quite soon. Anne kicked her cigarette stub into a dark corner. (*GSM*, 12)

The repetition provides some additional information, such as the name of Anne's interlocutor and both of their responses to the exchange, but the event is dramatised quite differently: although we start in the past tense – 'It was Greggie who had said' – the interchanges are now laid out as dialogue rather than being incorporated into a continuous paragraph, as though we are encountering them in the immediate present of the narration rather than as the repetition of something we have only just been told. The repetition thus disrupts the temporal sequence of the narrative, making the later rendition seem more immediate, more *present*, than its precursor, while, at the same time, underlining that the events do not take place in a narrative present in which we move forward in time as the events unfold but are the products of a recollection – 'Long ago in 1945 all the nice people in England were poor, allowing for exceptions' (*GSM*, 1) – which allows events to be revisited no matter what their place in the original sequence. Repetition establishes a relationship between the two repeated versions of an event by which they are both transformed: no longer confined to being a singular occurrence in time, it is as though, despite their triviality, they have escaped from the constrictions of time and can be replayed looking forward or looking backward. The repetition of this opening little encounter between Greggie and Anne prepares the way for a novel to which repetition and recollection will be central. Thus Selina repeats to herself daily two sentences from a manual on 'poise':

> The Two Sentences were a simple morning and evening exercise prescribed by the Chief Instructress of the Poise Course which Selina had recently taken, by correspondence, in twelve lessons for five guineas. The Poise Course believed strongly in auto-suggestion and had advised, for the maintenance of poise in the working woman, a repetition of the following two sentences twice a day:
>
> Poise is the perfect balance, an equanimity of body and mind, complete composure whatever the social scene. Elegant dress, immaculate grooming, and perfect deportment all contribute to the attainment of self-confidence.
>
> (*GSM*, 59–60)

Selina's equivalent of a secular daily prayer is juxtaposed, on the following page, with Joanna's teaching of poetry, which for her, too, has become a substitute for prayer:

> At the top of the house the apples are laid in rows
> And the skylight lets the moonlight in, and those
> Apples are deep-sea apples of green. There goes
>   A cloud on the moon in the autumn night.
>
> (*GSM*, 61)

The apples of John Drinkwater's poem are transformed from the products of time into an apparently timeless state, in which they represent an innocence – a suspension of the original eating of the apple – that will be overthrown when Selina escapes from the 'top of the house' by virtue of the slenderness that allows her to pass through the window not once but several times, first in order to save herself and then in order to recover the Schiaparelli dress. Selina's 'body' – both her flesh and its favourite clothing – is twice saved from the fires of time, a salvation that appears to Nicholas as a 'savagery so extreme that it forced him involuntarily to make an entirely unaccustomed gesture, the signing of the cross upon himself' (*GSM*, 73). Nicholas's action is first presented as a prefiguration in Chapter 4 and then presented in retrospect in Chapter 8, when its repetition becomes ambiguous:

> Later, reflecting on this lightning scene, he could not trust his memory as to whether he then involuntarily signed himself with the cross. It seemed to him, in recollection, that he did. Felix Dobell later said that Nicholas had crossed himself in superstitious relief that Selina was safe. (*GSM*, 161)

The narrative repetition of the event challenges recollection as to its real significance: what kind of sign has been given to the world of time? Nicholas is confronted by a Kierkegaardian paradox – is his signing of the cross a repetition of a childhood gesture or is it the recollection of the meaning of faith; is it a recollection of a fallen world from which there is no escape or, by the timelessness of the action, an invocation of a transcendent meaning? Given the impossibility of a reasoned decision, Nicholas, like Kierkegaard, will choose faith, even if it is a faith that can make no sense to a secular world.

The importance of Kierkegaard's account of 'recollection' and 'repetition' to the structuring of Spark's narratives is underlined in *Symposium*: the title, of course, presents the novel as itself a repetition and reinterpretation of Plato's dialogue of that name, a dialogue in which each of the characters who have gathered to celebrate Agathon's winning the prize with his first tragedy is challenged to deliver a speech about the nature and meaning of love. Plato's dialogue is also the intertext, however, of the opening section of Kierkegaard's *Stages on Life's Way*, in which Constantine Constantius, in a section entitled 'In Vino Veritas', organises a banquet attended by various editors, authors and characters from Kierkegaard's pseudonymous works who, once they have eaten and are, like Plato's characters, sufficiently intoxicated, make speeches on the topic of 'erotic love' (*SLW*, 30). The fact that Constantius is both the pseudonymous author of *Repetition* and the character who creates a modern repetition of Plato's *Symposium* in the Danish countryside is testimony to the importance of repetition in Kierkegaard's own writings – the *Concluding Unscientific Postscript*, for instance, is a recapitulation and extension of the ideas presented in *Philosophical Fragments* (or *Philosophical Crumbs*) in a section entitled 'The Issue in *Fragments*: How Can an Eternal Happiness be Built on Historical Knowledge', while an 'Appendix' to chapter II of the second part, entitled 'A Glance at a Contemporary Effort in Danish Literature', is actually a critical account and a recapitulation of Kierkegaard's previous pseudonymous writings. The 'Preface' to 'In Vino Veritas' – supposedly written by one William Afham, who is himself a character in a work compiled by 'Hilarius Bookbinder' – returns to the nature of 'recollection' that has been the starting point of *Repetition*:

> Although the difference between memory and recollection is great, they are frequently confused. In human life, this confusion lends itself to studying the depth of the individual. That is, recollection is ideality, but as such it is strenuous and conscientious in a way completely different from indiscriminate memory. Recollection wants to maintain for a person the eternal continuity in life and assure him that his earthly existence remains *una tenore* [uninterrupted], one breath, and expressible in one breath. (*SLW*, 10)

Recollection, according to Afham, provides the 'proceeds for eternity', for, 'in recollection, a person draws on the eternal' (*SLW*, 11) in providing the unity of a life in time. Lise, in *The Driver's Seat*, is a character who is incapable of turning repetition into recollection; she has no recollections to provide a continuity to her identity and must create the sequence of events by which she will in the end become a character in her own narrative, while the characters in *A Hothouse by the East River*, on the other hand, are moving from memory – the 'indiscriminate' memories of their lives during the war – to recollection – their realisation of the continuities of their existences which make possible not only their entry into eternity but an entry in which one has 'provided oneself with enough to recollect for a whole eternity' (*SLW*, 11).

In Plato's dialogue, the key issue is the justification of love between an older man and a male youth; in Kierkegaard's, it is whether erotic love is compatible with marriage; in Spark's, it is whether any kind of marriage is sustainable in the modern world. In Spark's *Symposium*, ten characters are gathered around the dinner table of Hurley Reed, 'an American painter in his early fifties', and Chris Donovan, 'a rich Australian in her late forties', who 'live together' in 'a union of great convenience and contentment' (*S*, 11). The invited dinner guests have been carefully chosen by Hurley and Chris for their intelligence – 'we've got an intelligent party' (*S*, 40) – and represent the variety of modern sexual and marital relationships – heterosexual, homosexual, bisexual, inter-familial, platonic, and, in the case of Ernst and Ella Untzinger, a shared passion for their home help, a young man by the name of Luke: 'Luke was the main thing they now had in common. It had positively begun to draw them together, so that they were actually further from separating than they had ever been in their married life' (*S*, 130). The strengths and weaknesses of these various kinds of relationships will be debated by the characters, both, as in Plato and in Kierkegaard, by statements at the banquet itself but also in discussions interspersed in conversations in the days leading up to the dinner party. Hurley, who lives with but is not married to Chris, insists to Ella, who is comfortably married to but not in love with Ernst, that,

> 'The vows of marriage [. . .] are mostly made under the influence of love-passion. I am talking of modern marriages where the partners have been free to choose for themselves. They are in love. I am not talking about arranged marriages where the parents, the families, have combined to bring about the union. Good. We have a love-match. Let me tell you,' says Hurley, 'that the vows of love-passion are like confession obtained under torture. Erotic love is a madness. Neither of the partners know what they are doing, saying. They are *in extremis*. The vows of love-passion should at least be liable to be discounted. That it is why it is possible, and in fact imperative, for a Catholic, who is supposed to belong to the most rational religion, to believe in divorce between people who have been in love, the marriage vows being made in a state of mental imbalance.' (*S*, 44)

Hurley is, of course, defending his own choice not to be married, but indirectly he indicates the tenuous knowledge upon which the marriage of two other guests at the dinner is based: Margaret Murchie, a young Scottish woman, and William Damien, the only son of an Australian businesswoman sufficiently rich that she can buy them a London flat for their wedding present and decorate it with a painting by Monet, have known each other for only four months before they marry. Margaret, however, has a history of which her new husband is unaware, for throughout her life she has been so regularly in close proximity to murders, disappearances and unexplained deaths that her family are terrified by her; her parents, Dan and Greta, were

> frightened, as they had every reason to be. Because Margaret's capacity for being near the scene of tragedy was truly inexplicable in any reasonable terms. If they had been able to see, as, to do them justice, nobody else was capable of seeing, that there was absolutely no link of any rational, physical or psychological nature between Margaret's personal activities and what went on around her, Dan and Greta might have felt a certain consolation. But still they would never have left well alone. (*S*, 142)

Margaret's life is shaped by the insistent repetition of sudden deaths among those close to her, but it is shaped, too, by the force of recollection, primarily the recollections of her mad Uncle Magnus who 'liked to quote the Border ballads' (*S*, 140), and who sees in Margaret a descendant of the 'Covenanting stock who refused to accept the rule of the bishops' (*S*, 107) and who might, therefore, 'be under divine orders' (*S*, 108). Magnus is himself possibly implicated in some of the deaths close to Margaret, since the woman who murdered Margaret's grandmother only days after she had altered her will in favour of Margaret's father had escaped from the same institution where Magnus was held, and the disappearance of Margaret's schoolteacher follows on a meeting with Magnus. Magnus's capacity for recollection, however, is also a source of divination: he anticipates the repetitions to come, as when he suspects (*S*, 106) the coming death of the Mother Superior in the convent to which Margaret has been sent in order to recover from her grandmother's murder. As it turns out, it is another nun who is murdered and the Mother Superior confesses to the crime, though she seems so weak it would have been impossible for her carry out such an act. While Plato's characters carouse and discourse on the virtues of love, Spark's characters, despite the various kinds of love that they declare or personify, are enmeshed in a world of evil: Lord Suzy makes a speech not about love – his third wife is thirty years younger than him and 'had frequently thought of flight' (*S*, 7) – but about the recent burglary and desecration of his home; Luke, the sexual focus of Ernst and Ella's relationship, is a waiter at the dinner but has sold the names of those attending to a gang who are on the lookout for empty properties to rob; Margaret is there by virtue of having arbitrarily selected William Damien from a list of rich unmarried men provided to her by Magnus and stalked him till she found an opportunity to accost him. By marrying a potentially rich husband Margaret has fulfilled what she had plotted with Magnus, but having proved her capacity for action and being tired of implied guilt in crimes she has not committed, she determines that she will do away with her rich mother-in-law so that her husband will come into his inheritance:

> 'Between the two of us', Margaret said, 'we could arrange an accident.'
>
> 'Impossible,' said Magnus. 'No guarantee, ever, of success. Too risky.'
>
> 'All those suspicions have fallen on me,' said Margaret. 'Why shouldn't I really do it? I'm tired of being made to feel guilty for no reason. I would like to feel guilty for a real case of guilt.' (*S*, 160)

Margaret's plans, however – 'I want to actively liquidate the woman. Compared with the evil eye, what I have in mind is just healthy criminality' (*S*, 159) – will be pre-empted by the gang who have been tipped off by Luke that Mrs Damien will be at Hurley and Chris's dinner party, when in fact she is, at that time, installing her secret wedding present in their flat. Magnus's anticipation that Margaret need not act on her own behalf because 'destiny might do it for you' (*S*, 160) turns out to be true: the force of repetition defies Margaret's effort to take control of at least one of the deaths by which she is afflicted. Her existential attempt to project the plan of her own future reveals only that the future is beyond her control: her life is not one of existential choices by which her future will be shaped but one in which apparent accidents determine the future through which she will have to live.

Margaret's life is thus the effective denial of Sartre's assertion that 'man will be what he will have planned to be',[3] a context which is invoked by Margaret's repeated appeal to the philosophy of '*Les Autres*' – a philosophy of which she asserts her mother-in-law to be an example:

> 'Hilda's a good sort,' said Hurley.
>
> 'Absolutely immersed in the philosophy of *Les Autres*,' said Margaret.
>
> 'What?'
>
> 'Have another drink,' said William, taking Hurley's glass to fill it with ice, vodka and tonic.
>
> 'The philosophy,' said Margaret 'of *Les Autres* is a revival of something old. Something very new and very old. It means we have to centre our thoughts and actions away from ourselves and entirely on to other people.'
>
> 'Oh, meaning the others. Why is it expressed in French?
>
> 'It's a French movement,' said Margaret. 'Well, Hilda as I say, exemplifies *La Philosophie des Autres*. She really does.' (*S*, 35)

That Hilda might have any interest in '*La Philosophie des Autres*' is scoffed at by Chris Donovan – 'what absolute rot. Hilda doesn't take up philosophies and ideas. She's a very busy active woman. The girl must be mad' (*S*, 41) – but Margaret's French philosophy echoes one of Sartre's most famous aphorisms, the statement from his play *In Camera* that 'L'enfer, c'est les autres' – 'Hell is other people'. Indeed, the first performance of *In Camera* in 1944 was done under the title of *Les Autres*.[4] In Part Three of *Being and Nothingness*, Sartre explores what he describes as *être-pour-autrui*, or being-for-others, but in what Arthur C. Danto describes as 'Sartre's curiously morbid psychology',[5] 'being-for-others' is not a matter of generosity or empathy towards others but of a profound mistrust produced by a fundamental fear of the ontological aims of the Other:

> Everything which may be said of me in my relations with the Other applies to him as well. While I attempt to free myself from the hold of the Other, the Other is trying to free himself from mine, while I seek to enslave the Other, the Other seeks to enslave me. We are by no means dealing with unilateral relations with an object-in-itself, but with reciprocal and moving relations. The following descriptions of concrete behaviour must therefore be envisaged within the perspective of conflict. Conflict is the original meaning of being-for-others. (*B&N*, 364)

Margaret's invocation of a beneficent commitment to *les autres* conceals her deep resistance to all of the 'others' who might represent an 'enslavement' of her life, from her grandmother, her parents and her sisters through to her mother-in-law and even to her Uncle Magnus – unless he does what she wants. For Sartre, as we have seen, the nothingness of human consciousness releases it from the causal sequence of the world and, therefore, into freedom; Margaret is equally freed from the normal causal sequence but is so by her apparent ability to defy causality and to attract supernatural interventions into her environment. As Magnus writes to her about her alibi for the death of the nun in the convent, 'Chronology is not causality' (*S*, 122). There are, he implies, forces which are not recognised in the ordinary world's conception of causality, and which produce outcomes that remain mysterious or are attributed to causes which are not their real determinants. The madwoman who kills Margaret's grandmother and the burglars who kill Hilda are the immediate causes of their deaths, but they are operating as though instructed by a more fundamental force. Margaret may appear to be 'perfectly innocent' (*S*, 181) but only because she is a conduit for the supernatural, chanting to her marriage bed with its collection of William's and her childhood toys,

> Now speak to me, blankets, and speak to me, bed,
> And speak, thou sheet, enchanted web.
>
> (*S*, 133)

The deaths by which she is surrounded reveal her life as an 'enchanted web' in which the recollection of the powers of the past invoked in such Border Ballads transforms her future; under the disguise of a concern for *les autres* lurks a savage spirit as unredeemed by a Christian concern for the Other as Sartre's atheism:

> 'It's a question of *les autres*,' Margaret says. 'One can't live unto oneself.' She is thinking how much she craves to be back in Scotland with her father looking terrorized through his smoke-glasses into the distance and her mother weakly trying to cope with her horse-racing debts and her menopause; there, Margaret is at home and feels it. She longs for the weekend, the coming Sunday, and sees quite clearly how easily Hilda can go into the pond, a push, with Uncle Magnus kneeling, holding her down. She thinks: What am I doing among these

> people, what am I doing here? And, while the chatter goes on around her, and William smiles lovingly and a little fearfully in her direction, it is a relief to let her mind dwell with savagery on Hilda. (*S*, 186–7)

In Spark's *Symposium*, reality is governed by unacknowledged psychic forces which are deeper and more determining than either the freedom of choice espoused by existentialism or the material causes by which, for secular science, the physical world is organised: the world around Margaret is governed by 'enchantment', and the enchantment which brings about Margaret's marriage starts with her apparently accidental, but in fact long-premeditated, meeting with William Damien 'in the fruit section of Marks & Spencer's, Oxford Street':

> 'Be careful, those grapefruits look a little bruised.'
>
> He was enchanted right away, having just broken rowdily with a girl he had been living with for almost two years. (*S*, 30)

The implication that William's break-up with his previous girlfriend was responsible for his 'enchantment' glosses over the fact that Margaret had waited precisely for the break-up of that relationship in order to make her move to introduce herself to him. From his perspective, it is an accidental event; from hers, part of a carefully planned search for a wealthy husband. The ambiguous status of the event – accident, destiny or plot? – turns the banality of the phrase 'in the fruit section of Marks & Spencer's' into the locus of an intersection between very different and competing versions of the nature of reality, and its subsequent repetition throughout the novel – it recurs ten times – lifts the moment of their meeting from the world of accident and/or causality into the alternative reality of 'enchantment': the repetition of the phrase transfigures it from a description of an event in time into a mystery – 'I'll never believe she met William in Marks & Spencer's fruit section by chance', Hilda Damien declares (*S*, 171) – that defies the order of temporality and causality. Textual repetition, by continually displacing the event into the subsequent time of the novel, underlines the extent to which its original place in the order of time was deeply ambiguous. Textual repetition, for the reader, initiates a process of recollection which transforms the banality of the phrase into a poetic chorus to the action, continually gesturing to the mystery on which love is based and the impossibility of accounting for the forces involved: 'William's such a fool, he keeps repeating the phrase, "Be careful, the grapefruit could be bruised," or something like that, which Margaret said to him when they first met in Marks & Spencer's. It's childish' (*S*, 181). The trivial phrase becomes an incantation, both for William *in* the novel and for the reader *of* the novel, as it accumulates, from its repetition, the significance of a recollection full of paradoxical meanings – it has escaped from time into a seeming timelessness, but a timelessness which only underlines how trapped are the novel's characters in a world of time which has no access to or understanding of the supernatural: 'William looks at his watch. "I don't expect Mother will be coming, now." "Oh, there's still time," says Hurley getting up to fill someone's glass' (*S*, 189). There is 'still time' – but for Hilda, time is done: she has entered the very different 'stillness' of death. The fact that she is killed while delivering the 'present' of a painting underlines the difference between art and life: art can outlast the life of its creator or its owner. Hilda's Monet may be a present but its value is precisely that it is not a part of the present that is lived either by Monet or by Hilda, or as it will be lived by Margaret and William: it belongs to a pseudo-eternity created by its unchanging stillness, a pseudo-eternity which, for Hilda, is the occasion for her own encounter with whatever eternity holds for a living being.

The relationship between the living and the eternal is presented by Socrates in Plato's *Symposium* as one aspect of recollection's relation to repetition. He recalls what he was taught by his female teacher Diotima:

> For what is implied in the word 'recollection,' but the departure of knowledge, which is ever being forgotten, and is renewed and preserved by recollection, and appears to be the same although in reality new, according to that law of succession by which all mortal things are preserved, not absolutely the same, but by substitution, the old worn-out mortality leaving another new and similar existence behind – unlike the divine, which is always the same and not another? And in this way, Socrates, the mortal body, or mortal anything, partakes of immortality; but the immortal in another way. Marvel not then at the love which all men have of their offspring; for that universal love and interest is for the sake of immortality.[6]

If knowledge is indeed 'recollection', then knowledge is always in decay, just as the earthly imitation of the Platonic notion of the forms in their eternal perfection are a declension from that perfection to the disfigured repetitions which are the daily world of our ordinary experience. Diotima's 'law of succession' produces a repetition – the offspring to which each generation gives birth – but such repetitions can never be more than blighted versions of a divinity which 'is always the same and not another'. Natural repetition produces a similitude of immortality but one which is in fact dependent on our individual mortality, and, therefore, on the impossibility of the individual becoming him- or herself immortal. Nature offers a 'substitution' for immortality which only reinforces our individual mortality.

The irony of the relationship between the mortal and the immortal is one which informs Kierkegaard's own repetition of Plato's *Symposium* in the section of *Stages on Life's Way* entitled 'In Vino Veritas', in which Victor Eremita – the fictional editor of the papers gathered in *Either/Or* – insists that he will only attend a banquet for others of Kierkegaard's fictional authors and editors if it could be of an opulence that could never be recreated; indeed, he declares that 'I am so far from wanting to talk about a repetition that I assume that it cannot be done even once' (*SLW*, 25). Of course, the banquet – at which speeches will be given about the nature of 'erotic love' – is already a repetition of the one in Plato's *Symposium*, but the implication is that the original never actually took place, or never took place as presented in Plato's text: it is a piece of art recollecting events which it acknowledges to have been relayed by Aristodemus, than whom 'there was no one who was a more devoted admirer of Socrates',[7] and unlikely, therefore, to be an impartial observer. Recollection transforms an event in time into an event in art, another version of that repetition by which human beings seek 'the immortal in another way', and when Constantine Constantius unexpectedly arranges the banquet he does so by pre-empting the relation of life to art by creating a stage for it that ensures that the banquet takes place not in the sequence of ordinary life but in the apparent timelessness of the aesthetic. When the guests arrive at a location in a forest near Copenhagen,

> The double doors were opened, the effect of the brilliant lighting, the coolness that flowed towards them, the spicy fascination of the scent,

> and the tasteful table setting overwhelmed the entering guests for a moment, and when at the same time the orchestra began playing the dance music from *Don Giovanni*, the forms of those entering were transfigured, and as if in deference to an invisible spirit encompassing them, they stood still a moment, like someone whom admiration has awakened and who has risen in order to admire. (*SLW*, 27)

Eremita's apparently impossible demand – 'I assume that it cannot be done even once' – has been given challenge by a construction designed for the combination of all the possibilities of the aesthetic – the visual, the aural, the olfactory, the gustatory and the tactile – and therefore as a setting appropriate to speeches on the nature of 'erotic love'. At the conclusion of the banquet, Constantius drained his glass and 'hurled it against the door in the back wall' (*SLW*, 80), which is the sign for the dismantling of the banquet scene: 'like someone who has presumptuously knocked on death's portal and when it is opened sees the forces of annihilation, we saw that demolition crew ready to destroy everything' (*SLW*, 81). The art which has turned nature into a dramatic setting for the repetition of Plato's *Symposium* is itself demolished so that the scene has been made quite literally unrepeatable – except, of course, that even its demolition is repeated in Kierkegaard's text. The artful banquet is, like every moment in time, uniquely unrepeatable and yet, by its transformation into a literary text, becomes a repeatable recollection of an event which could never have taken place because the guests, being the fictional creators or creations of Kierkegaard's texts, never existed: art, as in Diotima's account of biological reproduction, partakes of a paradoxically immortal mortality.

The irony of the interaction of these various forms of repetition as undertaken 'for the sake of immortality' is taken up in Spark's *The Takeover*, which contrasts biological reproduction – the central character, Hubert Malindaine, is a homosexual who worships women but would not engage himself in any sexual activity with them – with aesthetic reproduction – Hubert is having all the artworks and antiques of the house in which he lives copied so that he can sell the originals and leave the fakes behind 'as another new and similar existence'. Hubert's house looks out on to Lake Nemi, site of the ancient shrine of the goddess Diana, and Hubert claims to be directly descended from the goddess – from a coupling of the eternal with the finite – and therefore to be 'spiritually if not actually' (*T*, 11) the owner of the property, despite the fact that it was paid for and legally belongs to his wealthy friend Maggie who, having lost interest in Hubert after her third marriage, is attempting to have him evicted. Hubert's supposed descent from an immortal accurately reflects, however, the intertwining of life and art in his family background, since the story of the Malindaines' descent from Diana was the concoction of two old aunts who had been inspired by J. G. Frazer's *The Golden Bough* (*T*, 105), that immense study of ancient myth which, while claiming to be a scientific investigation into the origins of religion, was itself a vast construction of the imagination, a repetition of ancient lore disguised as a modern psychological investigation into the nature of the human mind. 'Infatuated' (*T*, 48) with Frazer's study in comparative religion, Hubert's spinster aunts infused the reality of their unreproductive lives with an imaginary primitive vitality drawn from Frazer's account of pre-Christian fertility cults. Just as those aunts had incorporated Frazer into their lives, so *The Takeover*, in its fifth chapter, incorporates Frazer's text into the body of its own:

> In the sacred grove there grew a certain tree round which at any time of the day, and probably far into the night, a grim figure might be seen to prowl. In his hand he carried a drawn sword, and he kept peering warily about him as if at every instant he expected to be set upon by an enemy. He was a priest and a murderer; and the man for whom he looked was sooner or later to murder him and hold the priesthood in his stead. Such was the rule of the sanctuary. A candidate for the priesthood could only succeed to office by slaying the priest, and having slain him, he retained office till he was himself slain by a stronger or craftier. (*T*, 56)

Repetition is of the essence of the priesthood at Nemi: the king awaits and fears his replacement by a repetition of the means by which he himself had acquired his kingship: 'surely no crowned head', Frazer comments, 'ever lay uneasier, or was visited by more evil dreams, than his' (*T*, 56). It is a condition replicated in Hubert's uncertain guardianship of Maggie's property, having reproductions made of her Louis XIV chairs and her artworks in order to insure his financial future against the consequences of eviction. Just as Hubert's aunts displaced the reality of their origins with a manufactured alternative, so Hubert replaces original artworks with their reproductions in a chain of repetitions which makes it impossible any longer to tell the fake from the real. Maggie, not knowing about this reproduction of the artworks, secretly sends Hubert a cache of gold coins to prevent him suffering too much while she goes through the legal process of eviction. The gold coins, however, point to the central paradox of the novel — what is the value of the repeatable? The gold coins have value only because, in the end, of the limited supply of the world's gold, which makes gold a medium by which the value of other things can be established: the value of gold is a fiction but a fiction based upon a material reality. After the abandonment of the 'gold standard', however, money is entirely fictional, something which Maggie discovers to her cost when she puts her fortune in the hands of an Argentinian lawyer, Coco de Renault: 'Brilliant Monsieur de Renault was now the overlord of Maggie's network. Mysterious and intangible, money of Maggie's sort was able to take lightning trips around the world without ever packing its bags or booking its seat on a plane' (*T*, 99), and it is able to do because it has become separated from the real things whose exchange it makes possible: her rich friends 'talked of hedges against inflation, as if mathematics could contain actual air and some row of hawthorn could stop an army of numbers from marching over it' (*T*, 90). The characters in *The Takeover* live in a world divided between the relics of an older religion — their houses are built on the foundations of ancient Roman constructions just as the value of modern money is based on relics of the gold standard – and the coming into existence of new kind of repetition based on a different model of reproduction, one in which the imitation is no less valuable than the original. The values of the older world are invoked when Agata, who is pregnant by a fellow servant, Lauro (who is in turn having sex both with Maggie and her daughter-in-law, Mary, and still planning a reluctant marriage to another local girl), stops on the main street of Nemi to talk to another servant, Clara:

> The two women were greeted occasionally by busy shoppers who passed and swept a glance, along with their smiles, at Agata's hard-done-by belly of shame, while the whole of eternal life carried on regardless, invisible and implacable, this being what no skinny craving cat with its gleaming eyes by night had ever pounced upon, no tender mole of the earth in the hills above had ever discovered down there under the damp soil, no lucky spider had caught, nor the white flocks of little clouds could reveal when they separated

> continually, eternal life untraceable and persistent, that not even the excavators, long dead, who had dug up the fields of Diana's sanctuary had found; they had taken away the statues and the effigies, the votive offerings to the goddess of fertility, terracotta replicas of private parts and public parts, but eternal life had never been shipped off with the loot [. . .] (*T*, 180–1)

The eternal, as Diotima suggested, secretes itself in the world of natural reproduction, while the world of money and wealth begins, in 1973, to evanesce into repetitions without substance: thus the friends of Maggie's third husband, Berto,

> spoke of the mood of the stock market, the health of the economy as if these were living creatures with moods and blood. And thus they personalized and demonologized the abstractions of their lives, believing them to be fundamentally real, indeed changeless. But it did not occur to one of those spirited and in various ways intelligent people round Berto's table that a complete mutation of our means of nourishment had already come into being where the concept of money and property were concerned, a complete mutation not merely to be defined as a collapse of the capitalist system, or a global recession, but such a sea-change in the nature of reality as could not have been envisaged by Karl Marx or Sigmund Freud. (*T*, 127)

The 'sea-change' is a world where 'assets were to be liabilities' (*T*, 127), open to blackmail and extortion that turn the surety of wealth and possession into an illusion, the reproduction of a former reality that no longer has any substance. Repetition is not the challenge that it proved to be for Constantine Constantius in *Repetition* because it is now fundamental to the denatured nature of the modern world,

The transformation of the historical circumstances in which the characters of *The Takeover* live in 1974 is revealed when the property of Maggie's new husband, Berto, is visited by two supposed art experts who are in fact thieves planning a raid to steal some of his art collection, but they bring with them a catalogue from a Swiss auction house which has, on its cover, an image that Maggie recognises:

> It bore on its lovely cover, in tasteful print, the name Neuilles-Pfortzheimer, a Swiss auction house famous among collectors of paintings and fine arts. Under this was a reproduction of an impressionist

painting. 'What's this?' Maggie shrieked, and the circle of friends around her stood back a little as if in holy dread. 'What's what?' said Berto looking over her shoulder.

'My Gauguin!' It was in my house at Nemi. What is it doing in this catalogue? Is it up for sale?'

The younger of the visiting art historians said, 'Why, that was sold last week. We were there. You must be mistaken, ma'am.' (*T*, 162)

Maggie's house and its contents are emblematic of a world where reproduction in the sense of mechanical imitation has displaced natural reproduction as the means by which a human being 'partakes of immortality'. Ironically, Hubert's reproduction of Maggie's work of art is accompanied by his turning the house into a place of worship for a fertility cult which is a recapitulation of pre-Christian celebrations of the reproduction which he denies himself:

'To us,' said Hubert, 'who are descended from the ancient gods, your Christianity is simply a passing phase. To us, even the God of the Old Testament is a complete upstart and his Son was merely a popular divergence. Diana the huntress, the goddess of nature, and ultimately of fertility, lives on.' (*T*, 107)

This fake religion has its roots in the ancient world just as the houses on Maggie's property are built on Roman foundations, but Hubert's cult finds itself in competition with a general return to ecstatic forms of religion, each a repetition and recapitulation of some previous movement; as a newspaper report incorporated into Chapter 14 announces, 'The Charismatic Movement, a predominantly lay movement claiming more than half a million followers, emerged in the main line Protestant churches in the early 1960s and in Roman Catholicism in 1967, among students and professors at Duquesne University in Pittsburgh' (*T*, 209). To Hubert, these celebrants of a revived Christianity are 'nothing but schismatics from the true and original pagan cult of Diana' (*T*, 206), but Hubert, of course, is the priest of a religion which claims to represent the 'the true and original' only in the context of its recreation from Frazer's account of the 'cult of Diana'. For Hubert, such a fiction is a release from the responsibilities of modern society: 'The concepts of property and material possession are the direct causes of such concepts as perjury, lying, deception and fraud. In the world of symbol and the worlds of magic, of allegory and of mysticism, deceit has no meaning, lies do not exist, fraud is impossible' (*T*, 138). In a world overwhelmed by repetition, it is impossible to distinguish between that which is repeated and that which it repeats, between that which exists and that which imitates existence. Hubert's house, he discovers, has been built on land that Maggie did not actually own but had been sold to her by a fake lawyer of whose existence there is no record, resulting in a metaphysical conundrum about a house which is '*abusivo*' (unauthorised) and therefore does not legally exist:

> '[. . .] The house does not exist.'
> 'I mean this house,' Hubert said.
> 'It does not exist. How can it exist? It is not on the records. In Italy if a house is not on the records, it has been constructed illegally, and we call it *abusivo*. An *abusivo* construction does not exist in legal terms [. . .].' (*T*, 191)

Like Maggie's Gauguin which is now a copy of what may itself be a copy, becoming ever more unprovably related to an original, so Hubert's house and Hubert with it vanish into a multitude of non-existences:

> '[. . .] There are many tenants in *abusivo* houses who cannot be put out and who need not pay rent, either. Because the house does not exist.'
> 'And the contents of the house?' Hubert said.
> 'It would be difficult,' said Massimo, moving his plump hands in the air as he spoke, 'to say anything about the contents of a house that does not exist. How can a non-existent house contain contents? How can it have a tenant? You don't exist when you inhabit a house that is *abusivo*.' (*T*, 192)

The non-existent is both the foundation and the endpoint of repetition: 'being' turns seamlessly into 'nothingness', a nothingness that can be the foundation of a spurious religious belief. Hubert's legal non-existence is an outcome which parallels the unreality of his life and personality, based as they are on a fiction dreamed up by his aunts, a fiction deriving from Frazer's claims to knowledge about the past which was itself a fiction. Hubert's cult of Diana is a repetition of a repetition, an *abusivo* construction which exists only because it does not exist.

It is symptomatic of the confusions of repetition that the American Jesuits who come to visit Hubert are fascinated by the pagan elements which were incorporated into early Christianity and see in the 'ecological' implications of Hubert's cult of Diana, 'the mother of nature' (*T*, 166), a repetition of that early blending of the pagan with the Christian. When Hubert goes for a last look at the Lake of Nemi before he departs for Rome (where he is planning to work with the ecologically minded Jesuits), he finds again that 'from every point appeared a different view, every view a picture postcard except that it was real' (*T*, 187) – the real is indistinguishable from its aesthetic reproduction. There in the woods, however, Hubert finds Maggie, now magically transformed into a gypsy, so that her wealth will not attract robbery or kidnap, but having also transformed herself into a kidnapper, holding her lawyer, de Renault, as a hostage until his family pay her back as a ransom the fortune which he had stolen from her. Just as Socrates' final words in Plato's *Symposium* are his attempt to prove to Agathon and Aristedemus that 'the genius of comedy was the same with that of tragedy, and that the true artist in tragedy was an artist in comedy also',[8] so Spark's comic inversions in *The Takeover* cannot conceal the tragedy that has overtaken the world in its transformation by repetition and by the desires that such repetition provokes in the search for material or religious delusions. Hubert's cult gets followers because 'the new world which was arising out of the ashes of the old, avid for immaterialism, had begun to sprout forth its responsive worshippers' (*T*, 148), among them the Jesuit priests:

> Father Cuthbert whispered to his fellow-Jesuit Gerard, 'There's a lot of truth in what he says.'
>
> 'I like the bit about the earth being our capital,' replied Gerard, ever ecologically minded, 'but he mixes it up with a lot of shit, doesn't he?'
>
> 'Oh well,' said Cuthbert, 'it's like manure and even if it's shit it gets people thinking about religion, doesn't it?' (*T*, 149)

This benign latitudinarianism does not stop the past from being evil as well as fertilising; one of those at Hubert's ritual is an English schoolteacher who uses the Bible to insist that the worship of Diana was in fact an evil which Christianity had attempted to suppress, thereby transforming a charismatic celebration into a violent melee, after which Hubert's 'secretaries' of an earlier summer return not for the pleasures he once offered them but as hired assassins – 'He doesn't think that certain people might have a certain reason to pay us to kill him' (*T*, 165). Hubert's self-induced belief in his cult of Diana has led to his 'wildly believing that her will not only existed but would certainly come to pass' and, as a result,

> like ministers of any other religion, he was estranged from reality in proportion as he mistook the nature of prayer, offering up his words of praise, of gratitude, penitence, intercession and urgent petition in the satisfaction that his god would reply in kind, hear, smile and wave a wand. (*T*, 145)

Hubert exemplifies Kierkegaard's assertion that 'parsons too are poets' because they are '"deceivers" in a far deeper sense than the sense in which Socrates long ago called the poets' (*J*, '1861', 280).

It is a thought which Kierkegaard dramatizes at the end of 'In Vino Veritas', when the characters who have attended the banquet depart into the countryside and encounter Judge Wilhelm and his wife breakfasting in an arbour in the garden of their house; the banqueters, unseen, listen in to a discussion between the couple about the nature of their marriage, a discussion which might have been a further contribution to their night's speeches on the subject of erotic love. Thus one group of fictional characters secretly listens to the discussion of another group of fictional characters, and while they do so Victor Eremita, the fictional editor of *Either/Or* in which Judge Wilhelm first appeared, slips through a window into the Judge's study to uncover a new manuscript that he might publish: 'He stuck it in his pocket, or rather he intended to stick it in his pocket, but as he bent his arms and already had his hand with the manuscript half in his pocket, I slipped it away from him' (*SLW*, 86). Naturally, we wonder who this 'I' is who intervenes but he refuses to disclose himself: 'I am like the line with the arithmetic problem above and the answer below – who cares about the line?' If reality, in *The Takeover*, is always disappearing behind its repetitions, so authorship, in Kierkegaard's texts, is always disappearing behind the pseudonymous authors and editors, who are themselves concealed behind the characters to which they give voice. We inhabit a world of repetitions, too few for some, too many for others, which is why Constantius, defeated in his search for repetition, adopts the 'post-horn' as his 'symbol': 'one never can be sure of eliciting from this instrument the same note. And he who puts it to his mouth and deposits his wisdom therein can never be guilty of repetition' (*Rep*, 78). But the fact that the post-horn cannot repeat its note from day to day does not prevent the post from being delivered, or Job from recovering his losses, or for the eternal to have manifested itself in time.

Notes

1. Job 1:21.
2. In a discussion of *Territorial Rights*, Matthew Wickman suggests that 'there is a deeply existential-phenomenological dimension to the sort of "originary repetition" that resounds in Spark's novel. It echoes such formulations as Kierkegaard's when he opposes repetition to memory, Nietzsche's when he writes of the eternal return or Derrida's on *différance* and the erasure of primordial traces. These are the types of dynamics which inspire scholars like McQuillan to assert a strong and even self-conscious rapport between Spark and literary theory': 'Muriel Spark, Modernism and Postmodernism', in Michael Gardiner and Willy Maley (eds), *The Edinburgh Companion to Muriel Spark* (Edinburgh: Edinburgh University Press, 2010), 66.
3. Jean-Paul Sartre, 'The Humanism of Existentialism', trans. Bernard Frechtman, from 'L'Existentialisme est un humanisme' (1947), in *Jean-Paul Sartre: Essays in Existentialism*, ed. Wade Baskin (New York: Citadel Press, 1965), 36.
4. Philip Thody, *Jean-Paul Sartre: A Literary and Political Study* (London: Hamish Hamilton, 1960), 80.
5. Arthur C. Danto, *Sartre* (London: Fontana/Collins, 1975), 116.
6. *Dialogues of Plato*, trans. and ed. Benjamin Jowett, 3rd edn (Oxford: Oxford University Press, 1893), vol. 1, 578.
7. Ibid. 542.
8. Ibid. 223.

Chapter 6

The Geopolitics of the Personal

Muriel Spark's story 'The First Year of My Life' declares the speaker to have been born 'on the first day of the second month of the last year of the First World War' – the same day on which Spark herself was born – but the speaker in the story has a distinctive first year in life:

> I was known as the baby whom nothing and no one could make smile. Everyone who knew me then has told me so. They tried very hard, singing and bouncing me up and down, jumping around, pulling faces. Many times I was told this later by my family and their friends but, anyway, I knew it at the time. (*CSS*, 303)

The child's refusal to smile was not accidental but the result of the fact – which the story claims is well known to those who experience ESP (extrasensory perception), as well as to 'the adults of some primitive tribes' and many 'poets and philosophers' – that babies 'are born omniscient' and that 'in their waking hours, know everything that is going on everywhere in the world'. As a result, the speaker's 'autobiography, as I very well perceived at the time, started in the very worst year that the world had ever seen so far' (*CSS*, 303). The baby's introduction into the world coincides with a global history apparently at its most destructive and the relation between the individual and that history is immediately apparent to the omnisciently unsmiling child; her personal life is already intertwined with the military conflicts of that year as a result of the fact that she is surrounded by 'careless women in black' who have 'lost their sons', or 'lost their husbands and their brothers' (*CSS*, 304):

> The Western Front on my frequency was sheer blood, mud, dismembered bodies, blistered crashes, hectic flashes of light in the night skies, explosions, total terror. Since it was plain I had been born into

> a bad moment in the history of the world, the future bothered me, unable as I was to raise my head from the pillow and as yet only twenty inches long. (*CSS*, 304–5)

At a year old, however, what finally brings a smile to her face – though her family think it is produced by the blowing out of the candle on her cake – is Asquith's speech to the House of Commons in which he declares, 'All things have become new. In this great cleansing and purging it has been the privilege of our country to play her part . . .' (*CSS*, 308). The smile is one of disbelief, of contempt, of wonder at the hypocrisy of those who lead the world. The intimate sociability of the smile is profoundly and causally connected to the vast military, imperial and political events of the time into which she happens to have been born: the smile is not merely a personal statement for those in her immediate environment but a response to the whole world of which they are a part.

Spark's story of the child who is the medium that allows the contemporary world in its totality to be present in her parents' home has its parallel in the events that Kierkegaard attributes to the childhood of Johannes Climacus in a story of 1842, which is copied into the *Journals*:

> His father was a very severe man, apparently dry and prosaic, but under his frieze coat he concealed a glowing imagination which even old age could not dim. When occasionally Johannes asked his permission to go out, he generally refused to give it, though once in a while he proposed instead that Johannes should take his hand and walk up and down the room. At first glance this would seem a poor substitute, and yet, as in the case of the frieze coat, there was something totally different concealed beneath it. The proposition was accepted, and it was left entirely to Johannes to determine where they should go. So they went out of doors to a nearby castle in Spain, or out to the seashore, about the streets, wherever Johannes wished to go, for his father was equal to anything. While they went up and down the room his father described all that they saw; they greeted passers-by, carriages rattled past them and drowned his father's voice, the cake woman's cakes were more enticing than ever. He described so accurately, so vividly [. . .] everything that was known to Johannes and so fully and perspicuously what was unknown to him, that after half an hour of such a walk with his father he was as much overwhelmed and fatigued as if he had been the whole day out of doors. (*J*, '413', 108)

With the father this time as the medium, the outside world – though a much more pleasant one than Spark's – is transferred wholesale into the domestic interior and experienced as though it were reality. It is a scene which Theodor Adorno in *Kierkegaard: Construction of the Aesthetic* takes to be emblematic of Kierkegaard's philosophy as a whole because, despite its emphasis on the existential nature of the self, the self as outlined by Kierkegaard, Adorno argues, can never in fact come into contact with the world beyond itself. Kierkegaard's dialectic is one which erases rather than reveals the real, an erasure which Adorno believes can only 'be correctly interpreted' in the light of Kierkegaard's position in Danish society and, therefore,

> by considering the relation between the flesh-and-blood Kierkegaard and the sociohistorical conditions in which he lived, and from which he was largely estranged. As an early nineteenth-century rentier involved in neither economic production nor capital accumulation, Kierkegaard lived off a fixed sum of invested money, and was thus highly subject to the market fluctuations of his age (such as the economic downturn caused by the worker revolts of 1848). He was a member of a declining economic class, and, as such, was externally powerless.[1]

For Adorno, a Marxist and a materialist, Kierkegaard's philosophy might be summarised in the section of *Concluding Unscientific Postscript* entitled 'Becoming Subjective': 'to become subjective should be the highest task assigned to every human being, just as the highest reward, an eternal happiness, exists only for the subjective person or, more correctly, comes into existence for the one who becomes subjective' (*CUP*, 163). Kierkegaard's insistence on 'becoming subjective' is, for Adorno, indicative of the fact that that his philosophy prioritises illusion over truth, inner feelings over external economic realities. In the *Journals*, Kierkegaard recounts the economic difficulties by which he was entrapped in 1848 after he had invested in government war bonds in the course of Schleswig-Holstein crisis of that year:

> Economic anxieties come upon me suddenly and all too near. Two such heterogeneous weights as the opposition of the world and anxiety about my own subsistence I am unable to lift at the same time. Then the confusion suddenly breaks loose. For a few months the situation was such that to-morrow I might own perhaps nothing at

> all but be actually in financial need. That went hard with me. All the more powerfully did my spirit react. I produced more powerfully than ever before, but more than ever like a dying man.[2]

The major political disturbances of 1848 are the stimulant to Kierkegaard's creativity, as if the productivity of his imagination – as Adorno might suggest – could make up for the lack of productivity of his government bonds. The substitution of imaginative activity for economic insecurity is something with which Spark herself was very familiar in the late 1940s and early 1950s: Martin Stannard suggests that she committed herself to leave her son with her parents in Edinburgh and make her career in London 'even though she plunged herself into poverty'.[3] The substitution of imaginative assertion for economic uncertainty is also reflected in many of Spark's novels: Jean Brodie, continually under threat of losing her job, is nonetheless confident about her judgements – 'Who is the greatest Italian painter?' 'Leonardo da Vinci, Miss Brodie'. 'That is incorrect. The answer is Giotto, he is my favourite' (*PJB*, 11). Brodie imposes her own subjective values on the external world in defiance of how fragile, as a spinster and a teacher, her own economic position in the world actually is. The world in which she lives is not the material world in which she finds herself, but the world she creates by virtue of her imagination, a subjectivity or subjectivism which is reflected not only in Kierkegaard's philosophy, as interpreted by Adorno, but also in the philosophy of Sartre:

> For the rest, there exist concretely alarm clocks, signboards, tax forms, policemen, so many guard-rails against anguish. But as soon as the enterprise is held at a distance from me, as soon as I am referred to myself because I must await myself in the future, then I discover myself suddenly as the one who gives meaning to the alarm clock, the one who by the signboard forbids himself to walk on a flower bed or on the lawn [. . .] I emerge alone and in anguish confronting the unique and original project which constitutes my being; all the barriers, all the guard-rails collapse, nihilated by the consciousness of my freedom. I do not have nor can I have recourse to any value against the fact that is I who sustain values in being. (*B&N*, 39)

The values of the world that I experience are the values which I have chosen: Sartre may not follow Berkeley into suggesting that I sustain, by my perception, the being of the external world, but that world would not exist as it does exist if it were not for the values by which it is ordered by and for me, by the project of my freedom. Brodie's world is ordered not by the values of the school in which she teaches – which emphasises 'team spirit' rather than individualism – but by the projection of her own values which structure the world of the school and her pupils as one that reflects back to her the 'truth' of those values. The 'Brodie set' is, in effect, the world remade in the image of Jean Brodie, and such mutuality between the self and the 'other' is something which has concerned critics of Sartre's analysis of the self and its relationship to what is other to the self: as Thomas Busch has suggested, Sartre's ontology implies that the self is formed through its rejection of the other, that 'Human consciousness, upon contact with what is other than itself, recoils into itself, constituting in fact a *self*'.[4] In encountering the existence of the other, the self retreats back into the selfhood from which, supposedly, it is able to escape in order to be with others; rather than respecting the otherness of the world it encounters, the self defends itself by projecting its own values upon that world, to remake it in terms of those values. As a consequence, there can be no such thing as 'objective knowledge': all knowledge is experienced in and through the 'inwardness' of subjectivity. Which is why Johannes Climacus in the *Unscientific Postscript* can offer as a 'definition of truth: *An objective uncertainty, held fast through appropriation with most passionate inwardness*' (*CUP*, 203). Truth belongs not to the objective world, but to the intensity with which it is appropriated by subjectivity.

Such a remaking of the world on the model of the self and its values is, however, as Jean Brodie exemplifies, fraught with danger. The inner world of the self displaces external reality at the cost of moral discrimination: the 'aesthetic' becomes a self-indulgent justification of its own presuppositions. To escape the apparent subjectivism – or, indeed, the potential solipsism – of building an ontology on the experience of the existential self, and of that self's capacity to reshape the world on the basis of its own freedom, almost all varieties of existentialism came to lay stress on what Heidegger describes as the 'thrownness' of our being in the world. We do not get to choose the nature of the world in which we discover ourselves (as is underlined by 'The First Year of My Life') but are thrown into it without having been consulted: it may be the nature of the human being to be ontologically free but it is a freedom which has to be exerted in a context we did not choose, an environment – a 'facticity' – which we cannot simply erase by a subjective act of will. We may be free to choose but that freedom has to be exerted in a world that in the first instance we did not choose and did not contribute to creating. As Heidegger puts it, 'The concept of "facticity" implies that an entity "within the world" has Being-in-the-world in such a way that it can understand itself as bound up in its "destiny" with the Being of those entities which it encounters within its own world';[5] Sartre, more insistent that 'it is through human reality that there is a world' (*B&N*, 307), nonetheless insists that the human being as the 'for-itself' exists

> in the manner of an event, in the sense in which I can say that Philip II has been, that my friend Pierre is or exists. The for-itself is, in so far as it appears in a condition which it had not chosen, as Pierre is a French bourgeois in 1942, as Schmitt was a Berlin worker in 1870; it is in so far as it is thrown into the world and abandoned in a 'situation'. (*B&N*, 79)

Being 'abandoned in a situation' implies both the isolation and the interrelatedness of the existential self. In this sense, the personal life – that is, the life of a person in the world – is played out not only in terms of its subjectivity and its relationship to the eternal – 'the union with God proceeds through personality, transfigured by that whole process' (*J*, '220', 63) – but in a historical context of social values and of economic and military conflict.[6] The self is not thrown only into an ontological mystery, for which religion *may* provide an answer, but into a historical mystery governed by forces which are inescapably obscure at the time of their occurrence. Thus Jean Brodie's fate turns on the death of her fiancé in the First World War: she is engaged and then disengaged by events beyond her control, which drives her to use her pupils as alternative lives to the one into which she has been thrown. Her desire for a controlling power over her pupils is also expressed in her admiration for leaders who exert control over their countries: 'Sandy recalled Miss Brodie's admiration for Mussolini's marching troops, and the picture she had brought back from Italy showing the triumphant march of the black uniforms in Rome' (*PJB*, 31). Jean Brodie's personal life is intimately connected to her historical circumstances, and her personal future to what she imagines to be the future development of those historical circumstances: fascism is not a pastime in which she indulges during the school holidays, it is the external image of her internal nature: 'She's a born Fascist' (*PJB*, 125), as Sandy insists to Miss Mackay. But, of course, Sandy, in her profound resentment of Miss Brodie, is wrong: she is not a 'born Fascist' but someone who has come to fascism through the impact on her of the First World War, and has come to it as a movement which was itself a product of that war. Miss Brodie and fascism are, as it were, made for each other by the history by which both have been shaped and by their similar efforts to transform reality by the imposition on it of an aesthetic order. Miss Brodie's personal life, in its simultaneous rebelliousness and desire for order, runs in parallel with the rise, establishment and destruction of fascism. Brodie is not simply Spark's depiction of a woman mistakenly enamoured by the aesthetic power of fascism: she is an instance of fascism's attraction to those, like many of the poets of the 1920s and 1930s, who see the imagination as threatened by modern democratic societies and see in fascist states places where the imagination is able actively and purposively to impose itself on reality. The personal is not simply subjectivity: the individual does not find herself in the world burdened with the ontological reality of her freedom of choice, for the choices by which she is confronted are not open-ended – they are constrained and constricted by the historical environment in which she discovers herself, and the consequences of events – like the death of her fiancé – over which she has no control.

If Sartrean existentialism, as Gabriel Marcel argued, 'vilified freedom' by making it a necessity of consciousness and therefore the foundation of all human actions under all circumstances, Christian existentialism of the kind proposed by Marcel or Jaspers was founded in an alternative conception of the individual, one that rejected the primacy of the *cogito*, a primacy which, they argued, still underpins Sartre's philosophy of the self. For Marcel, for instance, the person comes into existence not in the moment of the *cogito*'s self-consciousness of its own being over against a world which is other to it, but only through its recognition of being *with* others and thus participating not just in its own subjectivity but in an intersubjectivity:

> it is the relationship expressed by the preposition *with* that is eminently intersubjective. The relationship that *with* expresses, here, does not for instance really apply to the world of objects, which,

> taken as a whole, is a world merely of juxtaposition. A chair is *along-side* a table, or *beside* it, or we put the chair *by* the table, but the chair is never really *with* the table in this sense.[7]

For Marcel, intersubjectivity plays its part in the life of the subject even at moments when the latter's only intercourse is with itself, for 'in its own intrinsic structure subjectivity is already, and in the most profound sense, genuinely intersubjective'.[8] As a consequence, to start with the *cogito*, as Sartre does, is to make a fundamental mistake about the nature of consciousness and, therefore, about a human being's place in the world: in the words of Emmanuel Mounier, following in the foot-steps of Marcel, 'there is within the oneness of a fundamental intuition a *Sum ego es* [I am, therefore you are], which, from one particular aspect, might, in more specific terms, be a *Videor ergo es* [I seem to be therefore you are].'[9] Mounier quotes from Jaspers to explain that we cannot escape

> factors of place, time, family, environment and character – I am born into a place in the world, a place peculiar to me. I did not choose my ground to fight upon – I don't even clearly understand the meaning of the struggle, yet, this place is mine; it is my position. The world into which I am thrust by taking up my position is not the world, but *my world*.[10]

The 'my' of 'my world' is not the possessive singularity of the 'I' of the cogito, it is the 'I' of 'being with', it is the 'I' that only exists in and through our relationship with other persons, 'following which I do not treat another-person as an aspect of nature, but as an aspect of freedom, and by which, in addition, I contribute towards his free-dom in the same way as he contributes towards mine'.[11]

This participatory sense of the self, the notion of a 'we' rather than an 'I' as the foundation of human consciousness, had been pro-moted in the 1930s by the Personalist movement in France, of which Emmanuel Mounier was the leading figure. A committed Catholic, Mounier saw Personalism as a development of the Christian existen-tialism of Marcel and identified in the existentialism of the 1940s a reprise of some of the central elements that had been developed by Personalism in the 1930s:

> There is a close similarity between the preoccupations of Existentialists and Personalists. We find this common ground, not only in Gabriel Marcel, but also in Berdyaev. 'Existential Philosophy is a personal philosophy; the subject of enquiry is the human person.' The existent is presented in terms of a being in collision with the inertia or impersonality of the thing. Existentialists are unanimous on this point. They have sounded the call to a revival of Personalism in contemporary thought.
>
> That is to say, in general terms, Existentialism presents a picture of a kind of intensified Personalism.[12]

For Mounier, Personalism 'is the living activity of self-creation, of communication and of attachment, that grasps and knows itself, in the act, as the movement of becoming personal'.[13] The possibility of 'becoming personal' acknowledges that the 'person' in Personalism was a potentiality as well as an ontological reality; human beings are persons but their personhood can be developed by their becoming more fully personal, by increasing 'the existence of free and creative persons',[14] and thereby fulfilling the immanent purpose of the world:

> One can proceed from the study of the objective universe, to show that the personal mode of existing is the highest form of existence, and that the evolution of pre-human nature converges upon the creative moment at which this achievement of the universe is attained. One may say that its central reality is this act of personalisation; the impersonal realities, or those that are more or less depersonalized (matter, living species and the ideas) being only the effects of a loss of speed, of nature's lagging-behind upon the road to personalization.[15]

Personalism is, for Mounier, both a philosophy and a call to social action to increase the numbers of those who recognise the importance of the person and are prepared to 'experiment' in how to live a more personal life: 'one may openly live the experiment of personal life, hoping to convert to it a number of others who still live like trees, like animals or like machines'.[16]

When Jean-Paul Sartre proposed in *Qu'est-ce que la littérature?* in 1947 that writers had to be 'engaged' in the struggle for freedom, because literature itself could not exist except in the freedom of the writer and the reader, he was following a path that had been trodden by Mounier's journal *L'Esprit* since its founding in 1933: Mounier had insisted on both religion and literature being *engagé* and directed at transforming the spiritual condition of the bourgeoisie and social conditions of the workers – *L'Esprit* was one of the promoters of the notion of 'working' priests as a means of re-engaging the working classes with Catholicism.[17] The potential of Mounier's 'Personalism' was a matter of live debate in the circles in which Spark moved in London in the 1940s and 1950s: Stefan Schimanski and Henry Treece, co-editors of the Personalist anthology *Transformation*, are mentioned by Derek Stanford as among those 'who looked on themselves as Muriel's friends', not only supporting her in her conflict with the Poetry Society but among those who had 'been summoned to witness what was hoped would prove the birth of a new literary group'.[18] Personalism also appealed to those who were seeking a way forward from the kind of anarchism that Stanford – like Nicholas Farringdon in *The Girls of Slender Means* – had adopted under the influence of George Woodcock and Herbert Read and which seemed, in the aftermath of the Second World War, to have little positive to offer in a world increasingly organised by the state. In this context, religion – and especially Mounier's Catholicism – is not an escape from the world but the basis for engaging with it. If existentialism proposed an engagement with a godless world, Personalism viewed human relations on the model of the believer's relationship to God, as an 'I–Thou' relationship of mutual recognition. That is why Mounier, while insisting on the development of the person and the personal, was equally insistent that 'to be' is 'to-be-with-others':[19] it is to share the weight of facticity and to acknowledge what Jaspers described as the 'situatedness' – the '*being-in-a-situation*' – of human experience.

Spark's novels are characterised by plots that dramatise both 'being with others' and 'being-in-a-situation'. It is the dynamics of the group – whether the Brodie set, or the girls of slender means, or the servants in *Not to Disturb* – that shape individual identities in her novels, a group which is situated in a specific historical and social environment with its own burden of facticity:[20] the novels are not about the inward depths of her characters but about the 'we' through which they define themselves. Spark's novels continually emphasise the 'situatedness' of her characters, both their situatedness in terms of a 'we' rather than an isolated 'I' but also their situatedness in terms of a particular set of historical events. Radios throughout the May of Teck Club drown out Joanna's recitations as their volume is turned up to listen to Winston Churchill:

> Joanna ceased. The wireless spoke forth their Sinaitic predictions of what would befall the freedom-loving electorate should it vote for Labour in the forthcoming elections. The wireless suddenly started to reason humbly:
>
> We shall have civil servants . . .
>
> The wireless changed their tones, they roared:
>
> No longer civil . . .
>
> Then they were sad and slow:
>
> No longer . . .
>
> . . . *servants.*
>
> Nicholas imagined Joanna standing by her bed, put out of business as it were, but listening, drawing it into her bloodstream. As in a dream of his own that depicted a dream of hers, he thought of Joanna in this immovable attitude, given up to the cadences of the wireless as if it did not matter what was producing them, the politician or herself. She was a proclaiming statue in his mind. (*GSM*, 87)

The history through which she is living turns Joanna, in Nicholas's imagining of her, into a kind of receiving station for words which, as in Sartre's conception of language as action, aim to shape the future but which, for Joanna, are simply 'cadences', underlining that the particular vision of the future to which the radio is giving expression will never happen, but will remain merely a piece of rhetorical art. As though a prefiguration of Joanna's forthcoming death, her recitation is silenced by the political even as she seeks to hear the political as the music of language – music being the art which, according to Sartre, is least capable of political engagement. Joanna is the representative, at least until the moments before her death, of disengagement, both in the marital and the political senses, which is why her image is so important to Nicholas Farringdon as he moves towards his own religious commitment.

Even in the novel of Spark's in which the central character is most solitary, *The Driver's Seat*, Lise's life is, quite literally, trampled on by political conflicts in which she randomly becomes an unwilling participant. Her personal plot to find her killer is interrupted by a student demonstration that is halted by police firing rounds of tear gas; caught up in the confusion and separated from her companion, Mrs Fiedke, Lise becomes an accidental participant in the encounter between the rioters and the forces of law and order:

> Just before it reaches the end of the street which joins the circular intersection the crowd stops. A band of grey-clad policemen come running towards them, in formation, bearing tear-gas satchels and with their gasmasks at the ready. The traffic on the circular intersection has stopped. Lise swerves with her crowd into a garage where some mechanics in their overalls crouch behind the cars and others take refuge underneath a car which is raised on a cradle in the process of repair. (*DS*, 74)

Lise has no part in this confrontation, but it has become 'her crowd' and it will lead to her being harangued as one of the rebellious students by the garage owner when she emerges from the car in which she has taken refuge. A short time later, having escaped from the manager's attempt to have sex with her, she encounters another group of policemen:

> The police collect on either side of the hotel doorway, their faces picked out by the bright lights, while there emerge down the steps from the hotel two women who seem to be identical twins, wearing black dresses and high-styled black hair, followed by an important-looking Arabian figure, sheikh-like in his head dress and robes, with a lined face and glittering eyes, who descends the steps with a floating motion as if his feet are clearing the ground by an inch or two. (*DS*, 83)

The sheikh may seem to be floating but, as Lise learns from a bystander, he has just been deposed from his kingdom by a coup d'état and is headed into exile. Her personal mission seems to be continually deflected by political events over which she has no control. Attempting to take control again, she encounters in the hotel which the sheikh has just left one of the sheikh's friends who happens also to be one of the men who had sat close to her on the plane that morning, an accidental conjunction that she hopes indicates that she has found the 'necessary' person for whom she is in search: he, however, is only interested in bewailing the sheikh's political situation – 'Damn rotters in his country have taken over behind his back. Now he's lost his throne or whatever it is he sits on' (*DS*, 129–30) – and recounting their schooldays and a hunting trip they took together in 1938. The inconsequentiality of this meeting sends her off, however, to meet her inevitable end, as though the geopolitical can interfere with but cannot derail the determinedly personal.

Similarly, in *The Only Problem*, Harvey Gotham's retreat to work on Job is disrupted by a nearby robbery, apparently carried out by the Front de la Libération de l'Europe, a terrorist group which the police suspect his wife has joined, if she is not, indeed, its ringleader:

> 'It was a coincidence that you were in Epinal this morning visiting a museum while your estranged wife was also in Epinal engaged in an armed robbery?'
>
> 'If my wife was in Epinal, yes, that was a coincidence.' (*TOP*, 80)

The group's aim is the transformation of the whole international economic and political system:

> The gang was going to liberate Europe from its errors. 'Errors of society, errors of the system.' Most of all, liberation from the diabolical institution of the *gendarmerie* and the brutality of the *Brigade Criminelle*. It was much the same as every other terrorist announcement Harvey had ever read. 'The multinationals and the forces of the reactionary imperialist powers . . .' (*TOP*, 104)

If indeed Harvey's wife is one of the terrorists, then the political intervention is necessarily also a personal intervention, one that implicates Harvey in the politics of terrorism but also poses Harvey with the issue that he is studying in Job: should one accept patiently the world into which one is thrown or should one resist it? Is Harvey's lack of political commitment the consequence of his wealth, which means he has no need to commit to action on his own or on others' behalf, or is his adopting of Effie's daughter an act which implies a commitment to the value of the personal? In a situation where one's wife is a terrorist, how do you separate the personal from the political?

The intertwining of the political in the personal is also a feature of Margaret Murchie's experience in *Symposium*, when she is sent off to an Anglican nunnery after the murder of her grandmother, an arrival which, from the point of view of nunnery, seems to have been destined:

> 'You were *sent*. I can only say you were sent.'
> 'I feel sent,' said Margaret, 'It is a most extraordinary feeling.' (*S*, 103)

The supposedly ahistorical values of the nunnery, however, are in the process of being transformed by a commitment to Marxism – 'there is no power in Church or State that can stop the inexorable march of Marxism into the future' (*S*, 105) – which is celebrated in a mural depicting Lenin's arrival at in St Petersburg in 1917, a mural, which, to an outsider, confuses Christian traditions deriving from Michelangelo's Sistine Chapel with secular ones, Karl Marx appearing to play the role of God: 'The figure she referred to was up near the refectory's ceiling. Lenin was looking up at it with his raised arm, so that his finger touched the pointing finger of the bearded man' (*S*, 113). The artist-nun, like the 'liberation theologians' of Latin America in the 1970s and 1980s, have reframed their Judaeo-Christian inheritance in terms of the geopolitics of Marx's analysis of the worldwide exploitation of the poor by capitalism. The nuns' self-consciousness about what they see as their geopolitical situatedness is at the opposite end of the spectrum from the lives presented in *The Takeover*, in which the success of Hubert's cult of Diana, with its implied retreat from the modern world, is made possible by geopolitical crises to which Hubert pays no attention and which remain a mystery to Maggie and her wealthy friends:

> A little over a year had passed since the Middle East war of 1973, and Hubert was fairly flourishing on the ensuing crisis. He had founded a church. It cultivated the worship of Diana according to its final phases when Christianity began to overcast her image with Mary the Mother of God. It was the late Diana and the early Mary that Hubert now preached, and since the oil trauma had inaugurated the Dark Ages II he had acquired a following of a rich variety and ever more full of members. (*T*, 139)

The success of Hubert's personal system of belief is the reflex of geopolitical upheavals of which he has no understanding and over which he has no control.

Spark's novels are not *engagé* in Sartre's conception of existentialism, but her characters are always presented in terms of their 'thrownness' into specific social and historical environments. Thus *The Mandelbaum Gate* explores the conflicts and contradictions of Christian faith in the context of being 'thrown' into a variety of histories over which one has no control: its central character, Barbara Vaughan, is, like Spark, the offspring of a divided racial and cultural inheritance. Spark's father was Jewish, her mother English, a relationship reversed in the case of Barbara who is Jewish on her mother's side, part of an urban, intellectual family, while, on her father's side, she is the offshoot of a solid English and Anglican squirearchy. To both families of this doubled and divided inheritance, Barbara is not quite fully a 'person', because she cannot be integrated into the 'being-with-others' – the communal 'we' – that represents each family's sense of its own identity. Her Anglican grandmother tries to get her to give up going back to her Jewish family for the Feast of the Passover, as though it is something of no significance, but once the ritual is completed in the Aaronson family, Barbara is excluded from the cleaning up because, as her cousin Michael points out, 'you're not kosher', ironically mimicking his own relatives to declare, 'She is neither Yeed nor Goy ees mein cousin Barbara.' He put his arm around her shoulder. 'She ees a bit milk and meat in the same dish, vot you expect?' (*MG*, 36). The accusation of her being neither one thing nor another is one that she will in turn cast at the British Embassy official Freddy Hamilton whom she meets in her hotel in Jerusalem when she goes on a pilgrimage to the Holy Land:

> 'Do you know,' said this passionate spinster, in a cold and terrifying voice, 'a passage in the book of the Apocalypse that applies to your point of view?'
>
> 'I'm afraid the Apocalypse is beyond me,' Freddy said . . .
>
> 'It goes like this,' she said, enunciating her words slowly, almost like a chant:
>
> I know of thy doings, and find thee neither hot nor cold; cold or hot; I would thou wert one or the other. Being what thou art, lukewarm, neither cold nor hot, thou wilt make me vomit thee out of my mouth. (*MG*, 16)

The topic of their conversation had been Barbara's engagement to an archaeologist working on the Dead Sea Scrolls, whom she cannot marry because he is divorced; he, on her behalf rather than his own, is seeking an annulment by the Catholic Church of his previous marriage so that she can remain within the Church if she marries him. To Freddy, her insistence that 'she would never see the man again' (*MG*, 20), if his suit fails, 'seems a bit extreme' (*MG*, 20), which is what provokes her quotation from Scripture. Engagement cannot turn into marriage if it violates her Catholic commitment.

Three varieties of 'engagement' come into play in Barbara's situation. First, she is an 'engaged' Catholic – not just one who takes her faith for granted as the backdrop of her life, but one who sees her Catholicism as the very basis of her personhood, precisely because it displaces the annulment of that personhood in her divided family background. By being a believing and rigorous Catholic she has overcome two half-empty identities in order, as she thinks, to become a whole person. Her pilgrimage is proof in action of this belief. The contradictions of her engagement, however, again repeats how Kierkegaard presents his own religious belief as a matter of having been 'engaged', indeed 'pre-engaged', 'to a Love which infinitely surpasses my understanding' and which therefore pre-empts his engagement to a merely human marriage.[21] This religious sense of engagement leads Barbara to threaten to do what Kierkegaard had done when he renounced his fiancée for his religious beliefs: according to the Seducer in 'The Seducer's Diary', 'an engagement, however, does not have ethical reality in the stricter sense, as marriage does' (*E/O*, I, 305), and, in the *Journals*, Kierkegaard describes the impossibility of his marriage to Regine Olsen as the consequence of 'a divine protest, that is how I understood it' (*J*, '367', 93); nonetheless, he left whatever possessions he had at his death to Regine (by then Mrs Scheler) with the statement that, 'What I wish to give expression to is that to me an engagement was and is just as binding as a marriage, and that therefore my estate is her due, exactly as if I had been married to her.'[22] For Barbara, there is a similar conflict between her religion and her engagement and the problem of 'engagement' spills over from the personal – her relationship with Harry Clegg – to the doctrinal – will the Church allow its consummation? – and then to the wider issue of her own relationship to her part-Jewish background and of the relationship of Judaism to Christianity. The 'personal' cannot escape both the burden of the past and the past's reappearance in the present: her Jewish guides want to tell her about the virtues of modern Israel rather than about the holy sites she wishes to visit, and in this discontinuity 'Barbara had felt displaced, she felt her personal identity beginning to escape like smoke from among her bones' (*MG*, 27). Thirdly, however, there is her implicit engagement to her friend Miss Rickward, the headmistress of the school in which she works, and with whom she has drifted into the expectation of a shared life. The crisis of their relationship in the novel is Ricky's discovery that Barbara is in the Holy Land not simply because her Catholic faith has taken her on a pilgrimage, but because she is planning to meet the man to whom she has become engaged. An engagement, as Kierkegaard knew all too well, is a public event, withdrawal from which is a public scandal, but Barbara's engagement is a secret. Barbara has not told Ricky about it despite the fact that they seem, in effect, to have set up home together: 'I haven't written because I was afraid, and that's the truth. It's as if I were married to Ricky, only worse' (*MG*, 158). She has made an implicit engagement to Ricky for their shared future, but Barbara discovers only when her engagement to a man is revealed that, in terms of the possessiveness of their relationship, she might as well have been married rather than simply 'engaged' to Ricky: the freedom implied by 'existence precedes essence' (*MG*, 162) which Ricky expounds so forcefully has been withdrawn and the narrative of Barbara's future life is to be dictated by Ricky, who arrives in Jordan in pursuit of her with evidence of Harry Clegg's illegitimate birth and therefore of his inappropriateness as a husband. Her knowledge of existentialism does not prevent her trying to annul other people's freedom. In this context, Barbara's engagement is, ironically, a disengagement, not only in terms of distancing herself from Ricky but in terms of having made or articulated no clear choice about her future: she lingers in a hotel in Jerusalem not knowing whether she can marry the man to whom she is engaged if his previous marriage is upheld by the Catholic Church or whether she will be able to continue her pilgrimage into Jordan, where her Jewishness, even if she has a British passport, might make her suspect. The strange non-reality of her engagement is noted by Freddy, who 'had not felt that the ring referred to an engagement to marry anyone: such things were not unaccountable in an English spinster: it was probably someone killed in the war' (*MG*, 17). Barbara's violent response to Freddy is, in effect, the demand for a level of commitment – a commitment beyond the 'lukewarm' – which has proved beyond her own capacity for decision-making. She has drifted into her relationship with Ricky and is unable to break free of it; she has gone on a pilgrimage to the Holy Land but she has not committed to visiting her fiancé Harry Clegg in Jordan, for which the pilgrimage was partly a cover: because of her religious beliefs, she is a person who has found it impossible to commit to being engaged.

It is symptomatic of Barbara's drifting uncommitted existence that she attends the trial in Jerusalem of Adolf Eichmann for his part in the Holocaust but has no recollection of why she decided to go: 'for no reason at all, for some reason she could not remember' (*MG*, 176) – perhaps only because her cousin Michael has some role as a lawyer in the case – she attends the trial:

> Minute by minute throughout the hours the prisoner discoursed on the massacre without mentioning the word, covering all aspects of every question addressed to him with the meticulous undiscriminating reflex of a computing machine. Barbara turned the switch of her earphones to other simultaneous translations – French, Italian, then back to English. What was he talking about? The effect was the same in any language, and the terrible paradox remained, and the actual discourse was a dead mechanical tick, while its subject, the massacre, was living. She thought, it all feels like a familiar dream, and presently located the sensation as one that the anti-novelists induce. Or it is like, she thought, one of the new irrational films which people can't understand the point of, but continue to see; one can neither cope with them nor leave them alone. At school she usually took the novels and plays of the new French writers with the sixth form. She thought, repetition, boredom, despair, going nowhere for nothing, all of which conditions are enclosed in a tight, unremarkable statement of the times at hand. She had changed her mind, without awareness, at that moment, of any disruption in the logic of personal decisions, but merely allowing herself to recognize, in passing, that she would inevitably complete her pilgrimage to the Holy Land in Jordan. (*MG*, 177–8)

Eichmann's testimony switches, in Barbara's consciousness, from being an event in the world to being a version of the new art forms – the anti-novel, the films of the Nouvelle Vague – which are themselves designed to disrupt traditional expectations of the relationship between art and life. The 'inevitability' of the work of art, even one that tries to resist traditional notions of artistic form, crosses over into her sense of the narrative of her own journey to the holy sites – previously undecided, she now foresees that she will indeed enter Jordan and 'complete her pilgrimage'. The historical event to which she is witness and the vast destructive forces of the modern state which it invokes determine her commitment to a personal pilgrimage that is undertaken in defiance of the borders previous history has constructed in order to separate nations, races and religions.

Barbara will cross over into Jordan, risking arrest, but, as she does so, she is also crossing over from the time of history – both the immediate history of Israel and the history of the Second World War and the attempted genocide to which the Eichmann trial attests – into the places where history intersected with the eternal: 'There seemed no mental difficulty about these miracles, here on the spot. They seemed to be very historic and factual' (*MG*, 48); standing in the place where the transfiguration of Christ was supposed to have taken place, Barbara's only doubt is about the actual location, not about the event: 'Wherever it did take place, she thought, I believe it did take place all right. Transfigured, and in a radiant time of metamorphosis, was seen white and dazzling, to converse with Moses and Elias' (*MG*, 48).[23] Her entry into this different order of time is achieved by her apparent shedding of her historical identities: she travels disguised as the servant of her guide, Suzi Ramdez, and thus hidden from the world; is disengaged from Ricky (who has come to Jordan in pursuit of her); disengaged from Harry (who is in Rome pursuing the annulment of his marriage); disengaged from Freddy (who, after she contracts scarlet fever, leaves her hidden in the house of the Ramdez family); there, having been 'confined by the fever [. . .] Barbara Vaughan had taken one of her religious turns and was truly given to the love of God' (*MG*, 163), as if her identity has reached to its religious core. Having thus divested herself of the various relations which constituted her past identities, and the various histories which they embody, she is immediately confronted by Ruth Gardnor whom Suzi has arranged to look after Barbara while she and Freddy return to Jerusalem, not realising that Ruth and Barbara know each other and not yet having been informed that Freddy has just discovered Ruth's role in a spy-ring working on behalf of the Egyptians against the Israelis and the British. Apparently redeemed from the historical and in touch with the eternal, Barbara discovers herself to be at the centre of the political conflicts of the Middle East, in the company of a woman whose justification for betraying her country is her belief in a worldwide Jewish conspiracy: 'The Jews. They've got us in a net. If you knew how the banking system worked, you'd realize . . .' (*MG*, 294). Barbara's person is both a matter of international concern – the Jordanians and the Israelis are trying to track down her whereabouts – and she is attributed, by Ruth Gardnor, with the role of an important co-conspirator in her spying activities: what Barbara had thought was a casual personal acquaintanceship with Ruth has turned into part of an international political conflict, a conflict which is played out when Barbara attacks Ruth – defending her Jewishness against the other's anti-Semitism – but afterwards adopts the identity that Ruth has imposed on her:

> Then Ruth said, 'Have you been told to do this to me?' Barbara said nothing. Ruth said, 'Oh God! Don't they trust me? What have I done? Rupert will have to come over – I can't wait on and on.'
>
> Barbara said, 'Yes, you'll let them down alright.' She said this out of the dark, but meant it decidedly for a thrust, which it turned out to be. (*MG*, 294)

Come to seek the eternal, she finds herself not only caught up the conflicts of contemporary history but to be an actor – in both senses of the word – in the history that is being played out in those conflicts.

Completing her pilgrimage and then escaping from Jordan back to her life as Barbara Vaughan, engaged to be married to Harry Clegg, requires the joint efforts of Suzi and Abdul Ramdez, Suzi to organise the rest of the pilgrimage and Abdul to negotiate her re-entry into Jordan, once again disguised but this time as a Christian nun. Like Barbara, Abdul and Suzi are of mixed race, being of Arab stock but with blue eyes inherited from some Norman ancestor (*MG*, 94), and also of mixed or uncertain nationality, since their father, Joe Ramdez, a schoolteacher who had provided lessons in Arabic to British officials, had moved from Transjordan to Palestine when Jordan was granted autonomy in 1928 in order to be able to continue his business with the British. His children, therefore, grew up as Arabs in what has become Israel but in a prosperous environment based on their father's travel business in Jordan, a business based on legal and illegal border crossings in times when 'business connexions between Israel and Jordan were illegal in both countries' (*MG*, 63). This mixed inheritance releases them from commitment to any particular past or any particular modern polity as well as from traditional moral constrictions: at the age of nineteen Abdul is discovered to have tuberculosis and,

> It was at this time that the secret affinity ripened between Abdul and Suzi. Suzi was then fifteen, Abdul nineteen. He talked of new ways of life and outlook, undreamt of even by their modernized parents. His imagination went wild in most particulars, but Abdul conveyed to her, as only tubercular patients can, the excitement of what was in his mind. He said that the modernization of Joe Ramdez was simply a new form of the old exploiting mentality. In this way Suzi discovered the future as an idea, and together the brother and sister merged in a pact of personal anarchism: they started to fool everyone; they conformed to outward demands and resisted in spirit. (*MG*, 97)

They are 'merrily uncommitted at heart' (*MG*, 96); they represent the absolute antithesis of the values which Freddy represents in doing his best for 'the country' – which is, to him, 'Ours' (*MG*, 262) – and yet that lack of commitment will prove enticing to Freddy – who makes love to Suzi in part as an expression for his affection for Abdul – and also to Barbara, who finds her time with Suzi 'unforgettable': 'The whole week was unforgettable and Suzi most of all' (*MG*, 280). The holiness of the Holy Land is to be found not in the shrines – Barbara finds them of little interest – but in the personal relations which people establish in defiance of the political environment into which they have been cast. Abdul and Suzi represent a different kind of future which neither Freddy nor Barbara would have believed they could be engaged by, a future which has cut its ties with the past:

> 'It was a long time ago, my friend. Even yesterday was before our time, it's dead too.'
>
> 'The past has got nothing to do with you my friend, and nothing to do with me. It's all dead history.' (*MG*, 111)

Abdul and Suzi are the representatives of a world which wishes to deny the weight of facticity, while Barbara is engaged to an archaeologist whose job – like her pilgrimage – is to uncover the reality of the past. Abdul and Suzi are part of a general movement of people who 'belonged to nothing':

> At Acre the people he had known were gone, but as happens, the place itself, by some invisible influence or tradition, had drawn the same sort of people, the young or the young at heart who belonged to nothing but themselves, for whose temperament no scope existed in any society open to them, and who by day enacted the requirements of their society. These were lapsed Jews, lapsed Arabs, lapsed citizens, runaway Englishmen, dancing prostitutes, international messes, failed painters, intellectuals, homosexuals. (*MG*, 101)

Among such people, the personal survives by its evasion of the geopolitical but it does so only by escaping into drugs or sex or mere playfulness, and into a conception of the 'person' which has been narrowed to the indulgence in immediacy – to Kierkegaard's 'aesthetic'. To those burdened with the past the immediate is profoundly attractive, even if they cannot survive in its impermanency: when Freddy loses his memory after he returns from Joe Ramdez's house where he has spent the night with Suzi, it is because such immediacy leaves no trace: 'She wondered, later, how it was that Freddy had forgotten Suzi Ramdez. And, of course, the question answered itself: she was too memorable to remember' (*MG*, 280). This world of sensual immediacy is a secular equivalent of the eternal which Barbara seeks – both defy and negate time and history, but from entirely opposite directions, one by considering all time as irrelevant to the eternal which is always of the here and now; the other by living entirely in a here and now disconnected from the weight of the past. We are told at the end of the novel that Barbara and Suzi, with their respective husbands, saw each other 'many times in Athens and London' (*MG*, 303): the personal survives but survives only in defiance of a world in which the personal is no longer the basis of a shared communal world. Barbara is married to a non-believer, Suzi to someone from another culture: they have each, in their different ways, escaped from the constrictions of the history into which they were born but the escape is purely personal – the personal is not a model for how the world can be transformed or transfigured but a place of retreat from a world riven by the geopolitics of the past. The Dead Sea

Scrolls that Harry Clegg and his fellow archaeologists are investigating may preserve the original insights which led to the establishment of Christianity as a worldwide religion, but their preservation is also a symbol of the extinction of religious belief in a world which knows too much about the history of belief to be able any longer to believe – all of the characters in *The Mandelbaum Gate* have to survive in the Dead Sea of modernity, a time and a place 'bearing no breath of life' (*MG*, 220).

The Mandelbaum Gate is a novel built on a series of dialectical oppositions: not only the inner dialectic of Barbara's Jewish-Anglican heritage but between the eternal (the claim of Barbara's religious beliefs) and the shape of modern history (the conflicts created by the establishment of the Israeli state); between religious belief (Barbara's Catholicism and Ricky's eventual adoption of Islam) and secularisation (Abdul and Suzy's 'merry anarchy'); between duty to the state (Freddy's commitment to his role as a servant 'our country') and the legal consequences of working for a criminal state (the Eichmann trial); between tending the world that you have come, however temporarily, to inhabit (like Freddy's friend Joanna's tending of flowers) and the imposition of alien values in a colonised environment (those flowers are actually English flowers transplanted into Jordan). Such dialectical structures, as we have seen, were typical of Kierkegaard's pseudonymous works but the aim of those works was to reverse the loss of 'inwardness' in the modern world: as Johannes Climacus emphasises in his account of the works of the other pseudonymous authors – in a section of *Concluding Unscientific Postscript* entitled 'A Glance at a Contemporary Effort in Danish Literature', which is actually a glance at Kierkegaard's writings – 'the age has forgotten what it means to exist and what inwardness is. It no longer believes that inwardness enriches the apparently poor contents, whereas change in the external is only the diversion that world-weariness and life-emptiness clutch at' (*CUP*, 287). In *The Mandelbaum Gate*, the 'inwardness' of Barbara Vaughan's religious experience is balanced against the immediacy of Suzi and Abdul's commitment to living in the present, in the aesthetic, that balance being played out in Barbara's aesthetic immersion in the pilgrimage organised by the 'memorable' Suzi: the inwardness of religious experience is fulfilled in a world of action and sensory excitement. But Kierkegaard feared that in such interactions the very possibility of the ethical and the religious might be about to be erased from the world:

> Prior to the outbreak of cholera there usually appears a kind of fly not otherwise seen; in like manner might not these fabulous pure thinkers [that is, Hegelians] be a sign that a calamity is in store for humankind – for example, the loss of the ethical and the religious? (*CUP*, 307)

A world to which 'inwardness' has been lost is the world that Spark presents in *Territorial Rights*, a novel in which Lina Pance has been seduced into defecting from communist Bulgaria by a relative's tales of bohemian life in London. Trying to establish herself as an artist in Paris, however, she discovers that life in the capitalist West is not necessarily better than life in the communist East. Disenchantedly, she goes in search of the grave of the father she never knew but whom she believes died in Venice in the last days of the Second World War. This personal pilgrimage to a city famous in European literature as a place of wealth and decay will entangle her in two different narratives, one suburban and domestic – the flight from a stale marriage of Arnold Leaver, a retired headmaster, who travels to Venice on holiday with a former teacher in his school, Mrs Tiller, the winner of a small fortune on the football pools – and one cosmopolitan and flamboyant, the search by multimillionaire art dealer Mark Curran (known only as 'Curran', as though to strike out his Christian name) for Leaver's son Robert, with whom he has had a lengthy affair in Paris. Robert, in turn, is in search of Lina, whom he had first encountered in Paris. Each of these visitors to a city famed for its aesthetic value believes themselves to have been released from their past but ends up under surveillance by people or organisations from their past – on his arrival, Leaver is spied by his son, who queries his relationship with Mrs Tiller, and is later trailed by his former mistress, Grace Gregory, who has flown to Venice to provide Leaver's wife, Anthea, with an account of what is going on; Curran warns Robert that Lina is being followed by people he assumes are communist agents, but Curran himself is accused by Mrs Tiller of being a private detective employed to follow them, though he will, in fact, be followed by a private detective agency hired by Anthea to find out about the doings of her husband but an agency which judges, correctly, that Curran is a more valuable target for their real business, which is blackmail. The people who are apparently following Lina are, however, actually following Robert, with the aim of conscripting him to help blackmail Curran. Each of the characters is being trailed by a past from which they had thought to have set themselves free, free aesthetically to enjoy a present in which there is no requirement to search for 'inwardness' or, indeed, to make any commitment to personal relations other than as a source of present pleasure: deserted by Robert, Lina immediately takes up with Grace's travelling companion, Leo, a former student in Leaver's school, while Robert spends his days in the company of Anna, with whom he 'made love whenever they wanted to' (*TR*, 221). Their illusory freedoms are, however, trapped within the dynamics of their past personal and political commitments: Robert is pursued by Curran to whom he had said what he thought was a final 'goodbye'; the ironically named Grace points out that she kept Leaver's sexual urges under control while she was matron of his school – 'Anthea knows nothing about us'; 'When you had Anthea to go home to at nights you used to make the most of your days' (*TR*, 118, 119) – while Lina is so appalled to discover that Leo is part-Jewish, and therefore the carrier of a past that she cannot tolerate, that she leaps into a canal to cleanse herself; later, she is pursued by the cousin who first inspired her desire to escape to the West, and who eventually returns her to Bulgaria as a 'repentant dissident' (*TR*, 238).

The relation of present to past in *Territorial Rights* is symbolised by two buildings which are within sight of one another in Venice. The first is the 'bulbous and comely church' (*TR*, 8) of Santa Maria Formosa, a church visited by various of the characters but none of them for the purposes of religious devotion: to Robert Leaver it is an art object to which he might dedicate his thesis (*TR*, 23) but where he meets with the people who have been following him (*TR*, 129); to Lina it is the central feature of the dilapidated district in which she rents a room (*TR*, 10) but later the place where she will come 'every evening to look for Robert' (*TR*, 229); to Curran it is a place of exchange where he can leave the money for his blackmailers (*TR*, 228). From the church of Santa Maria Formosa 'you could, of course, see a short way down the side-path leading from the far end of the square to the street-gate and old-fashioned front garden of the

Pensione Sofia' (*TR*, 9), the pensione being a place where Curran had lodged during the war while it was still the Villa Sofia and before it became a hotel run by the sisters Eufemia and Katerina, who had inherited their property from an 'old count, who had no relatives at his death; it was supposed that they were his illegitimate daughters' (*TR*, 69). In the garden of the pensione is buried the body of Victor Pancev, a Bulgarian refugee in the Second World War with whom the sisters were both in love. After his death in the final days of the war, each claimed the body as her own, a dispute which was resolved by getting a fascist butcher to cut the body in two and having each half buried separately in adjacent sections of the garden which each sister thereafter regards as her own. In the case of the sisters, their business in running the hotel is also a memorial to their lost love: in the garden, time has been suspended, the personal become a permanent absence over which both continue to exert their territorial rights. The two buildings – the church and the hotel – are symbolic of a society to which religion has become redundant and in which Europe, like Pancev's body, is split between a capitalist West and a communist East, both equally committed to a materialism by which the world of the past is assumed to be redundant in the present and in which the only 'spirit' is the 'spirit stove' (*TR*, 111) which is Lina's most prized possession because she smuggles it into her impoverished lodgings in order to save money by doing her own cooking. Spirit as a Kierkegaardian 'inwardness' has entirely disappeared from the aesthetic world of modern Venice.

The action of *Territorial Rights* is focused on the extent to which the present can be divorced from the past. The sisters who guard Pancev's body preserve the past but only by ensuring that their relationship to him is not publicly known. The apprentice to the butcher who carved the body believes that it was Curran who murdered Pancev, and has tracked Robert down as the medium by which the story can be turned into effective blackmail, not only by implicating Curran and his friend Violet de Winter in the killing of Pancev and the secreting of the body, but in their involvement as Nazi agents in the war; equally, in letters delivered to his father's mistresses, Robert accuses one of them of poisoning previous husbands (Mrs Tiller, *TR*, 131) and the other of having been a 'vicar's concubine' during the war (Grace Gregory, *TR*, 152). Robert's fictional reconstruction of their various pasts proves dangerous because they are all people who have suppressed their pasts in order to conform to the world they now inhabit: 'there remained undoubted pieces of truth buried in the mixture, like the bones of Pancev under the garden-beds of the Pensione Sofia' (*TR*, 153). The material world of post-war modernity may have erased Christian inwardness but it cannot erase the past because, however limited the characters' sense of their own personal identity, the continuity of the self, as in the case of Adolf Eichmann, cannot be denied. Former apprentice butcher Giorgio declares of Curran and de Winter that, 'There are things those people won't even admit to themselves after thirty-five years of putting it behind them. They think they've become different persons' (*TR*, 221), a view which Violet de Winter wants to take of her own past:

> 'We were different people,' Violet said. 'Everything was different. Everyone else was different.'
>
> 'We're the same people,' Curran said. 'Any other point of view is foolish. We wouldn't be vulnerable if we were not the same people.' (*TR*, 223)

The aesthetic person, attempting to live entirely in the present, cannot annul the past or escape their geopolitical environment, whether it is the immediate geopolitics of capitalism versus communism, or the geopolitics of what seems like a totally different era, when the choice was between fascism and democracy. Equally, blackmail will be, for Robert Leaver, an initiation into crime which will lead on to violent bank and jewellery robberies (*T*, 233), violence which will in turn lead to training as a terrorist in the Middle East (*TR*, 238). The political evils of the past which make Curran a possible victim of Robert's blackmail will be repeated in Robert's own engagement with the geopolitics of his contemporary world.

There is, for Spark, no escape from the 'situatedness' of the lives into which we have been thrown, or from the consequences of choices made in an earlier time when the ultimate meanings and consequences of those choices were as yet unknown. If her characters are, on one level, the ontological puppets of an author who has scripted their lives, they are, on another level, the representation of people whose lives are lived as part of a larger narrative over which they have no control: they are actors in a history over whose direction and meaning they have very little say. This is the fundamental irony of

The Abbess of Crewe and its relationship to the Watergate scandal of the 1970s: Alexandra's effort to achieve an author-like omniscience over her abbey by the use of audio and video surveillance (just as Richard Nixon did in the White House) does not prevent it being invaded by the forces of change from a world beyond the boundaries of the abbey over which she has no control, whether in the dictates of the Catholic Church – 'the Lady Abbess ignores the latest reforms, rules her house as if the Vatican Council had never been' (*AC*, 10) – or the spirit of sexual licence that has emboldened her opponent in the election to Abbess, the symbolically named 'Felicity', proponent of the ethics of happiness and free love. For Alexandra, to be Abbess of Crewe may be her 'destiny' (*AC*, 32) but it is a destiny that must be managed and be made to happen, a plot that has to be shaped towards a successful end: life must become art – 'I am become an object of art' (*AC*, 105), the Abbess declares – and history must be transfused with the spirit of mythology: 'We are leaving the sphere of history and about to enter that of mythology. Mythology is nothing more than history garbled; likewise history is mythology garbled and it is nothing more in all the history of man' (*AC*, 87). Spark declares in her essay on Job that, 'Over the years I have begun to think more and more in terms of fiction, of myth' (*GF*, 191), and as in so many of the novels in which she transfers the guilt of authorial control from herself to one of her characters – Caroline Rose, in *The Comforters*, Jean Brodie in *The Prime of Miss Jean Brodie*, Fleur Talbot in *Loitering with Intent* – so in *The Abbess of Crewe* she transfers fiction's complicity with the confusions of myth and history from the author to her character, for Alexandra uses her author-like omniscience to shift the issues by which she is faced from the territory of doctrine to the territory of myth – enacting what Spark, in her essay 'An Unknown Author', quotes as Professor Scheindlin's explanation of the resolution of the narrative of Job: 'Since the narrative presents Job's complaint as rational and correct, there is no room left for a rational solution. Rather, poetry is used to shift the ground from reason, where life must lose, to emotion, where it at least has a chance' (*GF*, 198–9). This, Spark declares, 'is a poetic joy' (*GF*, 199), but if the principles of poetry are introduced into life, then life must be judged not in terms of veracity or morality but in terms of what 'need not be plausible, only hypnotic, like all good art' (*AC*, 89). Released from its self-contained environment, art, rather than doctrine or justice, becomes Alexandra's justification. To achieve this, however, she must operate in league with her supporters, Walburga and Mildred as well as the obtuse Winifrede, while, at the same time insisting that she knows nothing of what they are plotting: 'I can take no personal part in whatever you have in mind' (*AC*, 46). 'Being-with-others' is both necessary and to be discounted, a contradiction evidenced in the actions of Sister Gertrude, who is theoretically part of the order of nuns in the abbey but is only ever available by phone from some part of the world where she is sorting out conflicts between hostile religious communities – but where she never stays long enough to become responsible for the consequences of her actions. Gertrude, like the Abbess herself, is *engagée* but at the same time disengaged; the Abbess has all the information provided by her recordings but initially denies that she has knowledge of them – 'it seems it is they who have bugged the Abbey' (*AC*, 92) – and then, when she makes them available, suggests that any editing that has occurred is because 'the devil who goes about as a raging lion hath devoured them' (*AC*, 104); similarly, Gertrude ensures she is available only at a distance, at the end of a phone line which is often disengaged – 'Gertrude has hung up' (*AC*, 44) – when her advice is sought. For both of them, 'being-with-others' is a camouflage for a profound solipsism that has much in common with Sartre's account of the necessary conflict of the self with the other in his discussion, in *Being and Nothingness*, of 'être-pour-autrui'.

Spark's continuing interaction with Sartre, both in terms of his philosophy of the person and in terms of his conception of literature, is clear from her 'Address to the American Academy and Institute of Arts and Letters, New York', entitled 'The Desegregation of Art'. In terms which might well have been derived from *Qu'est-ce que la littérature?*, she argues that

> Literature, of all the arts, is the most penetrable into the human life of the world, for the simple reason that words are our common currency. We don't instinctively, from morning to night, paint pictures to each other, or play music to each other, in order to communicate; we talk, we write to each other. (*GF*, 26–7)

Not only are words different from the other artistic media but their specific power has been, throughout the twentieth century, that they directed the attention of readers to the victims of social and political injustice:

> We have in this century a marvellous tradition of socially conscious art. And especially now in the arts of drama and the novel we see and hear everywhere the representation of the victim against the oppressor, we have a literature and an artistic culture, one might almost say a civilisation, of depicted suffering, whether in social life or in family life. We have representations of the victim-oppressor complex, for instance, in the dramatic portrayal of the gross racial injustices of our world, or in the exposure of the tyrannies of family life on the individual. (*GF*, 28)

This is precisely the kind of literature that Sartre's *littérature engagée* sought to encourage but, instead of producing a commitment to freedom, its effect, Spark suggests, has been to encourage somnolence:

> but I suspect that a great number of the audience or of the readers feel that their moral responsibilities are sufficiently fulfilled by the emotions they have been induced to feel. A man may go to bed feeling less guilty after seeing such a play. He has undergone the experience of pity for the underdog. Salt tears have gone bowling down his cheeks. He has had a good dinner. He is absolved, he sleeps well. (*GF*, 28)

Littérature engagée is not a demand for commitment on the part of its audience but a substitute for commitment – the emotion of the aesthetic experience is sufficient to make the reader feel that s/he has sided with the victim and that nothing more is required. For Spark this kind of literature has become redundant and must be replaced with a literature that has more grip on reality, a literature that has more capacity to do what Sartre wanted literature to do – to effect change:

> I only say that the art and literature of sentiment and emotion, however beautiful in itself, however stirring in its depiction of actuality, has to go. It cheats us into a sense of involvement with life and society, but in reality it is a segregated activity. In its place I advocate the arts of satire and of ridicule. And I see no other living art form for the future. Ridicule is the only honourable weapon we have left. (*GF*, 28–9)

The literature of 'sentiment and emotion' is exhausted:

> The art of protest, the art which condemns violence and suffering by pathetic depiction is becoming a cult separated from the actions of our life. Our noble aspirations, our sympathies, our elevated feelings should not be inspired merely by visits to an art gallery, a theatre, or by reading a book, but rather the rhetoric of our times should persuade us to contemplate the ridiculous nature of the reality before us, and teach us to mock it. (*GF*, 30)

Spark adopts as the epigraph to *The Abbess of Crewe* W. B. Yeats's stern admonition to himself about what is possible for an artist in the modern world: 'Come let us mock at the great', but

> Mock mockers after
> That would not lift a hand maybe
> To help good, wise or great
> To bar that foul storm out, for we
> Traffic in mockery.[24]

The art of ridicule is an art which must also be applied to itself, which must acknowledge that it too is implicated in the world it ridicules. *The Abbess of Crewe* both celebrates and mocks the pretensions of the Alexandra who thinks she can defy the environment into which she has entered only to discover how powerful are the forces, both public and institutional, ranged against her. She is, like the world of which she is a part, both heroic and absurd, because she defies the 'normality' by which the world would judge her and in so doing reveals the world as ridiculous. As Kierkegaard puts it,

> The world has therefore substituted, as the thing most of all feared: ridicule, to be made the laughing-stock, which is, quite rightly, an aesthetic judgment. And so no one is afraid of having a false opinion – so long as they are in the majority; but they are afraid of an opinion, though it be the truth itself – if they are to hold it alone. (*J*, '1081', 385)

'Being with' is here not a recognition of interdependence but an escape route from personal responsibility. Ridicule, on the other hand, is the means of refusing 'being with' when we need to expose 'the ridiculous nature of the reality before us and teach us to mock it' (*GF*, 30). Ridicule wipes away the sentimental 'illusion that we are all essentially aspiring, affectionate and loving creatures' (*GF*, 30) and, in the case of the Abbess of Crewe, the sentimental illusion that religion is a safe-haven from the world; the Abbey of Crewe is a place of power, domination and wealth – the last bastion of aristocratic superiority over the commonplace bourgeoisie (*AC*, 74–5) – and as Alexandra departs to defend herself at Rome she has ensured that some of the wealth of the abbey has been transferred for her future use: the jewel-encrusted statue of the Infant of Prague, she tells Gertrude, 'is already in the bank' (*AC*, 106), a statement which Gertrude carefully does not hear (*AC*, 106). The Abbey, supposedly a place of retreat from the world, is utterly infiltrated by the forces from which it is in retreat, becoming a microcosm which allows us to 'contemplate the ridiculous nature of the reality before us, and teach us to mock it' (*GF*, 30).

Ridicule is also the pivot of the plot in *A Far Cry from Kensington*, in which Nancy Hawkins, a literary editor, insists on describing aspiring author Hector Bartlett as a *pisseur de copie*, a comment which is then echoed in the circles in which Hector is trying to establish himself as a serious writer. Nancy's characterisation comes to the attention of the novelist Emma Loy, whose relationship with Hector is partly based on his being a proponent of the literary value of her works: Emma twice gets Mrs Hawkins fired from her editorial jobs for her refusal to withdraw her judgement but nonetheless tries to get Nancy to take responsibility for Hector when she, Emma, is about to leave for the United States where her 'books are doing rather well' (*FCK*, 135). That Nancy's *bon mot* is French is no accident, since this is a novel shaped at every level by international interconnections: the landlady of the house in which Nancy rents a room is Irish; one of her fellow tenants is Wanda Podolak, a Polish refugee; her neighbour is a Cypriot (*FCK*, 11), and one of her fellow-workers at the Ullswater press 'had been in a German concentration camp in the 'thirties, and had got away' (*FCK*, 15). Eventually, through the help of Abigail, who had worked alongside her in the firm of Ullswater and York, Nancy gets an editorial job with a new magazine called *The Highgate Review*, which has been established by Americans who were 'refugees from Senator McCarthy's political persecutions' (*FCK*, 149), their left-wing threat compounded by the fact that they are homosexuals. The contents of the *Review*, as Nancy recalls them, reveal the international geopolitical dynamics of the period:

> The hydrogen bomb and the World Scientists' Appeal for peace, the question of atomic stations and the suspension of nuclear test explosions, a report on an Afro-Asian conference, universal copyright law, the need for smokeless zones in major cities, Germany's joining NATO, the reopening of the Vienna State Opera house, the case of Anglo-Catholicism as against Roman Catholicism, extra-sensory perception. (*FCK*, 173)

Nancy's personal life is situated in a geopolitical context of competing forces over which she has no control: she is herself a kind of refugee, being a war widow whose husband died at the attack on Arnhem only a few weeks after their marriage; she is burdened by the mystery of the death of Wanda Podolak, the impoverished Polish dressmaker who is a tenant in her house; she is the beneficiary of the arrival of the wealthy American refugees for whom she works. Her antagonist, Hector Bartlett, is equally the product of these international interactions: he has become involved in radionics – which 'had started in the United States in the early part of the twentieth century' and which claimed 'to diagnose and cure at any distance disorders and ailments in people animals and vegetables' (*FCK*, 152) – in order to ingratiate himself with publisher Ian Tooley, who believes that radionics is a practical version of spiritualism; Hector also masquerades as a Polish seminarian cousin of Wanda Podolak whom he has trained as a radionics operator; and he fawns on Emma Loy who, when she is trying to get his work published, declares that he 'may be described as the poor man's Kierkegaard' (*FCK*, 181). Bartlett is a medium for many different and often contradictory international flows of information: the comparison to Kierkegaard reveals only how far he is from the demanding Christian existentialism which the Dane sought to define.

The structure of *A Far Cry from Kensington* sets Nancy Hawkins and Hector Bartlett as opposing versions of 'being with'. In Nancy's case, her large bulk is symbolic of her willingness to accept 'being with' many others:

> There was something about me, Mrs Hawkins, that invited confidences. I was abundantly aware of it and indeed abundance was the expression I gave. I was massive in size, huge-bosomed, with wide

> hips, hefty long legs, a bulging belly and fat backside. I carried an ample weight with my five-foot-six of height, and was healthy with it. It was, of course, partly this physical factor that disposed people to confide in me. I looked comfortable. (*FCK*, 11)

The novel progresses through the changing environments in which Nancy lives and works, in each of which she establishes close relationships with those around her: she engages herself in the life of her fellow tenant Wanda Podolak sufficiently to become acquainted with the Polish community in London whom she meets at Catholic services, after which 'conversation consisted in exchanges of émigré survival-lore and items of information about practical aspects of the country they had come to settle in. Like other groups of war refugees, they brought their courage with them' (*FCK*, 27); she takes her landlady, Milly, off for a holiday in Paris; she arranges jobs for fellow workers made unemployed by the failure of the publishing company from which she had been fired because of her refusal to retract her comments on Hector Bartlett. Her 'ample weight' is the weight of her commitment to those alongside whom she lives – she 'felt the weight of so many people's difficulties' (*FCK*, 69) – and indicative of her commitment to a shared sense of relationship: after Wanda's death she organises 'a sort of wake' with Milly's tenants because 'Some show of solidarity was called for' (*FCK*, 163).

Nancy is solid in body and committed to solidarity; she is an exemplary case of someone who sees her life not in terms of the isolation of the individual subject but in terms of the subject's interrelationship with others. When she lies awake at night, she does not so much suffer from insomnia as benefit from the opportunity to reconsider her relation both to herself and to other people;

> at night I would like awake as long as possible with the sound in my mind's ear of soft voices and amusing stories and in my mind's eye an ambience of leafiness. Sometimes I thought of London and wondered where fate would take me in the future, and sometimes in those precious, silent waking hours I thought of Wanda. (*FCK*, 68–9)

Given her support for others, her animosity towards Hector Bartlett seems out of character – 'it's not at all like you, Mrs Hawkins', says Emma Loy (*FCK*, 136) – but Bartlett represents a way of relating to others that is entirely antithetic to Nancy's. Nancy exemplifies what Gabriel Marcel describes as fundamental to human experience – that our being is not that of the solitary *cogito* but is founded on 'intersubjectivity': 'intersubjectivity plays its part also within the life of the subject, even at moments when the latter's only intercourse is with itself.'[25] Even when meditatively waiting out her insomnia, Nancy's life is one of 'being with' others, rather than being for herself. In Marcel's terms, her life points back to older forms of living together:

> I would say that we are living in a world in which the proposition 'with' – and I might also mention Whitehead's noun, 'togetherness' – seems more and more to be losing its meaning: one might put the same idea in another way by saying that the very idea of a close human relationship (the intimate relationship of large families, of friends, of old neighbours, for instance) is becoming increasingly hard to put into practice, and is even being rather disparaged.[26]

What makes Nancy's response to Hector Bartlett so different is that he, as far as she is concerned – and she is proved right by the events of the narrative – is someone whose only interest in people is not for their potential intersubjectivity but for the use he can make of them to further his own projects: in Hector's relationships there is no 'being with' in Marcel's sense, there is only 'being for', not in Sartre's sense of the being which exists for itself but in the sense of 'being-of-use-for' or 'being-usable-for'. This instrumental appropriation of other people is enacted in Hector's adoption of radionics, of which he becomes a proponent in order to ingratiate himself with the publisher Ian Tooley, the appropriately named Tooley being a believer that radionics is an instrumental application of the traditional spiritualism and astrology in which he is also a believer. The radionics 'Box' is an instrument which is supposedly able to cure at a distance illnesses in people and animals, as well as increase the productivity of crops. Bartlett, though incapable of working 'the Box' himself, organises radionics operators on Tooley's behalf, producing results that seem to confirm its spiritual properties. Abigail, employed as an assistant to Tooley, tells Nancy that Bartlett is held to be 'a wonder at the box' even though 'he doesn't do it himself' but he 'does teach the operators' (*FCK*, 151), thereby deserving credit for its effectiveness. Hector's relationship to radionics is symptomatic of all his relationships: it is a means to further another purpose – his efforts to get published – and it treats other people as tools to that end. Since Hector is incapable himself of getting results from the radionics box, he needs to work through an operator who becomes in turn the tool of his own ambitions: relationships are not, for Hector, personal but entirely instrumental. Instead of the intersubjectivity of persons that Marcel describes as fundamental to human existence, Hector uses a machine to try to intervene in someone else's subjectivity, producing an 'inter-subjectivity' which has no human content but which is directed at disrupting human relations. Two different kinds of intersubjectivity are thus focused on the person of Wanda, the intersubjectivity of persons whose interactions are a matter of care for one another, and the inter-subjectivity produced by the machine which has no concern about the person or thing on which it is focused. The eventual irony of this opposition is that it is not the target of the machine's psychic disruptions – 'You are wasting. You will die', Wanda tells Nancy (*FCK*, 148) – but the machine's operator herself – Wanda – who is afflicted by the machine's illusory capacities. Abigail may insist that the Box 'was a complete fake' (*FCK*, 77), but it turns out to be only too dangerous to the psyche of its operator, stricken by guilt at the consequence of what she has been asked to perform. Bartlett's instrumentalism is aimed at destroying Nancy, but instead it destroys the medium by which he intended to achieve that aim. Ian Tooley may believe that radionics is beneficent but, as Nancy insists, 'If you believe it can affect your health beneficially, then you have to believe it can affect it malevolently' (*FCK*, 153). Radionics is a spoof version of the reality in which Nancy lives, one in which forces far removed from her personal life have a profound effect on the way that that life can be lived. The geopolitical is like a vast but effective radionics box, shaping the existence of people who have little or no knowledge of the forces by which their lives are governed.

Nancy's resistance to Hector may be based on his failure in art – a pretentious *pisseur de copie* – but what the novel reveals is that Hector not only turns the personal into the instrumental in his relationship with Wanda – 'Wanda had been blackmailed by Hector Bartlett, probably seduced, the foolish woman' (*FCK*, 149) – but transforms the one 'art' at which he has some success, the art of radionics, from its promise as a cure to the ills of life into an art of death.

Notes

1. David Sherman, *Sartre and Adorno: The Dialectics of Subjectivity* (New York: SUNY, 2007), 19.
2. Walter Lowrie, *Kierkegaard* (London: Oxford University Press, 1938), 392.
3. Martin Stannard, *Muriel Spark: The Biography* (London: Weidenfeld & Nicolson, 2009), 77.
4. Thomas Busch, 'Coming to Terms with Jean-Paul Sartre: A Critical Review of Recent Books about Sartre', *Philosophy Today*, Vol. XXIV, No. 3/4 (Fall 1980), 235.
5. Martin Heidegger, *Being and Time*, trans. John Macquarrie and Edward Robinson (Oxford: Blackwell, 1962), 82.
6. Bryan Cheyette argues that with *The Prime of Jean Brodie* there is a significant shift in Spark's technique: 'If the first five novels could easily have been situated anywhere at just about any time, her next three could only have been set in Edinburgh, London and Jerusalem in the 1930s, mid-1940s, and the early 1960s respectively', *Muriel Spark* (Tavistock: Northcote House, 2000), 53. This underplays the historical 'thrownness' and cultural specificity of the early novels, as, for instance in Laurence's profession of radio commentator on football, or the pre-First World War events in *Memento Mori*.
7. Gabriel Marcel, *The Mystery of Being*, vol. 1, *Reflection and Mystery*, trans. G. S. Fraser (London: Harvill Press, 1950), 177.
8. Ibid. 187.
9. Emmanuel Mounier, *Existentialist Philosophies: An Introduction*, trans. Eric Blow (London: Rockliff, 1948), 80.
10. Ibid. 65.
11. Ibid. 87.
12. Ibid. 50.
13. Emmanuel Mounier, *Personalism*, trans. Philip Mairet (London: Routledge and Kegan Paul), x.
14. Ibid. viii.
15. Ibid. x.
16. Ibid. xi.
17. See David L. Schalk, *The Spectrum of Political Engagement: Mounier, Benda, Brasillach, Sartre* (Princeton, NJ: Princeton University Press, 1979). Schalk suggests that 'Sartre is also predated by the Catholic personalists, who had been using the term engagement, again since 1932, when *Esprit* was founded under the editorship of Emmanuel Mounier. Mounier and the other contributors to *Esprit* deserve credit for persistent reference of engagement and for a number of efforts to delineate its significance' (10–11).

18. Derek Stanford, *Inside the Forties: Literary Memoirs, 1937–1957* (London: Sidgwick & Jackson, 1977), 160.
19. Mounier, *Personalism*, x.
20. Adam Piete's 'Muriel Spark and the Politics of the Contemporary', in Michael Gardiner and Willy Maley (eds), *The Edinburgh Companion to Muriel Spark* (Edinburgh: Edinburgh University Press, 2010), provides the best analysis of the nature of the situatedness of Spark's characters, who must be understood in terms of 'the three chronotopes of political contemporaneity, supra-mundane reality and psychosocial relations' (55).
21. Lowrie, *Kierkegaard*, 465.
22. Søren Kierkegaard, *Letters and Documents*, trans. Henrik Rosenmeier (Princeton: Princeton University Press, 1978), 33.
23. As Kierkegaard put it in *Philosophical Crumbs*, 'it is the perfection of the eternal not to have a history, to be the only thing that is and yet absolutely without a history' (*PC*, 143).
24. W. B. Yeats, 'Nineteen Hundred and Nineteen', *The Collected Poems of W. B. Yeats* (London: Macmillan, 1950), 236.
25. Marcel, *The Mystery of Being*, 182.
26. Ibid. 28; the reference to Whitehead is to Alfred North Whitehead and his *Process and Reality: An Essay in Cosmology* (Cambridge: Cambridge University Press, 1929), which was the published version of his Gifford Lectures delivered in Edinburgh in 1927–8.

Chapter 7

The Art of Death

In J. M. Barrie's first story about Peter Pan, *The Little White Bird* (1902), the male narrator is a former soldier who is known at his club as 'a confirmed spinster';[1] he plots, however, to gain a surrogate son by stealing the affection of a boy, David, from his mother Mary, as a result of making him the audience for stories about Peter Pan, as well as turning him into the protagonist of stories of people shipwrecked on a desert island. When Barrie came to write the play of *Peter Pan* (1906), he effectively crash-lands Peter with the Darling children on the island of the Neverland – Wendy is brought down by an arrow fired by one of the 'lost boys' – in what can be seen as a prefiguration of the airline crash which brings January Marlow to the island of Robinson in Spark's novel of that name. Barrie's 'neverland' and Robinson's human-shaped island[2] have both been for long the resort of 'pirates and smugglers' (*R*, 90) – places apparently set aside from the world but which are, nonetheless, continually invaded by the outside world. In *The Little White Bird*, however, the first question to be posed about Peter is not where he came from or whether he had a mother but whether or not he had a goat:

> If you ask your mother whether she knew about Peter Pan when she was a little girl, she will say, 'Why, of course I did child'; and if you ask whether he rode on a goat in those days, she will say, 'What a foolish question to ask; certainly he did.' Then if you ask your grandmother whether she knew about Peter Pan when she was a girl, she also says, 'Why of course I did, child,' but if you ask her whether he rode on a goat in those days, she says she never heard of his having a goat [. . .] Therefore there was no goat when your grandmother was a little girl.[3]

The question of the goat will also be crucial in *Robinson*, because after Robinson, the owner of the island, disappears there is blood and a scatter of clothes in the field beyond the house in which January and her two fellow survivors of the air crash are living: is this a murder scene or an artfully constructed representation of a murder scene?

> I said, 'Those blood-stained articles of clothing must have been planted by someone.'
> 'Oh, must they?'
> 'They wouldn't have been scattered about in quite such an obvious manner if they had been dropped accidentally.'
> 'Oh, wouldn't they?' (*R*, 109)

The dubiety turns on the issue of whether Robinson did or did not have a goat whose blood could be spattered around in imitation of violence against a human being: Robinson had supposedly shot the sick goat a couple of days before and disposed of the carcase, but was that a ruse? Did he still have the goat on the night of his disappearance? Is it goat's blood rather than Robinson's blood with which the field is stained and is the blood evidence of death or testimony to the artifice of death? The allusion to *Peter Pan* underlines that the island in *Robinson* is a place of the imagination, a possibility given increasing emphasis at the novel's conclusion when the island has been wiped off the map by a volcanic explosion and therefore exists only in the narrator's imaginative reconstruction. That Spark intends to build such an intertextual resonance between her novel and Barrie's most famous creation is suggested by further echoes of Barrie's works: Robinson's cat is named 'Bluebell', which is also the name of the ship which is driven ashore on a desert island in Barrie's *The Admirable Crichton* (1902), a play of social and gender reversals of a similar kind to those we see in *Robinson*. January tells us, for instance, that she is attracted to Jimmie because 'he appealed to a quality in my mind which I considered the most advanced I possessed, and which was also slightly masculine' (*R*, 26), and Act III of Barrie's play introduces what is apparently a new character:

> *A stalwart youth appears at the window, so handsome and tingling with vitality that, glad to depose CRICHTON, we cry thankfully, 'The hero at last.' But it is not the hero; it is the heroine. This splendid boy, clad in skins, is what Nature has done for* Lady Mary.[4]

Lady Mary has, as a result of the survivors' struggle to deal with their unanticipated environment, become an entirely new person of an ambiguous gender, her name echoed by Robinson's full name – Miles Mary Robinson. In her early fiction Spark regularly uses Barrie as an index of her characters' substitution of imagination for reality, as in Patrick Seton's fascination with Barrie's *Mary Rose*, or with Pierre's production of *Peter Pan* in *The Hothouse by the East River*. In Barrie's works, imagination appears to defy death – as, for instance, in *Farewell Miss Julie Logan*, in which a nineteenth century minister of the Church of Scotland is allowed to encounter and fall in love with an eighteenth-century Jacobite woman – but at the same time the imagination which defies death is also obsessed by death: Peter declares, 'To die will be an awfully big adventure'.[5] Barrie's narratives invite his readers not only to resist death by the power of the imagination but to revel in death as it is reproduced by the imagination: thus the narrator in the novel of *Peter Pan* invites us to participate in a killing – 'Let us now kill a pirate, to show Hook's method. Skylights will do' – and to treat that death as of no human significance, 'the hook shoots forth, there is a tearing sound and one screech, then the body is kicked aside, and the pirates pass on'.[6] An individual is killed simply in illustration of Hook's – and the reader's – carelessness about the deaths that take place in a work of fiction. Death, in art, is an aesthetic effect, not an existential reality: we do not need to care about death in a work of art because it has no finality – we can return to the beginning of the narrative and the dead are again living, acting out their lives as though unaware of the fate that awaits them.

The transformation of life into art was, for Kierkegaard, the prime deceit of systematic accounts of human history: the philosophy of history as practised by Hegelians transposed death as an existential reality into an aesthetic order, one in which death could not be seen in its individuality but simply as the fulfilment of a higher organisation of meaning into which every individual existence was incorporated. Death as the threat of extinction was translated into death as preservation because each individual death became a meaningful contribution to a narrative – in Hegelian terms the narrative of historical progress – which annulled the finality of death by each individual's contribution to a larger and more significant narrative of universal significance. It was against such an aestheticisation of death, its transformation into a consolatory contribution to a higher order of meaning, that Kierkegaard rebelled:

> If, however, the uncertainty of death is something in general, then my dying is also something in general. Perhaps dying is also something in general for systematicians, for absent-minded people. For the late bookseller Soldin, dying is said to have been something in general – 'When he was going to get up in the morning, he was not aware that he was dead.' But for me, *my* dying is by no means something in general; for others, my dying is some such thing in general. Nor am *I* for myself some such thing in general; perhaps for others I am some such thing in general. But if the task is to become subjective, then every subject become *for himself* exactly the opposite of some such thing in general. I think it is embarrassing to be so much for world history and then at home with oneself to be for oneself some such thing in general. (*CUP*, 167)

History, as an aesthetic reconstruction of life, denies the urgency of death as it is apprehended from the perspective of the existing individual, its finality absorbed into a higher order which continues to give an individual life meaning even if death were, for that individual, the extinction of meaning. Returning the *urgency* of death to our everyday experience, resisting its aestheticisation and systemisation, was Kierkegaard's aim, his indirect means of communication a way of advertising the falsehoods of the aesthetic with which his pseudonymous authors could not help being engaged, and thus opening up,

> the question about what death is and what it is for the living person, how the idea of it must change a person's whole life if he, in order to think its uncertainty, must think it every moment in order thereby to prepare himself for it. Then there is the question about what it means to prepare oneself for it, since here again a distinction is made between its actual coming and the idea of it (a distinction that seems to make all my preparation something meaningless if that which actually comes is not the same as that for which I have prepared myself, and if it is the same, the preparation, if consummate, is death itself) [. . .] (*CUP*, 168–9)

For Kierkegaard, faith is the answer to death: 'The believer possesses the eternally certain antidote to despair, viz. possibility; for with

God all things are possible every instant. This is the sound health of faith which resolves contradictions' (*SUD*, 61). But the world of Hegelianised Christianity removes the urgency of death not by contact with a God to whom 'all things are possible' but by translating death into the progressive order of meaning that is the development of 'Spirit' through history. The individual becomes part of a narrative that makes each individual life meaningful only by dissolving its individuality. The meaning of death to the individual was to become a central theme in the development of twentieth-century existentialism. Kierkegaard's 'uncertainty' about the 'when' of death and the need to be continually conscious of impending death implied that death was the context in which, and by which, each of our individual decisions and acts needs to be judged: we should – even if most of us do not – make our decisions about how we lead our lives in the awareness of what they will mean in the light of our coming death, in terms of what those decisions will contribute to the making of ourselves which is the necessary burden of being free to choose the life that we live. In *Being and Time*, Heidegger defines existential freedom in terms of 'anticipation' – our freedom rests in our continual orientation towards a future which anticipates the self that we wish to become – but such anticipation also has to be, in the end, an anticipation of our death, of the extinction of our possible futures; for 'Dasein' – Heidegger's term for self-conscious being – death has to be 'Dasein's *ownmost* possibility'.[7] We do not will our own death but we anticipate death as the determining horizon of what we can will for the fulfilment of our life in time. If we live authentically, rather than as creatures submerged in the common values of our society, our death will not be a mere accident but a consummation of what, despite the 'thrownness' of our existence, we have sought to make of ourselves. 'Being towards death' therefore becomes, for Heidegger, both an injunction as to how we live our lives and a way of valuing the outcomes of those lives: a life lived in the anticipation of death will be a life for which death is a consummation, bringing our existence to a meaningful closure. This is a view of death which Sartre rejected: in *Six Existentialist Thinkers* (1952), H. J. Blackham summarised the differences between the two thinkers as follows:

> Contrary to the conception of Heidegger that death is my sovereign possibility, death [according to Sartre] is not *my* possibility at all, it

> is 'a cancellation always possible of what I can be, which is outside my possibilities'. Death is accidental in its occurrence and therefore absurd: far from giving a life its meaning, it may leave that meaning in doubt and suspense [. . .] [8]

For Heidegger, if all our acts and decisions have been taken in the light of our coming death, then death will be that for which we have lived: our death, in effect, turns life into a completed work, having a structure similar to that of a completed work of art. For Sartre, on the other hand, death is an entirely accidental interruption of the narrative of a life, its 'absurdity' the result of its dislocation of any coherent relationship between the beginning, middle and end of our individual narratives:

> What must be noted first is the absurd character of death. In this sense every attempt to consider it as a resolved chord at the end of a melody must be sternly rejected. It has often been said that we are in the situation of a condemned man among other condemned men who is ignorant of the day of his execution but who sees each day that his fellow prisoners are being executed. This is not wholly exact. We ought rather to compare ourselves to a man condemned to death who is bravely preparing himself for the ultimate penalty, who is doing everything possible to make a good showing on the scaffold, and who meanwhile is carried off by a flu epidemic. (*B&N*, 533)

Spark's novels present us with versions of both of these existentialist accounts of death: Sartre's version of the absurdity of death is mirrored in the many deaths which are brought about by trivial accidents that make them contingent and unfulfilling in relation to the life that has preceded it. Death, in these cases, is not a fulfilment of life's choices but the ironic revelation of characters having died too soon, or having died too late, or having, by their death, brought about the deaths of others, as in Godfrey's death in *Memento Mori*: 'Godfrey died the same year as the result of a motor accident, his car having collided with another at a bend in Kensington Church Street. He was not killed outright, but died a few days later of pneumonia which had set in from the shock. It was the couple in the other car who were killed outright' (*MM*, 218–19). Death is meaningless in relation to the life for which it is a conclusion: in *The Girls of Slender Means*, for instance, Nicholas witnesses a murder as he and Jane and Rudi join in the celebrations outside Buckingham Palace on VJ night 1945:

> A seaman, pressing on Jane, kissed her passionately on the mouth; nothing whatever could be done about it. [. . .] another seaman, observed only by Nicholas, slid a knife silently between the ribs of a woman who was with him [. . .] The stabbed woman did not scream, but sagged immediately. Someone else screamed through the hush, a woman many yards away, some other victim. Or perhaps the screamer had had her toes trodden upon. (*GSM*, 141)

Jane's unwanted kiss is juxtaposed with another woman's stabbing: the celebration of achieved victory in war contains within it, even in the moment of its celebration, the absurdity of those sudden nearby deaths by which, ironically, the war has actually been won. The historical significance of the end of the war is not necessarily translated into a significant end for those who are celebrating it: the historical end and purpose of the war, which appears to give direction and purpose to the lives of those who have survived it, is founded on the accidental and absurd contingency of the many deaths which contributed to the outcome, lives which were – like the characters in *A Hothouse by the East River* – denied the individual futures that they had projected for themselves. From a Kierkegaardian perspective, the teleology of the narrative of history is meaningless to one who has had a knife slid silently between her ribs. On the other hand, many of Spark's characters are consciously involved in the art of death, in the sense of artfully constructing either their own or other characters' deaths, as in Frederick's carefully plotted suicide in *The Public Image*, which leaves behind a series of notes designed to destroy his wife's reputation, if not her life itself, or in Hector Bartlett's effort, in *A Fry Cry from Kensington*, to take revenge on Nancy Hawkins by means of Wanda Podolak's skill with radionics.

Such plotted deaths, however, also point to the ways in which art itself transforms the life which it seeks to represent. It is a paradox which is played out in *Loitering with Intent*, in which aspiring novelist, Fleur Talbot, finds that the events of her life as a secretary to the recently established Autobiographical Association run in parallel to the events of the novel she is writing. Is she using life as the material of her art or is art determining the nature of her life? Are the autobiographies of the members of the Autobiographical Association giving her material for her plot, or is her plot predicting the lives they are still to live? Her employer, Sir Quentin, believes she is abusing her position to steal the lives of his members and transform them into art, but her art begins to predict the unfolding plot of their lives, as when Lady Bernice 'Bucks' Gilbert commits suicide in fulfilment of the destiny of her equivalent character in Fleur's novel *Warrender Chase*, or when Sir Quentin is killed in a 'head-on' car crash (*LI*, 208) that repeats the death of the central character in her novel – as though the business of life, as Oscar Wilde had predicted,[9] is to imitate art. Thus Fleur discovers she is herself a character in a novel written by her married lover, Leslie (*LI*, 186), and that the text of her own novel has been copied by Sir Quentin into his version of the biographies of the members of his association: 'sheets of notes, some typed, some in Sir Quentin's hand had been inserted, familiar passages; they were lifted more or less directly from my *Warrender Chase*' (*LI*, 147).

Throughout *Loitering with Intent* art and life are in a continual process of mutual exchange, as is appropriate to its autobiographical premise, since an autobiography is an attempt to capture by art the life that its author has lived. The transfer of life into art which an autobiography seeks to achieve can only be done, however, by also mutely invoking the death towards which the autobiographer is moving, a tension rendered vividly in a passage which Fleur quotes from one of her (and Spark's) favourite autobiographies, that of Benvenuto Cellini:

> Some pleasant happenings I recall, and, again, some unspeakable misfortunes which, when I remember, strike terror into me and wonder that I have, indeed, come to this age of fifty-eight, from which, by God's grace, I am now going on my way rejoicing. (*LI*, 127)

The final phrase – 'I am now going on my way rejoicing' – is one which Fleur adopts for her own autobiographical narrative, covering as it does the transformation of her life as a result of the success of that first novel – 'Good-bye my poverty. Good-bye my youth' (*LI*, 220) – but Cellini's forward journey at the age of fifty-eight is, of course, already over by the time his autobiography is published (he completed it, or abandoned it, when he was sixty-three) so that the time it records is already long in the past and, for his readers, is the account of a life already consigned to death. Art transfigures life into permanence, but only as a prefiguration of the death that no autobiography can ever record, which is why Fleur's story of the Autobiographical Association begins in 'an old graveyard which had not yet been demolished' (*LI*, 7): autobiography as the transformation of life into art is inevitably haunted by the transformation of life into death. *Loitering with Intent* celebrates 'How wonderful it feels to be an artist and a woman in the twentieth century' (*LI*, 25), but it does so in the knowledge that the time it celebrates – the very mid-point of the twentieth century, midsummer's day 1950 – is also only a moment in the time that will ultimately consume the life being celebrated.

The interaction of the art of life as being necessarily transformed into an art of death is the kind of dialectical interchange on which Kierkegaard built his philosophy: in such an interchange the fact that life can become death implies that death can become life and this is precisely the reversal that Kierkegaard employs in *The Sickness unto Death*, published in 1849 and attributed to 'Anti-Climacus', in which the author proposes that the condition of 'despair' in which most human beings actually exist, whether they are conscious of it or not, is a consequence of regarding death as an end rather than a beginning. Life, Anti-Climacus suggests, does not end in death; rather, for a Christian, it begins with death:

> death itself is a transition unto life. In view of this, there is from the Christian standpoint no earthly, bodily sickness unto death. For death is doubtless the last phase of the sickness, but death is not the last thing. (*SUD*, 24)

The sickness of the body that leads to death is actually a sickness towards life, and the despair that afflicts the dying is not a despair at losing life but a despair at not being able to will the new life to come after death: 'This precisely is the reason why he despairs – not to say despaired – because he cannot consume himself, cannot get rid of himself, cannot become nothing' (*SUD*, 26). Despair is the psychological condition that follows from viewing death as 'the last thing' but, Anti-Climacus suggests, it is impossible to encounter this 'last thing' without also encountering the fact that there is more to a human being than a body, and the bodily illnesses which will end in its death:

> If one might die of despair as one dies of a sickness, then the eternal in him, the self, must be capable of dying in the same sense that the body dies of sickness. But this is an impossibility; the dying of despair transforms itself constantly into a living. The despairing man cannot die; no more than 'the dagger can slay thoughts' can despair consume the eternal thing, the self, which is the ground of despair [. . .] (*SUD*, 25–6)

Despair is, as it were, self-cancelling, because despair is the consequence of the body's sense of finality; but to fully engage with that sense of finality will necessarily result in an encounter with the 'eternal thing' without which despair itself would be impossible. As long as they do not live with the awareness of death as the realisation of their spiritual entry into eternity, human beings fail to fulfil their existential potential:

> In spite of the fact that a man is in despair he can perfectly well live on in the temporal, in fact all the better for it; he may be praised by men, be honoured and esteemed, and pursue all the aims of temporal life. What is called worldliness is made up of just such men, who (if one may use the expression) pawn themselves to the world. They use their talents, accumulate money, carry on worldly affair, calculate shrewdly etc., etc. are perhaps mentioned in history, but themselves they are not; spiritually understood they have no self, no self for which they could venture everything, no self before God – however *self*ish they may be for all that. (*SUD*, 53)

The arts of life, those for which the individual is praised by his fellows this side of death, are in fact no more than a 'being unto death', a preparation for the extinction of the self which has never been forced to encounter its eternal reality. 'Being unto death' is, for Kierkegaard, very different from the 'being unto death' that was developed in the philosophies of Heidegger and Sartre, because 'being unto death' is for Kierkegaard the expectation of a beginning rather than a conclusion: in the perspective of eternity, nothing of a life in time is lost through death. This paradox is enacted in the very nature of fiction: art appears to redeem a life in time by giving it permanence – 'But you must understand that everything happens to an artist: time is always redeemed, nothing is lost and wonders never cease' (*LI*, 87) – but that permanence is effectively the equivalent of death, because it prevents the 'being unto death' which promises a new and a different beginning. The very fixity of art, which makes it seem to be part of the eternal, reinforces the understanding of death as an end rather than as a beginning: art can represent a life in time only as a 'being unto death', not as a 'being unto life' or as 'being unto eternity'. For Kierkegaard, the paradox of life is that, even for most Christians, it is lived towards its end rather than towards its beginning; the equivalent paradox in art is that it has no end – a work of fiction is always available to be started over again and therefore never reaches the finality of death, whether that finality is an absolute end or an entirely new beginning. However much it intends to represent the reality of life, it will always fail because it is a pseudo-eternity which cannot imitate our lives in time and the ultimacy of death: Kierkegaard's adoption of fiction as the medium, through his pseudonymous authors, for the presentation of his philosophy dramatizes this paradox: existentialism as a philosophy of 'being towards death' can never articulate that death without, at the same time, negating it: the author writes on, the reader reads on, death has been pointed to, may even have been appointed, but it has not actually happened for it has been transfigured by the medium of the aesthetic.

Spark's fictions are an art of death not only because they involve so many deaths, so many struggles to overcome the consequences of death, but because they are designed to underline the paradox of death in a work of art: death in art cannot avoid belonging to that higher order of meaning which Kierkegaard rejected in favour of the urgency and immediacy of our individual 'being towards death'. The ironic contradiction between what art aims to represent and the medium of its representation is played out in *Not to Disturb*, a novel in which the arts of representation – writing, film, audio – are mobilised to transform the finality of death into the reproducibility of art. Set in the fake-Gothic castle of the Baron and Baroness Klopstock, which was built only eleven years previous to the time of the narration (*NTD*, 42) using materials sourced from other aristocratic houses – the castle and its characters are, like the novel itself, a piece of art created out of previous works of art. That the world of the novel is a world of art is underlined by the fact that the lives of the Baron and Baroness, on the single night of the action, have passed from the time of freedom and choice into the inevitability that is characteristic of art: 'They have placed themselves', the Butler Lister announces, 'unfortunately, within the realm of predestination' (*NTD*, 61). Though the Baron and Baroness have arrived at the castle to meet with their secretary, Victor Passerat, the outcome of their discussions is already certain in the minds of their servants: as he stores away a wad of banknotes which has just been slipped to him by Passerat, Lister, the head butler, evaluates it for the benefit of his fellow servants:

> 'Small change,' he says, 'compared with what is to come, or has already come, according as one's philosophy is temporal or eternal. To all intents and purposes they're already dead although as a matter of banal fact, the night's business has still to accomplish itself. (*NTD*, 17)

Lister's 'philosophy temporal or eternal' transforms the events of time, with their unidirectional unrepeatability, into the foreknowledge provided by a work of literature when it is being re-read, when the outcome is already known. As a consequence, Lister's account of what has not yet taken place is already complete:

> But what's done is about to be done and the future has come to pass. My memoirs up to the funeral are as a matter of fact more or less complete. At all events, it's out of our hands. I place the event at about three a.m. so prepare to stay awake. (*NTD*, 12)

The future has taken on the certainty of an event in the past or of an event re-played in the medium of art rather than one occurring in the medium of a time. The ironies of this reversal of the relationship of between art and futurity are not limited to Lister's memoirs but compounded by the fact that the servants of the house have already sold their stories of the events which have not yet happened to certain newspapers, and sold the film script of the events still to come to an American company on the agreement that individual servants will themselves get to play the parts of their employers, whom Lister describes as being involved in an 'eternal triangle which has come full circle' (*NTD*, 39), an image that codifies the repeatability within which the Baron, the Baroness and their secretary have become trapped. As they await the deaths that are to be the inevitable outcome of the night's events, the servants regularly have to deal with unexpected interruptions to their understanding of the plots in which they are engaged: first, Lister discovers that that the madman in the attic is not a relative of the Baroness but the Baron's younger brother, and, therefore, the inheritor of the estate (*NTD*, 63); second, there is the arrival of the Reverend, who has been summoned by the madman's nurse in the hope of being married to him and thus giving her a permanent role in a wealthy family; and, thirdly, the Reverend also brings with him a newspaper cutting about a drug for depressing sexual drives which he thinks might solve the Klopstock's problems (*NTD*, 83–4) – but if it did so, it would disrupt the necessity of the coming deaths by turning the inevitability of their tragedy back into a problem solvable in time. Preventing the events of time from interrupting the inevitability with which the lives of the Baron, Baroness and their secretary have been invested – and which now represents a significant investment for Lister and his fellow servants – means, as Lister declares, that 'There remain a good many things to be accomplished and more chaos effectively to organise' (*NTD*, 72). Part of that chaos is the uncertain paternity of the unborn child of the maid Heloise: in an establishment where sexuality has become the central focus of their social world, there are many possible candidates:

> Heloise comes to join them at the kitchen door.
>
> 'It's quickening,' she informs Clovis.
>
> 'Well it isn't my fault,' says the chef.
>
> 'Nor me neither, Heloise,' says Lister severely. 'I always took precautions the times I went with you.'
>
> 'It's Pablo,' says the girl, 'I could swear to it. Pablo's the father.'
>
> 'It could have been one of the visitors,' Lister says.
>
> Clovis looks up from his papers, spread out as they are on the kitchen table. 'The visitors never got Heloise, never.'
>
> 'There were one or two,' says Heloise reflectively. (*NTD*, 9–10)

This multiplicity of possible causes is reduced by Lister to one – the father is the mad brother in the attic – which brings order to chaos and further fulfils the aim of enriching the servants at the expense of their masters:

> 'Reverend,' says Lister, do you recall that night last June when the Klopstocks were away and him in the attic got loose? Remember we

> called you in to catch him and calm him down? [. . .] And I wish to draw the Reverend's attention to the result of that rampage last June.' Lister indicates Heloise who smiles at her stomach. (*NTD*, 112)

By identifying a single cause for Heloise's pregnancy, Lister re-establishes causal regularity in an otherwise chaotic world, but the fictionality of this order is reinforced by the recording on film and audio tape of the marriage ceremony between the mad brother and Heloise to ensure that the contingency of life is turned into the certainty of art. *Not to Disturb*'s translation of the uncertainties of life into the repeatable events of art allow those still living in time – the servants – not only to profit financially from their employers' deaths but also to allow some to be themselves translated into the permanence of art as they play out in film the lives of those whose deaths they have been anticipating. Spark's plot is thus an ironic reversal of Auguste Villiers de l'Isle-Adam's *Axel's Castle*, in which Axel declares, 'Live? Our servants will do that for us'. While Villiers' Axel retreats from the world into his Gothic castle, Lister and the other servants reverse that process by using the events in their castle as a means of negotiating with the world and of providing themselves with the kind of wealth that Axel and his lover Sara, having discovered Axel's father's treasure trove, did not bother to spend because it would have tarnished the ideality of their existence. Villiers' play was adopted as the symptomatic version of modernist art by Edmund Wilson in his book entitled *Axel's Castle* (1931), one of the earliest attempts in the period after the First World War to give an account of the development of what came to be known as modernist literature. Wilson used Axel as an example of the symbolists' retreat from the sordid utilitarianism of the modern world 'to a subjective world, from an experience shared with society to an experience savoured in solitude'.[10] In *Not to Disturb*, Spark reverses that process, by making the 'private' lives of the aristocrats in their castle into the stuff of an art that projects itself outwards on a world only too greedy to consume 'life as art': through their artistic recreation the aristocrats achieve an inevitability akin to eternity, a surrogate for the religious eternity for which their lives of hedonistic pleasure had shown no regard. The cause of their deaths may have been their private passions, fueled by unrestrained wealth, but the cause which they serve by their deaths is the cause of art, but a version of art that is itself in thrall to wealth – art as the representation of the lives of the wealthy and as an exercise in the accumulation of wealth for those who create such representations.

The transformation of the contingency of life into the necessity of art is achieved, of course, not only by Lister's ability to artfully create order out of chaos but by Spark's own narrative art, for which Lister is a surrogate, and which ensures that the contingency of life – and its ending in death – is transformed into the inevitability of art. This is underlined by scenes involving two of Victor Passerat's friends who brought him to the castle and then come to demand his release, but whose interruptions are dismissed by Lister on the basis that 'They don't come into the story' (*NTD*, 51), a dismissal repeated when they are found wandering in the storm that strikes just as the events within the locked room reach their climax, 'Forget them' says Mr Samuel, 'They're only extras' (*NTD*, 142), a description which is then fulfilled by the narrative itself because of 'the lightning, which strikes the clump of trees so that the two friends huddled there are killed instantly without pain' (*NTD*, 143). Their 'accidental' deaths confirm that in art, as in life, there are significant deaths and insignificant deaths; both may be equally a part of the plot but they represent different kinds of inevitability: Lister declares that 'There is a vast difference between events that arise from and those that merely follow after each other. Those that arise are preferable' (*NTD*, 63). At the same time there is a 'vast difference' between death in life and death in art, since art dispenses death 'without pain'. As compared with life, art is, in the words of W. B. Yeats's 'Sailing to Byzantium', the 'artifice of eternity';[11] as compared with a Christian eternity, however, art is *merely* artifice; like Axel's castle, it is the simulacrum of an eternity to which only death – real death – can provide access. As a consequence, death in art is an evasion rather than a representation of death in life, providing the consolatory transformation of life into a pseudo-eternity which is, in effect, another kind of death, since its characters are trapped in a world in which, with every reading, they endlessly repeat the same actions, actions which they do not have the power to change. Lister's organisation of chaos in *Not To Disturb* is a surrogate for Spark's organisation of chaos: Lister remains trapped – as Spark does not – within the 'artifice of eternity', a fact which he is allowed to acknowledge by quoting from Marvell that 'yonder all before us lie/Deserts of vast eternity' (*NTD*, 106) – a phrase which punningly suggests that the eternity offered by art is a 'lie', a desert compared with life in time or with what might be offered in a truly Christian conception of the hereafter. The characters of *Not to Disturb* are profoundly disturbed when viewed from an ethical or religious perspective but not from the perspective of the aesthetic, which cannot recognise either its potential or actual evil because it has not reached the ethical level which would make such a judgment possible. The aesthetic, cut loose from the ethical, seeks only sensation and the substitution of one novelty by another; though capable of good it is thoroughly imbued with the capacity for evil – as, for Spark, is the medium of the novel: the novelist necessarily commits herself to engaging in an art which is complicit with evil, rather than, as Sartre suggests, being necessarily on the side of freedom, justice and equality. In Spark's conception of the novel, the novelist must acknowledge rather than conceal the evil out of which the work of art creates its aesthetic pleasures, which also means acknowledging that its representation of death turns death from the extinction of the individual – or their translation to eternity – into their preservation within the repeatable structure of the aesthetic. The art of death reveals that the artifice of eternity is no escape from the world of time but its endless repetition: Spark's art of ridicule is also a revelation of how ridiculous are the claims made for art as the gateway to a transcendental reality.

In 1981 Arthur C. Danto adopted as the title of one of his many books on the problems of modern art the title that Muriel Spark had conferred on the psychological study produced by Sandy Stranger when she had been transformed into the person of Sister Helena – *The Transfiguration of the Commonplace*. Danto writes in his preface, 'Hers was a title I admired and coveted, resolving to take it for my own should I ever write a book it might suit':[12] the duplication of the title of Spark's fictional treatise in the title of Danto's own non-fictional treatise on art repeats a fundamental issue with which Danto's treatise is engaged – 'the possibility of two objects outwardly indiscernible, one of them an artwork and the other not',[13] as in the case of Duchamp's 'Fountain' (1917) which was an ordinary urinal, or Andy Warhol's 'Brillo Box'(1964), which looks to all intents and purposes like the box of metallic cleaning sponges one picks up in a supermarket. Danto's translation of Sandy Stranger's title from fiction into reality – the result is that there is indeed a book called *The Transfiguration of the*

Commonplace – parodies the ways in which much modern art adopts the 'commonplace' and transfigures it – perhaps only by putting it in an art gallery – into what we are asked to see as art. For Danto, such duplication reveals that art has ceased to be meaningful in itself but has come to be a space in which we encounter the displacement of meaning; in effect, a work of art is something that is out of its place in the ordinary world, shorn of its common meanings and so to be encountered purely for its aesthetic properties. What were once parts of a religious edifice, such as Greek statues or Renaissance paintings of the holy family, we now encounter in a museum or gallery – or, indeed, in a church which has come to be seen as a museum – and therefore in a setting to which their original religious purpose is no longer relevant: they become 'aesthetic' objects precisely by shearing away the significance they would have had to their original creators or audiences. The assumption of such a 'disinterested' point of view has been central to many theories of art since Kant proposed disinterestedness as fundamental to his account of beauty in the *Critique of Judgment*, but for Danto such disinterestedness has created a problem that has become more and more pressing in the development of modern art – art's loss of the significance that it once had when it is no longer, as it was for the Greeks, the medium through which a community engages with the most important truths that underpin its communal life. Warhol's 'Brillo Box' is art because it *displaces* an ordinary object from the purposes by which it was defined as a part of our everyday lives and makes it an object of display, but in doing so marginalises its significance within those everyday lives:

> that so base and *lumpen* an object should be enhanced by admission to the artworld seems out of the question. But then we recognize that we have confused the artwork – 'Brillo Box' – with its vulgar counterpart in commercial reality. The work vindicates its claim to be art by propounding a brash metaphor: the brillo-box-as-work-of-art. And in the end this transfiguration of the commonplace object transforms nothing in the artworld. It only brings to consciousness the structures of art which, to be sure, required a certain historical development before that metaphor was possible. The moment it was possible, something like the Brillo Box was inevitable and pointless. It was inevitable because the gesture had to be made, whether with this object or some other. It was pointless because, once it could be made, there was no reason to make it.[14]

We have finally reached the condition that Hegel had prefigured in his *Aesthetics* as the 'death of art', not in the sense that no art is being produced but that art has lost its original sense of purpose, which was its profound connection with religious belief and with ethics – art was the medium through which a community learned how best to conduct itself. In Danto's view, modern art has lost that purposiveness; as William Desmond has put it, 'The "aestheticizing" of art seems to reveal the highest glorification of art; yet this "aestheticizing" reveals art no longer immersed in but cut off from the sense of life's wholeness'.[15] As Danto is only too well aware, his argument reinforces what Hegel had proposed was inevitable in the aftermath of the rise of a scientific world view: art belongs fundamentally in the past where, as in classical Greece or in medieval Christianity, its purpose was to celebrate a community's highest understanding of itself. It can have no such purpose in the modern world.

The crisis of 'the death of art' is deeply inscribed in twentieth-century existentialism: in his *The Origin of the Work of Art* (1936), Heidegger appears to accept Hegel's account of the nature of art in the modern world suggesting, that although 'art is then the becoming and happening of truth',[16] it is a truth no longer available to modernity:

> To be sure, people speak of the immortal works of art and of art as an eternal value. Speaking this way means using that language which does not trouble itself with precision in all essential matters, for fear that in the end to be precise would call for – thinking. And is there any greater fear today than that of thinking? Does this talk about immortal works and the eternal value of art have any content or substance? Or are these merely the half-baked clichés of an age when great art, together with its nature, has departed from among men?[17]

In this context one might read Sartre's account of *littérature engagé* as the effort to give back to literature the kind of moral purposiveness that the 'aesthetic' annuls: real literature, for Sartre, is defined by 'freedom' as the modern equivalent of the value systems that made art significant in classical Greece or in medieval Christianity. Both, however, depend on what we might describe as 'art-as-truth' and it is precisely this which Kierkegaard, in his pseudonymous writings, refuses: art is no more than a stage on life's way towards a truth that can only be known through faith and, like death, faith has to be undertaken or undergone by an existing human being – an Abraham or a Job – whose experience, precisely because it defies universality, is incommunicable: it is a truth which can be known and communicated only indirectly. Hegel's 'death of art', George Pattison has argued, was the context that shaped Kierkegaard's pseudonymous writings:

> The exuberant and often excessive carnivalesque play of genres and styles that is constitutive of Kierkegaard's authorship is not just a sign of its author's quirkiness, though it may be that as well. It is also a sign of how he experienced the culture of his present age in its aesthetic self-manifestation, a manifestation that was postaesthetic in Hegel's sense of having passed from the sphere of the beautiful and ideal into the prose of everyday life. As such it was also a culture in which the clear contours of classical forms were chronically unable to hold the creative and destructive forces of the age in check [. . .][18]

Kierkegaard accepts that the 'aesthetic' cannot operate as it did in ancient Greece or in medieval Europe and therefore must operate indirectly to challenge the debased 'aesthetic' values of his contemporaries: the pseudonymous works must continually unveil their own artifice in order not to be mistaken as revelations of the 'truth' that had characterised art when it was the medium in which the shared values of a community were celebrated. The pseudonymous works are not art representing and affirming life; they are art demonstrating the falsities of contemporary life and its evasion of the necessity of death. The writers, editors and characters of Kierkegaard's pseudonymous works are not representations of life but artfully ironic enactments of the death of art.

By a similar dialectic, Spark ensures that her novels reveal rather than conceal their own artifice, and by doing so ensure that they cannot be taken either as attempted imitations of life or didactic assertions of any truth. They are governed not by the death of art but by the acceptance that art itself has more in common with death than it has with life. If death is the theme of much of her writing it is because death is where art is at home: literary creations, as compared with existing human beings, may seem to participate in some form of timelessness but it is a timelessness that has nothing in common with a Christian eternity. The aesthetic, as the context of everyday sensual life, leads only to the erasure that is death; the aesthetic, as an artwork, avoids that conclusion only by failing to turn timelessness into eternity. The art of death enacts the necessary failure of the aesthetic to redeem us from time by translating time into the endless repetition that is art: its 'truth' consists in unveiling the illusions through which its apparent defiance of time is constructed.

In Kierkegaard's *Journals* there are two entries for July 20 in 1839; the first is as follows:

> Just as in very nervous cases there are moments when the nerves of the eyes grow so microscopically sharp that they *see the air*, so that it is no longer a medium, so too in a spiritual sense there occur moments of ecstasy when the whole of existence is so poetic, stretched so tautly, so transparent to contemplation, that even the most insignificant part of infinity's mass-products seems, at least allegorically to suggest the profoundest truths [. . .] (*J*, '294', 76)

Such vividness of perception – to '*see the air*, so that it is no longer a medium' – is what art offers us, but alongside it Kierkegaard has added in the margin:

> It is characteristic of the present time always to be conscious of the medium. It is almost bound to end in madness, like a man who whenever he looked at the sun and the stars was conscious of the world going round. (*J*, '295', 76)

It is this double vision which Spark's novels invoke: an awareness of the medium which allows the world to be perceived with an unequalled intensity, but at the same time the consciousness that this cannot be a permanent substitute for our ordinary reality. The medium invokes a potential beyond our ordinary consciousness but it is a potential which must also be resisted if we are to know our lives as stages on the road not to art's timelessness, which is a form of death, but to eternity's paradoxical redemption.

Notes

1. J. M. Barrie, *Farewell Miss Julie Logan: A J. M. Barrie Omnibus*, ed. Andrew Nash (Edinburgh: Canongate, 200), 64.
2. A map at the beginning of the novel shows how the island of Robinson has what appears to be arms and legs.

3. Barrie, *Farewell Miss Julie Logan*, 99.
4. A. E. Wilson (ed.), *The Plays of J. M. Barrie* (London: Hodder & Stoughton, 1942), 390.
5. J. M. Barrie, *Peter Pan* (Harmondsworth: Penguin, 1967; 1911), 122.
6. Ibid. 74.
7. Martin Heidegger, *Being and Time*, trans. John Macquarrie and Edward Robinson (Oxford: Blackwell, 1962), 307.
8. H. J. Blackham, *Six Existentialist Thinkers* (London: Routledge and Kegan Paul, 1951). 135; an errata slip notes that it was actually published in 1952 as a result of production delays.
9. Oscar Wilde, 'The Decay of Lying': 'At present, people see fogs, not because there are fogs, but because poets and painters have taught them the mysterious loveliness of such effects. There may have been fogs for centuries in London. I dare say there were. But no one saw them. They did not exist till Art had invented them'; *Complete Works of Oscar Wilde* (London and Glasgow: Collins, 1966), 986.
10. Edmund Wilson, *Axel's Castle: A Study of the Imaginative Literature of 1870–1910* (London and Glasgow: Collins/Fontana, 1961; 1931), 211.
11. W. B. Yeats, *Collected Poems* (London: Macmillan, 1950), 218.
12. Arthur C. Danto, *The Transfiguration of the Commonplace: A Philosophy of Art* (Cambridge, MA: Harvard University Press, 1981), v.
13. Ibid. 201.
14. Ibid. 208.
15. William Desmond, *Art and the Absolute: A Study of Hegel's Aesthetics* (Albany: State University of New York Press, 1986), 53.
16. Martin Heidegger, 'The Origin of the Work of Art', *Poetry, Language, Thought*, trans Albert Hofstadter (New York: Harper & Row, 1971), 71.
17. Ibid. 'Epilogue', 79.
18. George Pattison, 'Kierkegaard's Literary Kaleidoscope', in Eric Ziolkowski (ed.), *Kierkegaard, Literature and the Arts* (Evanston: Northwestern University Press, 2018), 48.

Index

CPSIA information can be obtained
at www.ICGtesting.com
Printed in the USA
JSHW030346041120
9291JS00002B/51

9 781474 447218